D1374037

AMERICAN WOMEN
images and realities

AMERICAN WOMEN
Images and Realities

Advisory Editors
ANNETTE K. BAXTER
LEON STEIN

A Note About This Volume

A legion of ladies spent their lives earning bread and
board in domestic service. Lucy Maynard Salmon
(1853-1927) applied the meticulous research tech-
niques of a social scientist to produce this devastating
study of the anonymous thousands trapped in endless
days of servitude. In four decades of teaching at Vassar she was also concerned with the relationship of
college faculties to school faculties and of educational
institutions to communities. In her teaching she inno-
vated the project method, intensive student use of the
library, and the utilization of newspapers and artifacts
of everyday life as historical materials. She was the
first woman member of the executive council of the
American Historical Association.

DOMESTIC SERVICE

BY

LUCY MAYNARD SALMON

ARNO PRESS

A New York Times Company

New York • 1972

Reprint Edition 1972 by Arno Press Inc.

Reprinted from a copy in The Princeton University
Library

American Women: Images and Realities
ISBN for complete set: 0-405-04445-3
See last pages of this volume for titles.

Manufactured in the United States of America

- - - - - - - - - - - -

Library of Congress Cataloging in Publication Data

Salmon, Lucy Maynard, 1853-1927.
    Domestic service.

    (American women: images and realities)
    Reprint of the 1897 ed.
    Bibliography: p.
    1. Servants. I. Title. II. Series.
HD6072.S2 1972   301.44'44   72-2766
ISBN 0-405-04445-3

DOMESTIC SERVICE

DOMESTIC SERVICE

BY

LUCY MAYNARD SALMON

New York

THE MACMILLAN COMPANY

LONDON: MACMILLAN & CO., Ltd.

1897

Norwood Press
J. S. Cushing & Co. — Berwick & Smith
Norwood Mass. U.S.A.

" The reform that applies itself to the household must not be partial. It must correct the whole system of our social living. It must come with plain living and high thinking ; it must break up caste, and put domestic service on another foundation. It must come in connection with a true acceptance by each man of his vocation, — not chosen by his parents or friends, but by his genius, with earnestness and love."

EMERSON.

PREFACE

THE basis of the following discussion of the subject of domestic service is the information obtained through a series of blanks sent out during the years 1889 and 1890. Three schedules were prepared — one for employers, one for employees, and one asking for miscellaneous information in regard to the Woman's Exchange, the teaching of household employments, and kindred subjécts.[1] These schedules were submitted for criticism to several gentlemen prominent in statistical investigation, and after revision five thousand sets were distributed. These were sent out in packages containing from five to twenty-five sets through the members of the Classes of 1888 and 1889, Vassar College, and single sets were mailed, with a statement of the object of the work, to the members of different associations presumably interested in such investigations. These were the American Statistical Association, the American Economic Association, the Association of Collegiate Alumnæ, the Vassar Alumnæ, and the women graduates of the University of Michigan. They were also sent to various women's clubs, and many were distributed at the request of persons interested in the work.

[1] These schedules are given in Appendix I.

Of the five thousand sets of blanks thus sent out, 1025 were returned filled out by employers, twenty being received after the tabulation was completed. These gave the facts asked for with reference to 2545 employees. The returns received from employers thus bore about the same proportion to the blanks distributed as do the returns received in ordinary statistical investigation carried on without the aid of special agents or legal authority. The reasons why a larger number were not returned are the same as are found in all such inquiries, with a few peculiar to the nature of the case. The occupation investigated is one that does not bring either employer or employee into immediate contact with others in the same occupation, and it is therefore believed that the relations between employer and employee are purely personal, and thus not a proper subject for statistical inquiry. Another reason assigned was the fear that the agitation of the subject would cause employees to become dissatisfied, while a third reason was the large number of questions included in the blanks, and the fact that no immediate and possibly no remote benefit would accrue to those filling them out. Another reason frequently assigned was that all of the questions could not be answered, and that, therefore, replies to others could not be of service. Several of the questions, however, were framed with the understanding that in many cases they could not be definitely answered; as the question, " How many servants have you employed since you have been housekeeping? " The fact that often no reply could be given, was as significant of the condition of the service as a detailed statement could have been.

No success had been anticipated in securing replies from employees; but as any study of domestic service would be incomplete without looking at it from this point of view, the attempt was made. As a result, 719 blanks were returned filled out. In some instances employees, hearing of the inquiry, wrote for schedules and returned them answered. In a few cases correspondence was carried on with women who had formerly been in domestic service. The influences that operated to prevent employers from answering the inquiries made had even greater force in the case of employees. In addition, there was present a hesitation to commit anything to writing, or to sign a name to a document the import of which was not clearly understood by them.

The limited amount of information that could be given explains the small number of returns received to the third schedule, — about two hundred.

The returns received were sent to the Massachusetts Bureau of Statistics of Labor, where, by the courtesy of the chief of the bureau, they were collated during the spring and summer of 1890, under the special direction of the chief clerk, in accordance with a previously arranged scheme of tables. The general plan of arrangement adopted was to class the schedules with reference to employers, first alphabetically by states and towns, and second alphabetically by population. The schedules were then classed with reference to employees, first by men

and women, and second by place of birth. The various
statistical devices used in the Massachusetts Bureau were
employed in tabulating the material, and greatly facili-
tated the work.

Fifty large tables were thus prepared, and by various
combinations numerous smaller ones were made. The
classification thus adopted made it possible to give all the
results either in a general form or with special reference
to men and women employees, the native born and the
foreign born, and to all of the branches of the service.
It was also possible to study the conditions of the service
geographically, and with reference to the population and
to other industrial situations.

The most detailed tables made out concerned the wage
question, including a presentation of classified wages,
average wages with the percentage of employees receiving the same wages as the average, and also more or less
than the average, a comparison of wages paid at different
times and of wages received in domestic service and in
other employments. For the purposes of comparison,
the writer also classified the salaries paid to about six
thousand teachers in the public schools in sixteen representative cities, as indicated by the reports of city
superintendents for the year during which information
concerning domestic service had been given on the schedules. Through the courtesy of a large employment
bureau in Boston, the wages received by nearly three
thousand employees were ascertained and used for comparison. The most valuable results of the investigation

possibly were those growing out of the concensus of opinion obtained from employers and employees regarding the nature of the service considered as an occupation. The greater proportion of these tables can be found in Chapter V.

The question must naturally arise as to how far the returns received through such investigation can be considered representative. It has seemed to the writer that they could be considered fairly so. Investigations of this character must always be considered typical rather than comprehensive. It is difficult to fix the exact number to be considered typical as between a partial investigation and a census which is exhaustive. In some cases it is possible to obtain a majority in numbers, in others it is not. If the number of returns, however, passes the point where it would be considered trivial, the number between this and the majority may perhaps be regarded as representative. By the application of a similar principle, the expression at the polls of the wishes of the twentieth part of the inhabitants of a state is recognized as the will of the majority. But, while the returns can be considered only fairly representative as regards numbers, they seem entirely so as regards conditions. It is believed that every possible condition under which domestic service exists, as regards both employer and employee, is represented by the returns received, and that, therefore, the conclusions drawn from these results cannot be wholly unreasonable. Moreover, the circulars were sent out practically at random, and, therefore, do not

represent any particular class in society, except the class
sufficiently interested in the subject to answer the questions asked.   If the returns thus secured can be regarded
in any sense as representative, the results based on them
may be considered as indicating certain general conditions and tendencies, although the conclusions reached
may be modified by later and fuller researches.

The question must also arise as to what it is hoped
will be accomplished through this investigation.   It is
not expected that all, or even any one of the perplexing
questions connected with domestic service will be even
partially answered by it; it is not expected that any
individual housekeeper will have less trouble to-morrow
than to-day in adjusting the difficulties arising in her
household; it will not enable any employer whose incompetent cook leaves to-day without warning to secure
an efficient one without delay.   It is hoped, however, that
the tabulation and presentation of the facts will afford
a broader basis for general discussion than has been possible without them, that a knowledge of the conditions
of domestic service beyond their own localities and households will enable some housekeepers in time to decide
more easily the economic questions arising within every
home, that it will do a little something to stimulate discussion of the subject on other bases than the purely
personal one.   The hope has also come that writers on
economic theory and economic conditions will recognize
the place of domestic service among other industries, and
will give to the public the results of their scientific

investigations of the subject, that the great bureaus of labor — always ready to anticipate any demand of the public — will recognize a demand for facts in this field of work.

The writer has followed the presentation of facts by a theoretical discussion of doubtful and possible remedies. But if fuller and more searching official investigation, establishing a substantial basis for discussion, should point to conclusions entirely at variance with those here given, no one would more heartily rejoice than herself. It may reasonably be said that in view of the character of the investigation no conclusions at all should have been advanced by the investigator. Three things, however, seemed to justify the intrusion of personal views ; a recognition of the prevalent anxiety to find a way out of existing difficulties, a belief that improvement can come only as each one is willing to make some contribution to the general discussion, and a conviction that no one should criticise existing conditions unless prepared to suggest others that may be substituted for them.

The following discussion would have been impossible without the hearty co-operation of the thousand and more employers and the seven hundred employees who filled out the schedules distributed. The great majority of these were personally unknown to the writer, and she can express only in this public way her deep appreciation of their kindness, as she also wishes to do to the many friends, known and unknown, who assisted in distributing the schedules. She also desires to express her obli-

PREFACE

gation to the Hon. Carroll D. Wright, for help received in preparing the schedules and for the receipt of advance sheets from the Census of 1890; to the Hon. Horace G. Wadlin and Mr. Charles F. Pidgin, for the courtesies extended at the Massachusetts Bureau of Statistics of Labor, and also to Professor Davis R. Dewey, of the Massachusetts Institute of Technology; to Dean Marion Talbot of Chicago University, and to Professor Mary Roberts Smith, of the Leland Stanford University; to Mrs. John Wilkinson of Chicago, Mrs. John H. Converse of Philadelphia, and Mrs. Helen Hiscock Backus of Brooklyn, for their constant encouragement and assist-ance in the work. Most of all the writer is under obli-gation to Miss A. Underhill for her assistance in reading both the manuscript and the proof of the work, and for the preparation of the Index.

Articles bearing on the subject have at different times appeared in the *Papers of the American Statistical Asso-ciation, The New England Magazine, The Cosmopolitan,* and *The Forum.* These have been freely used in the work, and the writer acknowledges the courtesy of the publishers and editors of these periodicals in allowing this use of her papers.

JANUARY 18, 1897.

CONTENTS

CHAPTER I

INTRODUCTION

CHAPTER II

HISTORICAL ASPECTS OF DOMESTIC EMPLOYMENTS

CHAPTER III

DOMESTIC SERVICE DURING THE COLONIAL PERIOD

CHAPTER IV

DOMESTIC SERVICE SINCE THE COLONIAL PERIOD

CHAPTER V

ECONOMIC PHASES OF DOMESTIC SERVICE

CHAPTER VI

DIFFICULTIES IN DOMESTIC SERVICE FROM THE STANDPOINT OF THE EMPLOYER

CHAPTER VII

ADVANTAGES IN DOMESTIC SERVICE

CHAPTER VIII

THE INDUSTRIAL DISADVANTAGES OF DOMESTIC SERVICE

CHAPTER IX

THE SOCIAL DISADVANTAGES OF DOMESTIC SERVICE

CHAPTER X

DOUBTFUL REMEDIES

CHAPTER XIII

POSSIBLE REMEDIES — SPECIALIZATION OF HOUSEHOLD
EMPLOYMENTS

CHAPTER XIV

POSSIBLE REMEDIES — PROFIT SHARING

CHAPTER XV

POSSIBLE REMEDIES — EDUCATION IN HOUSEHOLD AFFAIRS

CHAPTER XVI

CONCLUSION

DOMESTIC SERVICE

CHAPTER I

INTRODUCTION

DOMESTIC service has been called "the great American question." If based on the frequency of its discussion in popular literature, foundation for this judgment exists. Few subjects have attracted greater attention, but its consideration has been confined to four general classes of periodicals, each treating it from a different point of view. The popular magazine article is theoretical in character, and often proposes remedies for existing evils without sufficient consideration of the causes of the difficulty. Household journals and the home departments of the secular and the religious press usually treat only of the personal relations existing between mistress and maid. The columns of the daily press given to "occasional correspondents" contain narrations of personal experiences. The humorous columns of the daily and the illustrated weekly papers caricature, on the one side, the ignorance and helplessness of the housekeeper, and, on the other side, the insolence and presumption of the servant. In addition to this, in many localities it has passed into a common proverb that, among housekeepers, with whatever topic conversation begins, it sooner or later gravitates towards the one fixed point of domestic service, while among domestic employees it is none the less certain that other phases of the same general subject are agitated.

This popular discussion, which has assumed so many forms, has been almost exclusively personal in character. A somewhat different aspect of the case is presented when the problem is stated to be "as momentous as that of capital and labor, and as complicated as that of individualism and socialism." This statement suggests that economic principles are involved, but the question of domestic service has been almost entirely omitted, not without reason, from theoretical, statistical, and historical discussions of economic problems. It has been omitted from theoretical discussions mainly because: (1) the occupation does not involve the investment of a large amount of capital on the part of the individual employer or employee; it therefore seems to be excluded from theoretical discussions of the relations of capital, wages, and labor; (2) no combinations have yet been formed among employers or employees; it is therefore exempt from such speculations as are involved in the consideration of trusts, monopolies, and trade unions; (3) the products of domestic service are more transient than are the results of other forms of labor; this fact must determine somewhat its relative position in economic discussion. Its exclusion, as a rule, from the statistical presentations of the labor question is also not surprising. The various bureaus of labor, both national and state, consider only those subjects for the investigation of which there is a recognized demand. They are the leaders of

public opinion in the accumulation of facts, but they are
its followers as regards the choice of questions to be
studied. Public opinion has not yet demanded a scientific treatise on domestic service, and until it does the
bureaus of labor cannot be expected to supply the material for such discussion.[1] Again, it is not surprising that
the historical side of the subject has been overlooked,
since household employments have been passive recipi-
ents, not active participants, in the industrial development of the past century. Yet it must be said that this
negative consideration of the subject by theoretical, practical, and historical economists, and the positive treatment
accorded it by popular writers, seems an unfair and unscientific disposition to make of an occupation in which
by the Census of 1890 one and a half millions of persons
are actively engaged,[2] to whom employers pay annually
at the lowest rough estimate in cash wages more than
$218,000,000,[3] for whose support they pay at the lowest

[1] Partial discussions of the subject can be found in the *First Biennial
Report of the Bureau of Labor Statistics of Minnesota*, pp. 131-196;
First Biennial Report of the Bureau of Labor Statistics of Colorado,
pp. 344-362 ; *Fifth Annual Report of the Bureau of Labor and Industrial
Statistics of Kansas*, pp. 281-326 ; *Third Biennial Report of the Bureau
of Labor Statistics of the State of California*, pp. 91-94 ; *Fifth Biennial
Report of the Department of Statistics, State of Indiana*, pp. 173-229.
The last is especially full and excellent.

[2] The total number of domestic servants is given as 1,454,791. This
does not include launderers and laundresses, paid housekeepers in private
families and hotels, or stewards and stewardesses. It excludes also the
very large number of persons performing the same duties as domestic
servants, but without receiving a fixed compensation.

[3] This estimate is based on the supposition that the average wages paid
are $3.00 per week, and that two weeks' vacation is given with loss of
wages. Both of these are probably underestimates, as will be seen farther
on. If the wages paid launderers and laundresses are included, and also

DOMESTIC SERVICE

estimate an equal amount,[1] and through whose hands
passes so large a part of the finished products of other
forms of labor.[2]

It is not difficult, however, to find reasons, in addition
to the specific ones suggested, for this somewhat cavalier
treatment of domestic service. The nature of the service
rendered, as well as the relation between employer and
employee, is largely personal; it is believed therefore that
all questions involved in the subject can be considered
and settled from the personal point of view. It follows
from this fact that it is extremely difficult to ascertain
the actual condition of the service outside of a single
family, or, at best, a locality very narrow in extent, and
therefore that it is almost impossible to treat the subject
in a comprehensive manner. It follows as a result of the

the fees paid for hotel and restaurant service, $300,000,000 seems a fair
estimate for the annual cash wages paid for domestic service.

[1] This estimate supposes the actual cost of board for each employee to
be $3.00 per week, which is probably less than would be paid by each
employee for table-board of the quality furnished by the employer. It
excludes the cost of house-rent furnished, and also fuel and light, all
of which are factors to be considered in computing the cost of service
received.

[2] It is difficult to estimate the value of the materials of which domestic
employees have the almost exclusive control. If the number of domestic
servants and launderers and laundresses in private families, hotels, and
restaurants is placed at 1,700,000, the number of employees in each family
as two, and the number of persons in each family, including servants, as
seven, it will be seen that at a rough estimate the food and laundried
articles of clothing of six million persons pass through the hands of this
class of employees. It was formerly a common saying, "a servant eats
her wages, breaks her wages, and wastes her wages." If this verdict of
experience is taken as approximately true rather than as scientifically
exact, it will be seen that the actual expense involved in domestic
service is probably double that included under the items of wages and
support.

two previous reasons that domestic service has never been considered a part of the great labor question, and that it has not been supposed to be affected by the political, social, and industrial development of the past century as other occupations have been.

These various explanations of the failure to consider domestic service in connection with other forms of labor are in reality but different phases of a fundamental reason — the isolation that has always attended household service and household employments. From the fact that other occupations are largely the result of association and combination they court investigation and the fullest and freest discussion of their underlying principles and their influence on each other. Household service, since it is based on the principle of isolation, is regarded as an affair of the individual with which the public at large has no concern. Other forms of industry are anxious to call to their assistance all the legislative, administrative, and judicial powers of the nation, all the forces that religion, philanthropy, society itself can exert in their behalf. The great majority of housekeepers, if the correspondent of a leading journal is to be trusted, "do not require outside assistance in the management of their affairs, and consequently resent any interference in the administration of their duties."

The question must arise, however, in view of the interdependence of all other forms of industry, whether it is possible to maintain this perfect separation with regard to any one employment, whether household employments are justified in resenting any intrusion into their domain, whether the individual employer is right in considering household service exclusively a personal affair. An answer to the question may be of help in deciding whether the difficulties that are found in the present system of domestic service arise in every case necessarily from the personal relations which exist between employer and employee, or are largely due to economic conditions over which the individual employer has no control. Still further, the conclusions reached must determine somewhat the nature of the forces to be set in motion to lessen these difficulties.

CHAPTER II

IT is impossible to understand the condition of domestic service as it exists to-day without a cursory glance at the changes in household employments resulting from the inventions of the latter part of the eighteenth century. These changes, unlike many others, came apparently without warning. At the middle of the last century steam was a plaything, electricity a curiosity of the laboratory, and wind and water the only known motive powers. From time immemorial the human hand unaided, except by the simplest machinery, had clothed the world. Iron could be smelted only with wood, and the English parliament had seriously discussed the suppression of the iron trade as the only means of preserving the forests. But during the last third of the century the brilliant inventions of Hargreaves, Arkwright, Crompton, and Cartwright had made possible the revolutionizing of all forms of cotton and woollen industries; Watt had given a new motive power to the world; the uses of coal had been multiplied, and soon after its mining rendered safe; while a thousand supplementary inventions had followed quickly in the train of these. A new era of inventive genius had dawned, which was to rival in importance that of the fifteenth century.

7

The immediate result of these inventions was seen in the rapid transference of all the processes of cotton and woollen manufactures from the home of the individual weaver and spinner to large industrial centres, the centralization of important interests in the hands of a few, and a division of labor that multiplied indefinitely the results previously accomplished.

But the factory system of manufactures that superseded the domestic system of previous generations has not been the product of inventions alone. It has been pointed out by Mr. Carroll D. Wright[1] that while these inventions have been the material forces through which the change was accomplished, other agencies co-operated with them. These co-operating influences have been physical, as illustrated in the discoveries of Watt; philosophical, as seen in the works of Adam Smith; commercial, or the industrial supremacy of England considered as a result of the loss of the American colonies; and philanthropical, or those connected with the work of the Wesleys, John Howard, Hannah More, and Wilberforce. All these acting in conjunction with the material force —invention— have operated on manufacturing industries to produce the factory system of to-day. It is, indeed, because the factory system is the resultant of so many forces working in the past that it touches in the present nearly every great economic, social, political, moral, and philanthropic question.

Although comparatively few of these inventions have been intended primarily to lessen household labor, this era of inventive activity has not been without its effects

[1] *The Factory System*, Tenth Census, II., 533-537.

on household employments. A hundred years ago the household occupations carried on in the average family included, in addition to whatever is now ordinarily done, every form of spinning and weaving cotton, wool and flax, carpet weaving and making, upholstering, knitting, tailoring, the making of boots, shoes, hats, gloves, collars, cuffs, men's underclothing, quilts, comfortables, mattresses, and pillows; also, the making of soap, starch, candles, yeast, perfumes, medicines, liniments, crackers, cheese, coffee-browning, the drying of fruits and vegetables, and salting and pickling meat. Every article in this list, which might be lengthened, can now be made or prepared for use out of the house of the consumer, not only better but more cheaply by the concentration of capital and labor in large industrial enterprises. Moreover, as a result of other forms of inventive genius, the so-called modern improvements have taken out of the ordinary household many forms of hard and disagreeable labor. The use of kerosene, gas, natural gas, and electricity [1] for all purposes of lighting, and to a certain extent for heating and cooking; the adoption of steam-cleaning for furniture and wearing apparel; the invention of the sewing-machine and other labor-saving contrivances; the improvement of city and village water-works, plumbing, heat-supplying companies, city and village sanitation measures, including the collection of ashes and garbage, — these are all the results of modern business enterprise.

These facts are familiar, but the effects more easily

[1] A. E. Kennelly, "Electricity in the Household," *Scribner's Magazine*, January, 1890 ; E. M. H. Merrill, "Electricity in the Kitchen," *American Kitchen Magazine*, November, 1895.

escape notice. The change from individual to collective enterprises, from the domestic to the factory system, has released a vast amount of labor formérly done within the house by women with three results : either this labor has been diverted to other places, or into other channels, or has become idle. The tendency at first was for labor thus released to be diverted to other places. The home spinners and weavers became the spinners and weavers in factories, and later the home workers in other lines became the operatives in other large establishments. As machinery became more simple, women were employed in larger numbers, until now, in several places and in several occupations, their numbers exceed those of men employees.[1] This fact has materially changed the condition of affairs within the household. Under the domestic system of manufactures nearly all women spent part of their time in their own homes in spinning, weaving, and the making of various articles of food and clothing in connection with

[1] In Massachusetts, in 1885, the number of women employed in manufacturing industries exceeded the number of men in eight towns. These were Dalton, Dudley, Easthampton, Hingham, Ipswich, Lowell, Tisbury, and Upton. *Census of Massachusetts*, II., 176–187.

A weaver in Lawrence, Massachusetts, reported in 1882 : "One of the evils existing in this city is the gradual extinction of the male operative." *Fall River, Lowell, and Lawrence*, p. 10. Reprinted from *Thirteenth Annual Report of the Massachusetts Bureau of Statistics of Labor*, p. 202.

In Massachusetts, in 1875, women predominated in fifteen occupations, eleven of them manufacturing industries. In 1885 there were also fifteen occupations in which women exceeded men in numbers, twelve of them manufacturing. These were manufacturers of buttons and dress-trimmings, carpetings, clothing, cotton goods, fancy articles, hair work, hosiery and knit goods, linen, mixed textiles, silk and silk goods, straw and palm-leaf goods, and worsted goods. *Report of the Bureau of Statistics of Labor*, 1889, pp. 556–557.

their more active household duties. When women came
to be employed in factories, the division of labor made
necessary a readjustment of work so that housekeeping
duties were performed by one person giving all her time
to them instead of by several persons each giving a part
of her time. The tendency of this was at first naturally
to decrease the number of women partially employed in
household duties, and to increase the demand for women
giving all their time to domestic work.

This readjustment of work in the home and in the factory brought also certain other changes that have an important bearing. The first employees were the daughters
of farmers, tradesmen, teachers, and professional men of
limited means, women of sturdy, energetic New England
character. They were women who, in their own homes,
had been the spinners and the weavers for the family and
who had sometimes eked out a slender income by doing
the same work in their homes.for others disqualified for
it. As machinery was simplified, and new occupations
more complex in character were opened to women, their
places were taken in factories by Irish immigrants as these
in turn have been displaced by the French Canadians.
All these changes in the personnel of factory operatives
have meant that while much labor has been taken out of
the household, that which remained has been performed
by fewer hands, and also that women of foreign nationalities have been pressed into household service.

Another and later result of the change from the domestic to the factory system was the diversion of much of the
labor at first performed within the household into entirely
different channels. The anti-slavery agitation beginning

about 1830 enlisted the energies of many women, and the
discussions growing out of it were undoubtedly the occasion for the opening of entirely new occupations to them.
Oberlin College was founded in 1833 and Mount Holyoke
Seminary in 1837, thus forming the entering wedge for
the entrance of women into higher educational work.
Medical schools for women were organized and professional life made possible, while business interests began to
attract the attention of many.

Another part of the labor released by mechanical inventions and labor-saving contrivances became in time idle
labor.   By idle labor is meant not only absolute idleness,
but labor which is unproductive and adds neither to the
comfort nor to the intelligence of society.   Work that had
previously been performed within the home without money
remuneration came to be considered unworthy of the same
women when performed for persons outside their own household and for a fixed compensation.   The era of so-called
fancy-work, which includes all forms of work in hair, wax,
leather, beads, rice, feathers, cardboard, and canvas, so
offensive to the artistic sense of to-day, was one product
of this labor released from necessary productive processes.
It was a necessary result because some outlet was needed
for the energies of women, society as yet demanded that
this outlet should be within the household, and the mechanical instincts were strong while the artistic sense had not
been developed.   It is an era not to be looked upon with
derision, but as an interesting phase in the history of the
evolution of woman's occupation.[1]

[1] George Eliot in *Felix Holt* speaks of Mrs. Transome as engaged in
"a little daily embroidery — that soothing occupation of taking stitches

Still another channel for this idle labor was found in what has been called "intellectual fancy-work." Literary clubs and classes sprang up and multiplied, affording occupation to their members, but producing nothing and giving at first only the semblance of education and culture. Many of them became in time a stimulus for more thorough systematic work, but in their origin they were often but a manifestation of aimless activity, of labor released from productive channels.

The era of inventions and resulting business activity has therefore changed materially the condition of affairs within the household. Before this time all women shared in preparing and cooking food; they spun, wove, and made the clothing, and were domestic manufacturers in the sense that they changed the raw material into forms suitable for consumption. But modern inventions and the resulting change in the system of manufactures, as has been seen, necessarily affected household employments. The change has been the same in kind, though not in degree, as has come in the occupations of men. In the last analysis every man is a tiller of the soil, but division of labor has left only a small proportion of men in this employment. So in the last analysis every woman is a housekeeper who "does her own work," but division of labor has come into the household as well as into the field, though in a more imperfect form. It has left many women in the upper and middle classes unemployed, while many in the lower classes are too heavily burdened; in three of the four great industries which absorb

to produce what neither she nor any one else wanted was then the resource of many a well-born and unhappy woman."

the energies of the majority of women working for remuneration—manufacturing, work in shops, and teaching—
the supply of workers is greater than the demand, while
in the fourth—domestic service—the reverse is the case.
But it cannot be assumed that all of those in the first
three classes have necessarily been taken from the fourth
class. It has been well said that "through the introduction of machinery, ignorant labor is utilized, not
created." Many who under the old order would have
been able to live only under the most primitive conditions, and whose labor can be used under the new order
only in the simplest forms of manufacturing, would be
entirely unfit to have the care of an ordinary household
in its present complex form.

One more effect must be noted of this transference of
many forms of household labor to large centres through
the operation of inventive genius. It has been seen that
many women have thus been left comparatively free from
the necessity of labor. The pernicious theory has therefore grown up that women who are rich or well-to-do
ought not to work, at least for compensation, since by
so doing they crowd out of remunerative employment
others who need it. It is a theory that overlooks the
historical fact that every person should be in the last
analysis a producer, it is based wholly on the assumption
that work is a curse and not a blessing, and it does not
take into consideration the fact that every woman who
works without remuneration, or for less than the market
rates, thereby lowers the wages of every person who is a
bread-winner. It is a theory which if applied to men
engaged in business occupations would check all indus-

trial progress. It is equally a hindrance when applied to women.

This revolutionizing of manufacturing processes through the substitution of the factory for the domestic system has thus rendered necessary a shifting of all forms of household labor. The division of labor here is but partially accomplished, and out of this fact arises a part of the friction that is found in household service.

Household employers and employees may be indifferent to the changes that the industrial revolutions of a century have brought, they may be ignorant of them all, but they have not been unaffected by them, nor can they remain unaffected by changes that may subsequently come in the industrial system. The interdependence of all forms of industry is so complete, that a change cannot revolutionize one without in time revolutionizing all. The old industrial régime cannot be restored, nor can household employments of to-day be put back to their condition of a hundred years ago.

CHAPTER III

DOMESTIC SERVICE DURING THE COLONIAL PERIOD

IT has been seen how great a change the inventions of the past century have made in the character of household employments. A change in the nature of household service no less important has taken place by virtue of the political revolutions of the century, acting in connection with certain economic and social forces. The subject of domestic service looms up so prominently in the foreground to-day that there is danger of forgetting that it has a past as well as a present. Yet it is impossible to understand its present condition without comprehending, in a measure, the manner in which it has been affected by its own history. It is equally impossible to forecast its future without due regard to this history.

Domestic service in America has passed through three distinct phases. The first extends from the early colonization to the time of the Revolution; the second, from the Revolution to about 1850; the third, from 1850 to the present time.

During the colonial period service of every kind was performed by transported convicts, indented white servants or "redemptioners," "free willers," negroes, and Indians.[1]

[1] Eddis, p. 63.

The first three classes — convicts, redemptioners, and free willers — were of European, at first generally of English, birth. The colonization of the new world gave opportunity for the transportation and subsequent employment in the colonies of large numbers of persons who, as a rule, belonged to a low class in the social scale.[1] The mother country looked with satisfaction on this method of disposing of those " such, as had there been no *English* foreign Plantation in the World, could probably never have lived at home to do service for their Country, but must have come to be hanged, or starved, or dyed untimely of some of those miserable Diseases, that proceed from want, and vice."[2] She regarded her "plantations abroad as a good effect proceeding from many evil causes," and congratulated herself on being freed from " such sort of people, as their crimes and debaucheries would quickly destroy at home, or whom their wants would confine in prisons or force to beg, and so render them useless, and consequently a burthen to the public."[3]

From the very first the advantage to England of this method of disposing of her undesirable population had been urged. The author of *Nova Britannia* wrote in 1609 : " You see it no new thing, but most profitable for our State, to rid our multitudes of such as lie at home,

[1] DeFoe, *Moll Flanders, Colonel Jack ;* Mrs. Alpha Behn, *The Widow Ranter.*

[2] Sir Joshua Child, pp. 183-184.

[3] Charles Davenant, II., 3. Velasco, the minister of Spain to England, writes to Philip III. from London, March 22, 1611 : " Their principal reason for colonizing these parts is to give an outlet to so many idle and wretched people as they have in England, and thus to prevent the dangers that might be feared from them." Brown, p. 456.

pestering the land with pestilence and penury, and infecting one another with vice and villanie, worse than the plague it selfe."[1] So admirable did the plan seem in time that between the years 1661 and 1668 various proposals were made to the King and Council to constitute an office for transporting to the Plantations all vagrants, rogues, and idle persons that could give no account of themselves, felons who had the benefit of clergy, and such as were convicted of petty larceny — such persons to be transported to the nearest seaport and to serve four years if over twenty years of age, and seven years if under twenty.[2] Virginia and Maryland[3] were the colonies to which the majority of these servants were sent, though they were not unknown elsewhere.[4]

Protests were often made against this method of settlement, both by the colonists themselves[5] and by Englishmen,[6] but it was long before the English government

[1] Force, *Tracts*, I., 19.

[2] *Calendar of State Papers, Colonial Series*, 1661-1668. Abstracts 101, 772, 791, 858. An admirable discussion of "British Convicts Shipped to American Colonies," by James D. Butler, is found in *The American Historical Review*, October, 1896.

[3] Eddis says, p. 66, that Maryland was the only colony where convicts were freely imported ; but Virginia seems to have shared equally in the importation.

[4] In Pennsylvania and Virginia transported criminals were so numerous that laws were passed to prevent their importation.

[5] William Smith, *History of the Province of New York from its Discovery to the Appointment of Governor Colden in 1762*, pp. 207-210. John Watson, pp. 485-486, quotes from contemporaneous writers in opposition to the practice in Pennsylvania, *circa* 1750 ; Hening, II., 509-511.

[6] " It is a shameful and unblessed thing to take the scum of people and wicked, condemned men, to be the people with whom you plant ; and not only so, but it spoileth the plantation ; for they ever live like rogues, and not fall to work ; but be lazy, and do mischief, and spend

abandoned the practice of transporting criminals to the American colonies.[1]

Of the three classes of white, or Christian servants, as they were called to distinguish them from Indians and negroes, the free willers were evidently found only in Maryland. This class was considered even more unfortunate than that of the indented servants or convicts. They were received under the condition that they be allowed a certain number of days in which to dispose of themselves to the greatest advantage. But since servants could be procured for a trifling consideration on absolute terms, there was no disposition to take a class of servants who wished to make their own terms. If they did not succeed in making terms within a certain number of days, they were sold to pay for their passage.[2] The colonists saw very little difference between the transported criminals and political prisoners, the free willers, and the redemptioners who sold themselves into slavery, and as between the two classes — redemptioners and convicted felons — they at first considered the felons the more profitable as their term of service was for seven years, while that of the indented servants was for five years only.[3]

victuals, and be quickly weary, and then certify over to their country to the discredit of the plantation." Bacon, *Essays, Of Plantations.*

[1] Bruce, I., 606, says that the order of the General Court of Virginia prohibiting the introduction of English criminals after January 20, 1671 (Hening, II., 509–511), was confirmed by a royal order announcing that the importation of Newgate criminals was to cease, and that this rule was to apply to all the Colonies. But the frequent protests against the practice found in other Colonies at a much later date would seem to show that it could not have been generally observed.

[2] Eddis, pp. 71–75.   [3] *Ibid.*, pp. 69–71.

It is impossible to state the proportion of servants belonging to the two classes of transported convicts and redemptioners, but the statement is apparently fair that the redemptioners who sold themselves into service to pay for the cost of their passage constituted by far the larger proportion. These were found in all the colonies, though more numerous in the Southern and Middle colonies than in New England. In Virginia and Maryland they outnumbered negro slaves until the latter part of the seventeenth century.[1] In Massachusetts, apprenticed servants bound for a term of years were sold from ships in Boston as late as 1730,[2] while the general trade in bound white servants lasted until the time of the Revolution,[3] and in Pennsylvania even until this century.[4]

The first redemptioners were naturally of English birth, but after a time they were supplanted by those of other nationalities, particularly by the Germans and Irish. As early as 1718 there was a complaint of the Irish immigrants in Massachusetts.[5] In Connecticut "a parcel of Irish servants, both men and women," just imported from Dublin, was advertised to be sold cheap in 1764.[6] In

---

[1] Berkeley's Report, Hening, II., 515. Brantly, in Winsor, III., 545.

[2] "In the year 1730 . . . Colonel Josiah Willard was invited to view some transports who had just landed from Ireland. My uncle spied a boy of some vivacity, of about ten years of age, and who was the only one in the crew who spoke English. He bargained for him." — "Mrs. Johnson's Captivity" in *Indian Narratives*, p. 130.

[3] Hildreth, III., 395.

[4] Samuel Breck writes under date of August 1, 1817, "I went on board the ship John from Amsterdam, . . . and I purchased one German Swiss for Mrs. Ross and two French Swiss for myself." *Recollections*, pp. 296–297.

[5] *Winthrop Papers*, Pt. VI., p. 387, note.

[6] Barber, *Connecticut Collections*, p. 166.

1783 large numbers of Irish and German redemptioners entered Maryland, and a society was formed to assist the Germans who could not speak English.[1]

It has been said that a great majority of the redemptioners belonged at first to a low class in the social scale. A considerable number, however, both men and women, belonged to the respectable, even to the so-called upper classes of society.[2] They were sent over to prevent disadvantageous marriages,[3] to secure inheritances to other members of a family,[4] or to further some criminal scheme.

[1] Scharf, p. 209.

[2] Some improvement was soon seen in Virginia. "There haue beene sent thither this last yeare, and are now presently in going, twelue hundred persons and vpward, and there are neere one thousand more remaining of those that were gone before. The men lately sent, haue beene most of them choise men, borne and bred vp to labour and industry." *Declaration of the State of the Colonie and Affairs in Virginia, 1620.* Force, III., 5. Hammond in *Leah and Rachel*, p. 7, also speaks of the improvement.

[3] A well-known case was that of Thomas, son of Sir Edward Verney, who at the age of nineteen wished to marry some one of lower rank than himself. He was sent to Virginia to prevent the marriage, not, however, as himself a servant. *Verney Papers, Camden Society Publications*, vol. 56, pp. 160–162.

A niece of Daniel DeFoe is said to have been sent to America as a redemptioner for the same reason.

The Sot-Weed Factor says of a maid in a Maryland inn,

> "Kidnap'd and Fool'd, I hither fled,
> To shun a hated Nuptial* Bed,
> And to my cost already find,
> Worse Plagues than those I left behind.

>   * These are the general Excuses made by *English* Women, which are sold or sell themselves to *Mary-land*." p. 7.

[4] James Annesley when twelve years old was transported to Pennsylvania. His father died soon after, and his uncle succeeded to the peerage. The boy was sold to a planter in Newcastle County, but his title to the peerage was subsequently proved. Anglesea Peerage Trial, Howell, *State Trials*, XVII., 1443–1454.

Many of these bond servants sold themselves into servitude, others were disposed of through emigration brokers,[1] and still others were kidnapped, being enticed on shipboard by persons called "spirits."[2]

The form of indenture was simple, and varied but little in the different colonies. Stripped of its cumbersome legal phraseology, it included the three main points of time of service, the nature of the service to be performed, although this was usually specified to be "in any such service as his employer shall employ him," and the compensation to be given.[3]

It sometimes happened that servants came without

[1] Neill, *Virginia Carolorum*, p. 108 ; *The Verney Papers, Camden Society Publications*, vol. 56, pp. 160–162, give a long and detailed account of the method of obtaining and transporting servants.

[2] Neill, *Terra Mariae*, pp. 201, 202,
          " In better Times, e're to this Land,
          I was unhappily Trapann'd."
                              Sot - Weed Factor, p. 6.
A young woman in search of employment was told that by going on board ship she would find it in Virginia, a few miles below on the Thames.   Another young woman was persuaded to enter the ship, and was then sold into service.   Cited by Bruce, I., 614, from *Interregnum Entry Book*, vol. 106, p. 84, and *British State Papers, Colonial*, vol. XIII., No. 29, 1.
The evil of "spiriting away" both children and adults became so great that in 1664 the Committee for Foreign Plantations interposed, and the Council created the office of Register, charged with the duty of keeping a record of all persons going to America as servants, and the statement that they had voluntarily left England.   This act was soon followed by another fixing the penalty of death, without benefit of clergy, in every case where persons were found guilty of kidnapping children or adults.   But even these extreme measures did not put an end to the evil ; and it is stated that ten thousand persons were annually kidnapped after the passage of the act.   Bruce, I., 614–619.

[3] " The Forme of Binding a Servant " is given in *A Relation of Maryland*, pp. 62–63, and reads as follows :

indenture. In such cases the law expressly and definitely fixed their status, though it was found extremely difficult to decide upon a status that could be permanent. Virginia, in particular, for a long time found it impossible to pass a law free from objections, and its experience will illustrate the difficulties encountered elsewhere. An early law in Virginia provided that if a servant came without indenture, he or she was to serve four years if more than twenty years old, five years if between twelve and twenty years of age, and seven years if under twelve.[1] Subsequently it was provided that all Irish servants without indenture should serve six years

> " This Indenture *made the   day of   in the yeere of our Soveraigne Lord King* Charles, *&c. betweene   of the one party, and   on the other party,* Witnesseth, *that the said   doth hereby covenant promise, and grant to, and with the said   his Executors and Assignes, to serve him from the day of the date hereof, untill his first and next arrivall in* Maryland ; *and after for and during the tearme of yeeres, in such service and imployment as the said   or his assignes shall there imploy him, according to the custome of the countrey in the like kind. In consideration whereof, the said   doth promise and grant, to and with the said   to pay for his passing, and to find him with Meat, Drinke, Apparell and Lodging, with other necessaries during the said terme; and at the end of the said terme, to give him one whole yeeres provision of Corne, and fifty acres of Land, according to the order of the countrey. In witnesse whereof, the said   hath hereunto put his hand and seale, the day and yeere above written.*
>   *Sealed and delivered* ⎱
>   *in the presence of* ⎰

Neill, *Virginia Carolorum*, pp. 5–7, gives a similar copy. Bruce, II., 2, gives the indenture of one Mary Polly whose master was to " maintain ye s[d] Mary noe other ways than he doth his own in all things as dyett, cloathing and lodging, the s[d] Mary to obey the s[d] John Porter in all his lawful commands within ye s[d] term of years."

[1] Hening, I., 257, 1642.

if over sixteen and that all under sixteen should serve until the age of twenty-four,[1] and this was again modified into a provision requiring those above sixteen years to serve four years and those under fifteen to serve until twenty-one, the Court to be the judge of their ages.[2] It was soon found, however, that the term of six years " carried with it both rigour and inconvenience " and that thus many were discouraged from coming to the country, and " the peopling of the country retarded." It was therefore enacted that in the future no servant of any Christian nation coming without indenture should serve longer than those of the same age born in the country.[3] But as the law was also made retroactive, it was soon ordained that all aliens without indenture could serve five years if above sixteen years of age and all under that until they were twenty-four years old, " that being the time lymitted by the laws of England."[4] This arrangement was equally unsatisfactory, since it was found that under it " a servant if adjudged never soe little under sixteene yeares pays for that small tyme three yeares service, and if he be adjudged more the master looseth the like." It was then resolved that if the person were adjudged nineteen years or over he or she should serve five years, and if under that age then as many years as he should lack of being twenty-four.[5] This provision was apparently satisfactory, subsequent laws varying only in minor provisions concerning the details of the Act.[6]

[1] Hening, I., 411, 1655.
[2] *Ibid.*, I., 441–442, 1657.
[3] *Ibid.*, I., 538–539, 1659.
[6] *Ibid.*, 1705, 1748, 1753.
[4] *Ibid.*, II., 113–114, 1661.
[5] *Ibid.*, II., 240, 1666.

In North Carolina no "imported Christian" was to be considered a

The condition of the redemptioners seems to have been, for the most part, an unenviable one. George Alsop, it is true, writes in glowing terms of the advantages enjoyed in Maryland:

" For know," he says, " That the Servants here in *Mary-land* of all Colonies, distant or remote Plantations, have the least cause to complain, either for strictness of Servitude, want of Provisions, or need of Apparel: Five dayes and a half in the Summer weeks is the alotted time that they work in; and for two months when the Sun predominates in the highest pitch of his heat, they claim an antient and customary Priviledge, to repose themselves three hours in the day within the house, and this is undeniably granted to them that work in the Fields.

In the Winter time, which lasteth three months (viz.), *December*, *January*, and *February*, they do little or no work or employment, save cutting of wood to make good fires to sit by, unless their Ingenuity will prompt them to hunt the Deer, or Bear, or recreate themselves in Fowling, to slaughter the Swans, Geese, and Turkeys (which this Country affords in a most plentiful manner): For every Servant has a Gun, Powder and Shot allowed him, to sport him withall on all Holidayes and leasurable times, if he be capable of using it, or be willing to learn." [1]

Hammond also says of Virginia:

" The Women are not (as is reported) put into the ground to worke, but occupie such domestique employments and houswifery as in *England*, that is dressing victuals, righting up the house, milking,

servant unless the person importing him could procure an indenture. Iredell, 1741, chap. 24.

In West New Jersey servants over twenty-one without indenture were to serve four years, and all under twenty-one to serve at the discretion of the Court. Leaming and Spicer, 1682, chap. XI.

In Maryland servants without indenture of over twenty-one years of age were to serve five years; if between eighteen and twenty-two, six years; if between fifteen and eighteen, seven years; if under fifteen, until twenty-two years old. Browne, 1692.

[1] Alsop, pp. 57–58.

imployed about dayries, washing, sowing, &c. and both men and women have times of recreations, as much or more than in any part of the world besides. . . . And whereas it is rumoured that Servants have no lodging other then on boards, or by the Fire side, it is contrary to reason to believe it: First, as we are Christians; next as people living under a law, which compels as well the Master as the Servant to perform his duty; nor can true labour be either expected or exacted without sufficient cloathing, diet, and lodging; all which both their Indentures (which must inviolably be observed) and the Justice of the Country requires." [1]

A Glasgow merchant under date of January 19, 1714, also writes: " The servants are all well cloathed and provided with bedding as ye will see," adding that some servants prefer " Mariland, the reason whereof is that Virginia is a little odious to the people here." [2]

But these enthusiastic descriptions must be taken *cum grano salis*. The object of Alsop's book was to stimulate emigration to Maryland, as is evident from the dedication to Lord Baltimore and to " all the Merchant Adventures for Mary-land." The object of *Leah and Rachel* was the same, and others who wrote in a similar strain had evidently little personal knowledge of the condition of the redemptioners. The real life is more truly portrayed in the accounts given by the redemptioners themselves, and many of these are preserved.

The Anglesea Peerage Trial brings out the facts that the redemptioners fared ill, worked hard, lived on a coarse diet, and drank only water sweetened with a little molasses and flavored with ginger.[3] Eddis says the redemptioners were treated worse than the negroes, since the loss of a negro fell on his master; inflexible severity

---

[1] *Leah and Rachel*, pp. 12,14.   [2] Neill, *Terra Mariae*, pp. 201–202.
[3] Howell, *State Trials*, XVII., 1443–1454.

was exercised over the European servants who "groaned beneath a worse than Egyptian bondage."[1]

Richard Frethorne, writing from Martin's Hundred, gives a pitiful tale of the sufferings of the indented servants. "Oh! that you did see my daily and hourly sighs, groans, tears and thumps that I afford my own breast, and rue and curse the time of my birth with holy Job. I thought no head had been able to hold so much water as hath, and doth daily flow from mine eyes."[2]

The maid who waited on the Sot-Weed Factor says:

> "In better Times, e're to this Land,
> I was unhappily Trapann'd;
> Perchance as well I did appear,
> As any Lord or Lady here,
> Not then a slave for twice two Year.
> My Cloaths were fashionably new,
> Nor were my Shifts of Linnen Blue;
> But things are changed, now at the Hoe,
> I daily work, and Bare-foot go,
> In weeding Corn or feeding Swine,
> I spend my melancholy Time."[3]

Undoubtedly, in time, servants of all kinds received more consideration than had at first been given them;[4]

[1] Eddis, pp. 69–70.

[2] Neill, *Virginia Carolorum*, p. 58. Neill adds: "While some of these servants were treated with kindness, others received no more consideration than dumb, driven cattle."

[3] P. 7.

[4] A negro servant in the family of Judge Sewall died in 1729, and the latter writing of the funeral says: "I made a good Fire, set Chairs, and gave Sack." *Diary*, III., 394. *The New England Weekly Journal*, February 24, 1729, has a detailed account of the funeral: "A long train followed him to the grave, it's said about 150 black, and about 50 whites, several magistrates, ministers, gentlemen, etc. His funeral was attended with uncommon respect and his death much lamented."

in 1704 Madame Knight even complained of what she considered too great indulgence on the part of the Connecticut farmers towards their slaves.[1] Yet, even at the North, the lot of a servant was not an enviable one, though much was done by the laws of all the colonies to mitigate the condition of the redemptioners, as will be seen later in discussing the legal relations of masters and servants.

The wages paid were, as a rule, small, though some complaints are found, especially in New England, of high wages and poor service.[2] More often the wages were a mere pittance. Elizabeth Evans came from Ireland to serve John Wheelwright for three years. Her wages were to be three pounds a year and passage paid.[3]

[1] She complains of the great familiarity in permitting the slaves to sit at table with their masters " as they say to save time " and adds, " into the dish goes the black hoof, as freely as the white hand." She relates a difficulty between a master and a slave which was referred to arbitration, each party binding himself to accept the decision. The arbitrators ordered the master to pay 40 shillings to the slave and to acknowledge his fault. " And so the matter ended : the poor master very honestly standing to the award." — *The Journal of Madame Knight.*

[2] John Winter writes from Maine, " I Can not Conceaue which way their masters Can pay yt, but yf yt Continue this rates the servants will be masters & the masters servants." *Trelawny Papers,* p. 164. John Winthrop makes a similar comment in narrating " a passage between one Rowley and his servant. The master, being forced to sell a pair of oxen to pay his servant his wages, told his servant he could keep him no longer, not knowing how to pay him the next year. The servant answered, he would serve him for more of his cattle. But how shall I do (saith the master) when all my cattle are gone ? The servant replied, you shall then serve me, and so you may have your cattle again." Winthrop gives as a reason for high wages the fact that "the wars in England kept servants from coming to us, so as those we had could not be hired, when their times were out, but upon unreasonable terms, and we found it very difficult to pay their wages to their content, (for money was very scarce)." — *History of New England,* II., 219-220.

[3] Lechford, *Note-book,* p. 107.

Margery Batman, after five years of service in Charles-town, was to receive a she-goat to help her in starting life.[1] Mary Polly, according to the terms of her indent-ure, was to serve ten years and then receive "three barrells of corn and one suit of penistone and one suit of good serge with one black hood, two shifts of dowlas and shoes and hose convenient."[2]

Peter Kalm writes of Pennsylvania in 1748: "A servant maid gets eight or ten pounds a year: these servants have their food besides their wages, but must buy their own clothes, and what they get of these they must thank their master's goodness for." He adds that it was cheaper to buy indented servants since "this kind of servants may be got for half the money, and even for less; for they commonly pay fourteen pounds *Pennsylvania* currency, for a person who is to serve four years."[3] Even at the beginning of the present century wages had scarcely risen. Samuel Breck writes of two redemptioners whom he purchased in 1817: "I gave for the woman seventy-six dollars, which is her passage-money, with a promise of twenty dollars at the end of three years if she serves me faithfully; clothing and main-tenance of course. The boy had paid twenty-six guilders toward his passage-money, which I agreed to give him at the end of three years; in addition to which I paid fifty-three dollars and sixty cents for his passage, and for two years he is to have six weeks' schooling each year."[4]

[1] Lechford, *Note-book*, p. 81. [2] Bruce, II., 2. [3] *Travels*, I., 303–304.
[4] *Recollections*, p. 297.
"Before the Revolution no hired man or woman wore any shoes so fine as calf-skins; course neats leather was their every day wear. Men and women then hired by the year, — men got 16 to 20*l*., and a servant

For the protection of both masters and servants the law sometimes interfered and attempted to regulate the matter of wages received at the end of an indenture. In Virginia by the code of 1705 every woman servant was to receive fifteen bushels of Indian corn and forty shillings in money, or the value thereof in goods.[1] In 1748 it was enacted "that every servant, male or female, not having wages, shall, at the expiration of his, or her time of service, have and receive three pounds ten shillings current money, for freedom dues, to be paid by his, or her master, or owner,"[2] and in 1758 the same law was re-enacted, but excepting convicts from the provisions of the Act.[3] In South Carolina all women servants at the expiration of their time were to have "a Wastcoat and Petticoat of new Half-thick or Pennistone, a new Shift of white Linnen, a new Pair of shoes and stockings, a blue apron and two caps of white Linnen."[4] The laws of Pennsylvania provided that every servant who served faithfully four years should at the expiration of the term of servitude have a discharge and be duly clothed with two complete suits of apparel, one of which should be new,[5] while in Massachusetts and New York it was provided that all servants who had served diligently and faithfully to the benefit of their masters should not be sent away empty.[6] In North Carolina every servant

woman 8 to 10*l*. Out of that it was their custom to lay up money, to buy before their marriage a bed and bedding, silver teaspoons, and a spinning-wheel, &c." — Watson, *Annals*, p. 165.

[1] Hening, III., 451.
[2] *Ibid.*, V., 550.
[3] *Ibid.*, VI., 359.
[4] Trott, 1736.
[5] Purdon, Act of 1700 ; Carey and Bioren.
[6] *Body of Liberties*, chap. 88, Laws of 1672 ; *Laws of the Duke of York.*

not having yearly wages was to be allowed at the expiration of the term of service three pounds Proclama-
tion money, besides one sufficient suit of wearing clothes.[1]
In East New Jersey the law was more liberal and gave
every servant two suits of apparel suitable for a servant,
one good felling axe, a good hoe, and seven bushels of
good Indian corn.[2] West New Jersey gave ten bushels
of corn, necessary apparel, two horses, and one axe.[3] In
Maryland a woman at the expiration of her term was to
have the same provision of corn and clothes as men servants, namely, "a good Cloath suite either of Kersey or
broad Cloath, a shift of white Linnen to be new, one
new pair of shoes and stockings, two hoes one Ax and
three barr[lls] of Indian corn."[4] A later act specified that
women servants were to have "a Waist-coat and Petty-
coat of new Half-thick, or Pennistone, a new Shift of
White Linen, Shoes and Stockings, a blue Apron, Two
Caps of White Linen, and Three Barrells of Indian
Corn."[5]

The test question to be applied to any system of service is — Is the service secured through it satisfactory?
It has been seen that a considerable number of servants
could be secured through the system of indenture, though
probably less than the colonists desired, and that the
wages paid them were, as a rule, remarkably low. But
it must be said that the service received from indented
servants was, as a rule, what might be expected from
the class that came to America in that capacity.

[1] Iredell, Acts of 1741, chap. XXIV.
[2] Leaming and Spicer, Acts of 1682, chap. VIII.
[3] *Ibid.*, chap. X.   [4] Browne, 1692.   [5] Bacon, 1715.

It is easy to surmise the character of the service rendered at first in Virginia and the difficulties encountered by employers. Many of the redemptioners had been idlers and vagabonds, and for idlers and vagabonds, there as elsewhere, stringent laws were necessary. In 1610, under the administration of Sir Thomas Gates, various orders were passed with reference to pilfering on the part of launderers, laundresses, bakers, cooks, and dressers of fish.

"What man or woman soeuer, Laundrer or Laundresse appointed to wash the foule linnen of any one labourer or souldier, or any one else as it is their duties so to doe, performing little, or no other seruice for their allowance out of the store, and daily prouisions, and supply of other necessaries, vnto the Colonie, and shall from the said labourer or souldier, or any one else, of what qualitie whatsoeuer, either take any thing for washing, or withhold or steale from him any such linnen committed to her charge to wash, or change the same willingly and wittingly, with purpose to giue him worse, old or torne linnen for his good, and proofe shall be made thereof, she shall be whipped for the same, and lie in prison till she make restitution of such linnen, withheld or changed."[1]

Even more stringent penalties are attached to purloining from the flour and meal given out for baking purposes.[2]

[1] Force, *Tracts*, III.: "Articles, Lavves, and Orders, Diuine, Politique, and Martiall, for the Colony in Virginea Brittania."

[2] "All such Bakers as are appointed to bake bread, or what else, either for the store to be giuen out in generall, or for any one in particular, shall not steale nor imbezell, loose, or defraud any man of his due and proper weight and measure, nor vse any dishonest and deceiptfull tricke to make the bread weigh heauier, or make it courser vpon purpose to keepe backe any part or measure of the flower or meale committed vnto him, nor aske, take, or detaine any one loafe more or lesse for his hire or paines for so baking, since whilest he who deliuered vnto him such meale or flower, being to attend the businesse of the Colonie, such baker or bakers are imposed vpon no other seruice or duties, but onely so to bake for such as

But it is not alone in Virginia that perplexed employers were found. John Winter, writing to Trelawny from Richmond Island, Maine, under date of July 10, 1639, says of a certain Priscilla:

"You write me of some yll reports is given of my Wyfe for beatinge the maid; yf a faire waye will not do yt, beatinge must, sometimes, vppon such Idlle girrells as she is. Yf you think yt fitte for my wyfe to do all the worke & the maide sitt still, she must forbeare her hands to strike, for then the worke will ly vndonn. She hath bin now 2 yeares ½ in the house, & I do not thinke she hath risen 20 times before my Wyfe hath bin vp to Call her, & many tymes light the fire before she Comes out of her bed. She hath twize gon a mechinge in the woodes, which we haue bin faine to send all our Company to seeke. We Cann hardly keep her within doores after we ar gonn to beed, except we Carry the kay of the doore to beed with us. She never Could melke Cow nor goat since she Came hither. Our men do not desire to haue her boyle the kittle for them she is so sluttish. She Cannot be trusted to serue a few piggs, but my wyfe most Commonly must be with her. She hath written home, I heare, that she was faine to ly vppon goates skins. She might take som goates skins to ly in her bedd, but not given to her for her lodginge. For a yeare & quarter or more she lay with my daughter vppon a good feather bed before my daughter being lacke 3 or 4 daies to Sacco, the maid goes into beed with her Cloth & stockins, & would not take the paines to plucke of her Cloths: her bedd after was a doust bedd & she had 2 Coverletts to ly on her, but sheets she had none after that tyme she was found to be so sluttish. Her beating that she hath had hath never hurt her body nor limes. She is so fatt & soggy she Cann hardly do any worke. This I write all the Company will Justify. Yf this

do worke, and this shall hee take notice of, vpon paine for the first time offending herein of losing his eares, and for the second time to be condemned a yeare to the Gallies, and for the third time offending to be condemned to the Gallies for three yeares." The same penalties are attached in case cooks or those who dress fish withhold any part of the provision given them. Every minister was to read these laws publicly every Sunday before catechising. Force, *Tracts*, III.: "Articles . . . for the Colony in Virginea."

D

maid at her lasy tymes, when she hath bin found in her ill accyons, do not deserue 2 or 3 blowes, I pray Judge You who hath most reason to Complaine, my wyfe or the maid. . . . She hath an vnthankefull office to do this she doth, for I thinke their was never that steward yt amonge such people as we haue Could giue them all Content. Yt does not pleas me well being she hath taken so much paines & Care to order things as well as she Could, & ryse in the morning rath, & go to bed soe latte, & to haue hard speches for yt." [1]

Winter's letters and reports to the London Company are as full of his trials with his servants indoors and out, as are the conferences to-day between perplexed employers. Even when fortune smiled on him and one promised well, misfortune overtook her.

" The maid Tomson had a hard fortune. Yt was her Chance to be drowned Cominge over the barr after our Cowes, & very little water on the barr, not aboue ½ foote, & we Cannot Judge how yt should be, accept that her hatt did blow from her head, & she to saue her hatt stept on the side of the barr. . . . I thinke yf she had lived she would haue proved a good servant in the house : she would do more worke then 3 such maides as Pryssyllea is." [2]

It is true that Maine was a remote colony and the difficulty of obtaining good servants was presumably greater than in places more accessible. Yet the same tale of trial comes from Boston and from those whose means, character, and position in society would seem to exempt them from the difficulties more naturally to be expected in other places. Mrs. Mary Winthrop Dudley writes repeatedly in 1636 to her mother, Mrs. Margaret Winthrop, begging her to send her a maid, " on that should be a

[1] *Trelawny Papers, Collections of Maine Historical Society*, III., 166–168.
[2] *Ibid.*, 169.

good lusty seruant that hath skille in a dairy."[1] But how unsatisfactory the "lusty servant" proved a later letter of Mrs. Dudley shows:

"I thought it convenient," she writes, "to acquaint you and my father what a great affliction I haue met withal by my maide servant, and how I am like through God his mercie to be freed from it; at her first coming me she carried her selfe dutifully as became a servant; but since through mine and my husbands forbearance towards her for small faults, she hath got such a head and is growen soe insolent that her carriage towards vs, especially myselfe is vnsufferable. If I bid her doe a thinge shee will bid me to doe it my selfe, and she sayes how shee can give content as wel as any servant but shee will not, and sayes if I loue not quietnes I was never so fitted in my life, for shee would make mee haue enough of it. If I should write to you of all the reviling speeches and filthie language shee hath vsed towards me I should but grieue you. My husband hath vsed all meanes for to reforme her, reasons and perswasions, but shee doth professe that her heart and her nature will not suffer her to confesse her faults. If I tell my husband of her behauiour towards me, vpon examination shee will denie all that she hath done or spoken: so that we know not how to proceede against her: but my husband now hath hired another maide and is resolved to put her away the next weeke."[2]

Other members of the Winthrop family also have left an account of their trials of this kind. A generation later, July 7, 1682, Wait Winthrop wrote to Fitz-John Winthrop, "I feare black Tom will do but little seruis. He used to make a show of hanging himselfe before folkes, but I believe he is not very nimble about it when he is alone. Tis good to haue an eye to him, and if you think it not worth while to keep him, eyther sell him

[1] *Mass. Hist. Soc. Coll.*, Fifth Series, I., 64-67.
[2] *Ibid.*, 68.

or send him to Virginia or the West Indies before winter. He can do something as a smith." [1] In the third generation John Winthrop, the son of Wait Winthrop, wrote to his father from New London, Connecticut, 1717:

"It is not convenient now to write the trouble & plague we have had wth this Irish creature the year past. Lying & unfaithfull; w^d doe things on purpose in contradiction & vexation to her mistress; lye out of the house anights, and have contrivances wth fellows that have been stealing from o^r estate & gett drink out of ye cellar for them; saucy & impudent, as when we have taken her to task for her wickedness she has gon away to complain of cruell usage. I can truly say we have used this base creature wth a great deal of kindness & lenity. She w^d frequently take her mistresses capps & stockins, hanckerchers &c., and dress herselfe, and away wthout leave among her companions. I may have said some time or other when she has been in fault, that she was fitt to live nowhere butt in Virginia, and if she w^d not mend her ways I should send her thither; thô I am sure no body w^d give her passage thither to have her service for 20 yeares, she is such a high spirited pernicious jade. Robin has been run away near ten days, as you will see by the inclosed, and this creature knew of his going and of his carrying out 4 dozen bottles of cyder, metheglin, & palme wine out of the cellar amongst the servants of the towne, and meat and I know not w^t." [2]

The trials of at least one Connecticut housekeeper are hinted at in an Order of the General Court in 1645, providing that a certain "Susan C., for her rebellious carriage toward her mistress, is to be sent to the house of correction and be kept to hard labor and coarse diet, to be brought forth the next lecture day to be publicly corrected, and so to be corrected weekly, until order be given to the contrary." [3]

[1] *Mass. Hist. Soc. Coll.*, Fifth Series, VIII., 427.
[2] *Winthrop Papers*, Pt. VI., 353–354, note.
[3] Trumbull, *Blue Laws*, p. 155.

But it is undoubtedly in the legislation of the colonial period that one finds the best reflection of colonial service, and one may say of it, as Judge Sewall wrote to a friend when sending him a copy of the Statutes at Large for 1684, "You will find much pleasant and profitable Reading in it."[1] Numerous acts were passed in all the colonies determining the relation between masters and servants, and these laws were most explicit in protecting the interests of both parties — a fact often indicated by the very name of the act, as that of 1700 in Pennsylvania, entitled "For the just encouragement of servants in the discharge of their duty, and the prevention of their deserting their master's or owner's service."[2]

In the legislation in regard to service and servants, it is impossible always to discriminate between the general class of either bound or life servants and the particular class of domestic employees. But the smaller class was comprised in the larger, and household servants had the benefit of all legislation affecting servants as a whole. Few or no laws were passed specifically for the benefit of domestic employees.

These laws worked both ways. On the one hand, they were intended to protect the servant from the selfishness and cruelty of those masters who would be inclined to take advantage of their position; on the other hand, they protected the master who had invested his capital in servants, and asked protection for it at the hands of the law, as he sought protection for any other form of property.

[1] *Mass. Hist. Soc. Coll.*, Sixth Series, II., 112.
[2] Purdon, *Digest.*

Several general classes of laws are found for the protection of servants. The first provides that no servant, bound to serve his or her time in a province, could be sold out of the province, without his or her consent.[1] A second class of laws compelled masters and mistresses to provide their servants with wholesome and sufficient food, clothing, and lodging;[2] and a third provided that if a servant became ill during the time of his service, his master should be under obligation to care for him, and heavy penalties were sometimes incurred by a master who discharged a servant when sick.[3]

[1] Purdon, *Digest*, Act of 1700. In East New Jersey the privilege was restricted to white servants. Leaming and Spicer, *Acts of East New Jersey, 1682*. In Massachusetts no servant was to be put off for more than a year to another master without the consent of the Court. *Body of Liberties*, § 86, Act of 1672. In New York no servant, except one bound for life, could be assigned to another master for more than one year, except for good reason. — *Laws of the Duke of York.*

[2] Iredell, Acts of 1741, chap. XXIV., § 4; Leaming and Spicer, *Acts of East New Jersey, 1682*, chap. XXVI. Any white servant burdened beyond his strength, or deprived of necessary rest and sleep, could complain to the justice of the peace. This officer was empowered, first, to admonish the offending master; second, to levy on his goods to an amount not exceeding ten pounds; and third, to sell the servant's time. Trott, Act of 1717. In New York and Massachusetts servants were to have convenient time for food and rest. — *Laws of the Duke of York;* Massachusetts, Act of 1672. In Maryland the penalty for insufficient meat, drink, lodging, and clothing, burdens beyond their strength, or more than ten lashes for one offence, was for the first and second offence a fine of not more than a thousand pounds of tobacco, and on the third offence the servant recovered his liberty. Permission to exceed ten lashes could be obtained from the Court, but the master could not inflict more than thirty-nine lashes. — Dorsey, *Laws of 1715*, chap. LXIV.

[3] Trumbull, *Public Records*, p. 263 ; Massachusetts, Act of 1700 ; Iredell, Acts of 1741, chap. XXIV. In North Carolina if a master did not use means for the recovery of a servant when ill, and turned him away, he forfeited five pounds for each servant so turned away, and if this was not

The law went even further and protected servants against unjust cruelty, especially against every form of bodily maiming. If a white servant lost an eye or a tooth at the hands of his master or mistress, he gained his freedom, and could sometimes recover further compensation, if the Court so adjudged.[1] If servants fled from the cruelty of their master, they were to be protected, though notice of such protection was to be sent to the master and the magistrate.[2] In New York if a master or dame tyrannically and cruelly abused a servant, the latter could complain to the constable and overseers, who were instructed to admonish the master on the first offence, and on the second, to protect the servant in the house until relief could be obtained through the Courts.[3] In North Carolina no Christian servant could be whipped without an order from the justice of the peace; if any one presumed so to do, the person offending was to pay forty shillings to the party injured.[4] Immoderate punishment

sufficient the Court was empowered to levy an additional amount. Such servants on their recovery were to have their freedom, provided they had not brought the illness on themselves. In Connecticut if the injury came at the hands of the master or any member of his family, the master was obliged to provide for the maintenance of the servant, even after the expiration of his term of service, according to the judgment of the Court. But if the injury "came by any providence of God without the default of the family of the governor," the master was released from the obligation of providing for him after his term of service expired. In South Carolina masters turning away sick or infirm servants were to forfeit twenty pounds.

[1] Leaming and Spicer, *East New Jersey, 1682; Body of Liberties*, § 87, Act of 1672; *Laws of the Duke of York.* In Maryland the Act of 1692 freed a mulatto girl whose master had cut off both her ears.

[2] *Body of Liberties*, § 85, Act of 1672; *Laws of Connecticut, 1673.*

[3] *Laws of the Duke of York.*

[4] Iredell, 1741, chap. XXIV.

also subjected the master to appear before the County
Court to answer for his conduct.[1] When New Jersey
became a royal province in 1702, the instructions of the
Crown to Lord Cornbury included a provision that he
should " endeavor to get a Law past for the restraining of
any inhuman Severity, which by ill Masters or Overseers,
may be used towards their Christian Servants, and their
Slaves, and that Provision be made therein, that the wil-
full killing of Indians and Negroes may be punished with
Death, and that a fit Penalty be imposed for the maiming
of them." [2] Moreover, in North Carolina complaints of
servants against their masters could be heard without
formal process of action.[3] In Pennsylvania the law of
1771 provided that every indented servant should obtain
a legal residence in the city or place where he or she had
first served his or her master sixty days, or if he had
afterwards served twelve months in any other place, he
was at liberty to choose his residence in either place. In
South Carolina a master denying a certificate at the expiration of a servant's time was to forfeit two pounds.[4]

Important as these provisions were in the interest of
the servant, the law protected the master even more care-
fully and specifically. The great danger to him was
in the loss of servants through their escaping from service
and being harbored by friendly sympathizers or rival
employers. The law dealt rigorously with both classes
of offenders. In South Carolina stubborn, refractory,

---

[1] Leaming and Spicer, *East New Jersey, 1682*, chap. VIII.
[2] *Instructions of the Crown*, November 16, 1702.
[3] Iredell, 1741, chap. XXIV.
[4] Carey and Bioren, chap. 635.

and discontented servants, who ran away before their term of service expired, were obliged to serve their masters three times the period of their absence.[1] In Pennsylvania every servant absenting himself without leave for one day or more was to serve, at the expiration of his time, five days for every day's absence, and in addition, to give satisfaction to his master for any damages or charges incurred through his absence.[2] In East New Jersey runaways were to serve double the time of their absence, and also to give satisfaction for the costs and damages caused by their absence.[3] In North Carolina runaways who would not tell the name of their master, either because unable to speak English or through obstinacy, were to be committed to jail and advertised for two months. Servants absenting themselves were to serve double time.[4] In South Carolina a servant who ran away was to serve one week for every day's absence, but the whole time was not to exceed two years.[5] Servants running away with slaves were to be considered felons. In Maryland absenting servants were to serve additional time at the discretion of the Court, ten days, or not exceeding that, for every day's absence, and to give satisfaction for costs incurred.[6]

The temptation to harbor runaways was great, not so much from philanthropic motives as because of the scar-

[1] Trott, Act of 1717.
[2] Act of 1673.
[3] Leaming and Spicer, Act of 1682. This is practically the re-enactment of a similar law in Carteret's time, 1668, and of the law of 1675.
[4] Iredell, Act of 1741.
[5] Trott, Act of 1717.
[6] Browne, 1692; Dorsey, 1715, chap. XLIV.

city of labor, and every colony supplemented its legislation
against runaways by corresponding acts carrying penalties
for harboring them. In East New Jersey the offender
was fined five pounds and was to make full satisfaction
to the master or mistress for costs and damages sustained
because of the absence, while any person who knowingly
harbored or entertained a runaway, " except of real charity," was to pay the master or mistress of the servant ten
shillings for every day's entertainment and concealment
and to be fined at the discretion of the Court.[1] In Connecticut the presumption was that if servants were entertained after nine o'clock at night they were runaways,
and the head of the family so entertaining them was to
forfeit five shillings to the complainer and five shillings
to the town treasurer. Any Indian hiding a runaway
was to forfeit forty shillings for every such offence or
suffer a month's imprisonment.[2] In South Carolina runaways were not to be harbored under a penalty of two
pounds for every day and night the servant was so entertained, but the total amount forfeited was not to exceed
treble the value of the servant's time remaining to be
served.[3] In New York any one proved to have connived
at the absence of a servant was to forfeit twenty pounds
to the master or dame and five pounds to the Court.
Any one knowingly harboring a runaway was to forfeit
ten shillings for every day's entertainment.[4] In Pennsylvania any one concealing a servant forfeited twenty

[1] Leaming and Spicer, Act of 1682. The Acts of 1682 and 1675 had
similar provisions.
[2] Act *circa* 1784 ; Trumbull, *Public Records*, 1665–1678.
[3] Trott, Act of 1717.
[4] *Laws of the Duke of York.*

shillings for each day's concealment.[1] In Rhode Island any person entertaining a servant after nine o'clock at night forfeited five shillings for each offence.[2] In Maryland, by an act of 1692, persons harboring runaways were to forfeit five hundred pounds of tobacco for every hour's entertainment, one half to the government and one half to the informer.[3] By a later act the person harboring runaways was to forfeit one hundred pounds of tobacco for every hour's entertainment, one half to go to the public schools and one half to the party aggrieved.[4] This was intended to meet evasions of the previous laws on the part of those who harbored runaways a few hours at a time and then helped them on their way. Free negroes or mulattoes harboring runaways were to forfeit one thousand pounds of tobacco for every such offence, one half for the use of free schools and one half to the party aggrieved.[5] By a later act, servants harboring runaways were to be punished by the magistrate by lashes, not to exceed thirty-nine, on the bare back.[6]

On the other hand, every incentive was held out to assist in the return of runaways. In North Carolina any person who assisted in taking up runaways was rewarded, the reward being gauged by the number of miles away from the master's house that the servant was taken.[7] In Pennsylvania any one apprehending a runaway servant and returning him or her to the sheriff of the county was to receive ten shillings if the runaway was taken within

[1] Purdon, *Digest*, Act of 1700.
[2] Act of 1704.
[3] Browne, 1692; Dorsey, 1715.
[4] Bacon, 1748.
[5] Browne, 1692; Dorsey, 1715.
[6] Bacon, 1748.
[7] Iredell, Act of 1741.

ten miles of the master's house and twenty shillings if at
a distance of more than ten miles.[1] In Connecticut any
Indian who returned a runaway to the nearest authority
was to receive as a reward two yards of cloth.[2] In
Maryland the allowance was two hundred pounds of
tobacco, while Indians were to receive a match coat or its
value.[3] Persons in Virginia, Delaware, or the northern
parts of America, who apprehended runaways from Maryland, were to receive four hundred pounds of tobacco, and
the servant was to reimburse his master by additional
servitude.[4] Every precaution to prevent runaways was
taken. Indian, negro, and mulatto servants were not to
travel without a pass,[5] nor were slaves to leave their plantation without leave, except negroes wearing liveries.[6]
In Connecticut servants were not to go abroad after nine
o'clock at night,[7] in Massachusetts they were not to frequent public houses,[8] and in South Carolina and Massachusetts innkeepers were not to harbor them.[9]

Yet the life under a master or mistress was often such
as to tempt a servant to escape; added to a condition
that often involved hard work, poor lodging, and insufficient food and clothing, was the infliction of humiliating
corporal punishment in case of disobedience or disorder.

[1] Carey and Bioren, Act of 1700.
[2] Trumbull, *Public Records.*
[3] Acts of 1692 and 1715.
[4] Act of 1692.
[5] Connecticut, *circa* 1784; New York, Act of 1672; Maryland, Acts of
1692, 1715.
[6] Iredell, Act of 1741.
[7] Act *circa* 1784.
[8] Act of 1646.
[9] Trott, 1717; Massachusetts, Act of 1698.

In Connecticut a servant could be punished by the magistrate not to exceed ten stripes for one offence.[1] The Rhode Island law was similar.[2] In North Carolina runaways were to receive from the constable as many lashes as the justice of the peace should think fit, "not exceeding the Number of thirty-nine, well laid on, on the Back of such Runaway," while disobedient servants were to be punished with corporal punishment, not to exceed twenty-one lashes. In cases where free persons suffered punishment by being fined, servants were whipped.[3] In South Carolina a servant for striking his master or mistress was to serve not more than six months' additional time, or be punished with not more than twenty-one stripes.[4] In Massachusetts and New York any servants who had been unfaithful, negligent, or unprofitable in their service, notwithstanding good usage from their masters, were not to be dismissed until they had made satisfaction according to the judgment of the civil authorities.[5]

In nearly every colony heavy penalties followed attempts to carry on trade or barter with servants. In North Carolina a freeman trading with a servant forfeited treble the value of the goods traded for and six pounds in addition ; if unable to pay the fine he was himself sold as a servant. A servant trading or selling the property of his master was to serve his master additional time, the

[1] Act of 1646.
[2] Act of 1728.
[3] Iredell, Act of 1741. But corporal punishment was not to deprive the master of such other satisfaction as he might be entitled to by the Act.
[4] Act of 1717.
[5] *Body of Liberties*, § 88, Act of 1672 ; *Laws of the Duke of York.*

length to be fixed by the Court.[1] In East New Jersey
the penalty was five pounds for the first offence and ten
pounds for each subsequent one ; the offending servant
was to be whipped by the person to whom he had ten-
dered such sale, the reward of half a crown being paid by
the master or mistress to the person administering the
punishment.[2] In Pennsylvania any one trading secretly
with a servant was to forfeit to the master three times the
value of the goods, and the servant at the expiration of his
time was to render satisfaction to the master to double
the value of the goods, and, if black, was to be whipped
in the most public place in the township.[3] Trading with
servants was prohibited in Connecticut[4] and in Massachusetts.[5] In South Carolina any one buying, selling, or
bartering with a servant was to forfeit treble the value of
the goods and ten pounds to the informer ; the offending
servant was to be whipped on the bare back in the watch-
house at Charleston.[6] In New York servants were forbidden to trade under penalty of fine or corporal punishment. Those trading with servants were to restore the
commodities to the master and to forfeit double their
value to the poor of the parish.[7] In Maryland the penalty was two thousand pounds of tobacco, one half to go
to the king and one half to the master.[8]

Many miscellaneous provisions in different colonies
must have seemed oppressive. In New Jersey and South
Carolina servants could not marry without the consent of

---

[1] Iredell, 1741.
[2] Leaming and Spicer. Act of 1682.
[3] Purdon, *Digest*, 1700.
[4] Act *circa* 1784.
[5] Laws of 1672.
[6] Act governing white servants, 1717.
[7] *Laws of the Duke of York.*
[8] Browne, 1692 ; Dorsey, 1715.

their masters.[1] In Massachusetts no covenant servant in the household with any other could be an office holder.[2] In Pennsylvania innkeepers were forbidden to trust them.[3] In North Carolina servants making false complaints in regard to illness were to serve double the time lost, and the same penalty followed if they were sent to jail for any offence.[4] No slave was to go armed in North Carolina, and if one was found offending, the person making the discovery was to appropriate the weapon for his own use, and the servant was to receive twenty lashes on his or her bare back. One servant on each plantation, however, was exempted from the law, but such an one must carry a certificate of permission.[5] In Massachusetts servants were to be catechised once a week[6] and were not to wear apparel exceeding the quality and condition of their persons or estates under penalty of admonition for the first offence, a fine of twenty shillings for the second, and forty shillings for the third offence.[7]

The obligation of the master to a servant-owning and slave-owning community was recognized in North Carolina in a positive law prohibiting a master from setting free a negro or mulatto on any pretence whatsoever, except for meritorious services to be judged and allowed by the County Court, and even in this case a license was to be previously obtained.[8] In Massachusetts Bay servants were not to be set free until they had served out

[1] Leaming and Spicer, Acts of 1668, 1675 ; Trott, Act of 1717.
[2] Massachusetts Bay, Act of 1636.
[3] Carey and Bioren, Act of 1721.
[4] Iredell, 1741.   [5] *Ibid.*
[6] Laws of 1672.   [7] *Ibid.*
[8] Iredell, 1741.

their time.[1] In Connecticut a slave set free was to be
maintained by his master if he came to want.[2]

In view of all these restrictions on servants of a personal, industrial, and political character it seems strange
that even any from their number should have been able,
at the expiration of their term of service, to break away
from the spirit of this bondage and reach a higher position in the social scale; yet many of the redemptioners
became in time, especially at the North, respectable
and even prominent members of the community.[3] The
women often married planters[4] and in turn became the
employers of servants.   Yet these are the exceptions.
For a long time the redemptioners were considered the

[1] Act of 1636.

[2] Act of 1784.

[3] Neill, *Founders of Maryland*, pp. 77–79, gives the names of eighty
servants brought over by Cornwallis between 1634 and 1651; and of
these, five became members of the Assembly, one became a sheriff, and
two were signers of the Protestant Declaration. Other noteworthy instances are found in Virginia. Neill, *Virginia Carolorum*, p. 297. Sometimes, however, the trail of the serpent remained. R. G., in a treatise
published about 1661, says of the burgesses that they "were usually such
as went over servants thither, and though by time, and industry, they
may have attained competent estates, yet by reason of their poor and
mean condition, were unskilful in judging of a good estate, either of
church or Commonwealth, or by the means of procuring it."— *Virginia
Carolorum*, p. 290. George Taylor, a Pennsylvania redemptioner, was
one of the signers of the Declaration of Independence.

[4] The Sot-Weed Factor describes a quarrel in which one says:

> ". . . tho' now so brave,
> I knew you late a Four-Years Slave ;
> What if for Planter's Wife you go,
> Nature designed you for the Hoe." — P. 21.

DeFoe says : " When their Time is expir'd, sometimes before it,
(they) get marri'd and settl'd ; turn Planters, and by Industry grow
rich ; or get to be Yearly Servants in good Families upon Terms." — *Behaviour of Servants*, p. 140.

off-scourings of English cities, and they formed a distinct class in the social order lower than their masters or employers. In view of this fact, a reproach was of necessity attached to all belonging to the class and to the designation applied to them. Their descendants ultimately formed the class of poor whites, — the lowest stratum in the social order whose members were held in contempt even by the negroes.

It has been said that the redemptioners were found in all the colonies, though they were more numerous in the Middle and Southern colonies than in New England. But it was difficult to keep white servants for any length of time in a country where land was cheap and the servant soon in turn became a master.[1] It was undoubtedly this difficulty that led to the substitution for white servants of Indians and negro slaves. Indian servants were apparently more numerous in the New England colonies, while negro slavery gained its strongest foothold in the South.

The employment of Indians as servants grew up naturally in New England and was continued for at least a hundred years.[2] Their presence was regarded as

[1] Elkanah Watson, writing from London in 1782, compares the silent attention given by English servants with the volubility of those in France, and then adds : " In America, our domestic feels the consciousness, that he may in turn become a master. This feeling may, perhaps, impair his usefulness as a servant, but cannot be deprecated, whilst it adds to his self-respect as a man." — *Men and Times of the Revolution,* pp. 169–170.

[2] Numberless advertisements are found like the following: " An Indian maid about 19 years of Age, brought up from a Child to all sorts of Household work, can handle her Needle very well and Sew or Flower and ingenious about her Work : To be sold on reasonable terms." — *Boston News Letter,* June 8, 1719.

" An Indian Woman Aged about 30 Years fit for all manner of House-

E

almost providential by the New Englanders, hard pressed
for assistance in house and field. When the question of
the right and wrong of the matter was suggested by the
troubled conscience, an easy answer was found : was it
not sin to suffer them longer to maintain the worship of
the devil when they were needed so sorely as slaves?[1]
But like the redemptioners, their service so eagerly
sought often proved unsatisfactory. Hugh Peter wrote
to John Winthrop, September 4, 1639, " My wife desires
my daughter to send to Hanna that was her mayd, now at
Charltowne, to know if shee would dwell with vs, for
truly wee are so destitute (hauing now but an Indian)

hold work either for Town or Country, can Sew, Wash, Brew, Bake,
Spin, and Milk Cows, to be sold by Mr. Henry Hill." — *Ibid.*, January
4, 1720.

" A Very likely Indian Womans Time for Eleven Years and Five
Months to be disposed of ; she's a very good Servant, and can do any
Household work, either for Town or Country." — *Ibid.*, March 21, 1720.

" An Indian Woman aged Sixteen Years, that speaks good English ;
to be sold." — *Ibid.*, February 20, 1715.

"A Stray Spanish Indian Woman named Sarah, Aged about 40 Years
taken up, which the Owner may have paying the Charges." — *Ibid.*,
January 4, 1720.

[1] "A warr with the Narraganset is verie considerable to this plantation, ffor I doubt whither yt be not synne in vs, hauing power in our
hands, to suffer them to maynteyne the worship of the devill which
theire paw wawes often doe ; 2lie, If vpon a Just warre the Lord should
deliuer them into our hands, wee might easily haue men woemen and
children enough to exchange for Moores, which wilbe more gaynefull
pilladge for vs than wee conceive, for I doe not see how wee can thrive
vntill wee gett into a stock of slaves sufficient to doe all our buisines, for
our children's children will hardly see this great Continent filled with
people, soe that our servants will still desire freedome to plant for them
selues, and not stay but for verie great wages. And I suppose you know
verie well how wee shall maynteyne 20 Moores cheaper than one Eng-
lishe servant." — Emanuel Downing to John Winthrop, 1645. *Mass.
Hist. Soc. Coll.*, Fourth Series, vol. VI., p. 65.

that wee know not what to doe." [1] More unfortunate
still was the young clergyman, the Rev. Peter Thatcher.
He records in his diary at Barnstable, May 7, 1679, " I
bought an Indian of Mr. Checkley and was to pay 5£ a
month after I received her and five pound more in a quarter of a year." A week later he writes, " Came home
and found my Indian girl had liked to have knocked my
Theodora on head by letting her fall, whereupon I took
a good walnut stick and beat the Indian to purpose till
she promised to do so no more." [2]

In every section negro slavery grew up side by side
with white and Indian slavery, [3] though its hold even

[1] *Mass. Hist. Soc. Coll.*, Fourth Series, vol. VI., p. 101.

James Russell Lowell commenting on this letter says, " Let any housewife of our day, who does not find the Keltic element in domestic life so
refreshing as to Mr. Arnold in literature, imagine a household with one
wild Pequot woman, communicated with by signs, for its maid of all
work, and take courage. Those were serious times indeed, when your
cook might give warning by taking your scalp, or *chignon*, as the case
might be, and making off with it into the woods." — "New England
Two Centuries Ago," in *Among My Books*, I., 263.

[2] Teele, *History of Milton, Massachusetts, 1640–1887*, Journal of
Rev. Peter Thatcher, Appendix B, pp. 641–642.

[3] *The Report of a French Protestant Refugee in Boston, 1687*, evidently submitted to guide friends in France thinking of coming to America,
says : " You may also own negroes and negresses ; there is not a house in
Boston, however small may be its means, that has not one or two. There
are those that have five or six, and all make a good living." — Pp. 19–20.

The New England papers, even in the first part of the eighteenth century, are full of advertisements like the following : " A Negro Wench
with a Girl Four Years old both born in the Country, used to all Family
work on a Farm, to be sold on reasonable Terms." — *Boston News Letter*,
October 5, 1719.

" A very likely young Negro Wench that can do any Household Work
to be sold, inquire of Mr. Samuel Sewall." — *Ibid.*, April 9, 1716.

" Lately arrived from Jamaica several Negro boys and girls, to be sold
by Mr. John Charnock & Co." — *Ibid.*, May 11, 1719.

upon the South was far from strong until the end of
the seventeenth century.   It is both unnecessary and
impossible to discuss in this place the question of slavery[1]
and its relation to the larger subject of service.   The
close of the colonial period saw it firmly established at
the South, where it supplanted the system of white servitude, while at the North both black and white slavery
gave place to free labor.

The details of the history of domestic service during
the colonial period may seem unnecessary to an understanding of domestic service as it is to-day, but an examination of them must show the existence during that
period of principles and conditions that must modify
the judgment concerning the conditions of to-day.   No
wish is more often expressed than that it might be possible to return to the Arcadian days when service was

Most of the advertisements describe those offered for sale as "very
likely," and add the specially desirable qualification that he or she "speaks
good English."   Judge Sewall, in 1700, gives this account of his first protest against negro slavery: "Having been long and much dissatisfied
with the Trade of fetching Negros from Guinea; at last I had a strong
Inclination to Write something about it; but it wore off.   At last reading Bayne, Ephes. about servants, who mentions Blackmoors; I began
to be uneasy that I had so long neglected doing anything." — Diary,
II., 16.

[1] But it is of interest in passing to note two contemporaneous judgments on the effect of slavery.   Elkanah Watson, writing of his journey
through the South in 1778, says: "The influence of slavery upon southern
habits is peculiarly exhibited in the prevailing indolence of the people.   It
would seem as if the poor white man had almost rather starve than work,
because the negro works." — Men and Times, p. 72.

Thomas Anburey writes, "Most of the planters consign the care of
their plantations and negroes to an overseer, even the man whose house
we rent, has his overseer, though he could with ease superintend it himself; but if they possess a few negroes, they think it beneath their dignity,
added to which, they are so abominably lazy." — Travels, II., 328.

abundant, excellent, and cheap. But those days did not exist in America during the colonial period. The conditions at that time bear a marked resemblance to those of to-day. The social position of all servants was lower than that of their employers, and the gulf between the two was more difficult to span. Service was difficult to obtain and unsatisfactory when secured. Servants complained of hard work and ill treatment, and masters of ungrateful servants and inefficient service, and both masters and servants were justified in their complaints. The legal relations between master and servant were explicitly defined as regards length of service, wages paid, and the mutual obligations of both parties to the contract during the period of service. But this very definiteness of the contract was due to the fact that the relationship between the two parties was an arbitrary one and could not have been preserved without this legal assistance. In default of a better one, the system of white servitude may have served its age fairly well; but its restoration, if the restoration were possible, would do nothing to relieve in any way the strain and pressure of present conditions.

CHAPTER IV

DOMESTIC SERVICE SINCE THE COLONIAL PERIOD

It has been said that domestic service in America has passed through three distinct phases. The second phase began about the time of the Revolution, when at the North the indented servants as a class were gradually supplanted by free laborers, and at the South by negro slaves who inherited with large interest the reproach attached to the redemptioners. The social chasm that had existed at the North between employer and employee, under the system of bonded servants, disappeared. The free laborers, whether employed in domestic service or otherwise, were socially the equal of their employers, especially in New England and in the smaller towns. They belonged by birth to the same section of the country, probably to the same community; they had the same religious belief, attended the same church, sat at the same fireside, ate at the same table, had the same associates; they were often married from the homes [1] and buried in the family lots of

---

[1] A New England woman writes : "In several instances our ' help ' was married from our parlor with my sisters for bridesmaids. I correspond with a woman doctor in Florida whose sister was our cook when I was a child, and who shared her sister's room at our home while she earned her education, alternating work in the cotton mills and going to school." This is but one illustration of hundreds that have doubtless come within the experience of most persons living in New England fifty years ago.

their employers.[1] They were in every sense of the word
" help."[2] A survival of this condition is seen to-day in
farming communities, especially at the West. In the
South, on the contrary, the social chasm became impassable as negro slavery entirely displaced white labor.

This democratic condition at the North seemed especially noteworthy to European travellers,[3] and it was one
to which they apparently never became accustomed.
Harriet Martineau, in planning for her American journey,
was perplexed by the difficulty of securing a travelling
companion. " It would never do," she says, " as I was
aware, to take a servant, to suffer from the proud Yan-
kees on the one hand and the debased slaves on the
other."[4] On arriving here, she found " the study of
domestic service a continual amusement," and what she
saw " would fill a volume."[5] " Boarding-house life," she
says, " has been rendered compulsory by the scarcity of

---

[1] A visit to many New England burying grounds will illustrate this
statement. It was doubtless a survival of the English custom. A curious
and interesting collection of epitaphs of servants has been made by Arthur
J. Munby. •

[2] " . . . Help, for I love our Yankee word, teaching, as it does, the
true relation, and its being equally binding on master and servant."
—J. R. Lowell, *Letters*, I., 105.

[3] Even Americans commented on it. John Watson writes : " One of
the remarkable incidents of our republican principles of equality is the
hirelings, who in times before the war of Independence were accustomed
to accept the names of servants and to be drest according to their condition, will now no longer suffer the former appellation ; and all affect the
dress and the air, when abroad, of genteeler people than their business
warrants. Those, therefore, who from affluence have many dependents,
find it a constant subject of perplexity to manage their pride and assumption." — *Annals*, p. 165.

[4] *Autobiography*, I., 331.

[5] *Society in America*, II., 248.

labour, — the difficulty of obtaining domestic service." [1]
But she was quick to appreciate the difference between
the spirit of service she found in America and that with
which she was familiar in the old world.   She writes :

"I had rather suffer any inconvenience from having to work occasionally in chambers and kitchen, and from having little hospitable
designs frustrated, than witness the subservience in which the menial
class is held in Europe.   In England, servants have been so long
accustomed to this subservience; it is so completely the established
custom for the mistress to regulate their manners, their clothes, their
intercourse with friends, and many other things which they ought to
manage for themselves, that it has become difficult to treat them any
better.   Mistresses who abstain from such regulation find that they
are spoiling their servants; and heads of families who would make
friends of their domestics find them little fitted to reciprocate the duty.
In America it is otherwise : and may it ever be so ! . . . One of the
pleasures of travelling through a democratic country is the seeing no
liveries.   No such badge of menial service is to be met with throughout the States, except in the houses of the foreign ambassadors at
Washington."

She then gives illustrations to show "of how much
higher a character American domestic service is than any
which would endure to be distinguished by a badge." [2]

[1] *Society in America*, II., 245.

[2] *Ibid.*, II., 254-255.

It is of interest to contrast this picture of service in America by an
Englishwoman with one given a little earlier of service in England by an
American.   Elkanah Watson writes from London in 1782 : "The servants
attending upon my friend's table were neatly dressed, and extremely
active and adroit in performing their offices, and glided about the room
silent and attentive.   Their silence was in striking contrast with the volubility of the French attendants, who, to my utter astonishment, I have
often observed in France, intermingling in the conversation of the table.
Here, the servant, however cherished, is held at an awful distance.   The
English servant is generally an ignorant and servile being, who has no
aspiration beyond his present condition." — *Men and Times of the Revolution*, p. 169.

De Tocqueville, also, found that "the condition of domestic service does not degrade the character of those who enter upon it, because it is freely chosen, and adopted for a time only; because it is not stigmatized by public opinion and creates no permanent inequality between the servant and the master." [1]

Francis J. Grund was also able to appreciate the difference between external servility and true self-respect, for he writes in 1837: "There are but few native Americans who would submit to the degradation of wearing a livery, or any other badge of servitude. This they would call becoming a man's man. But, on the other hand, there are also but few American gentlemen who would feel any happier for their servants wearing coats of more than one color. The inhabitants of New England are quite as willing to call their servants 'helps,' or 'domestics,' as the latter repudiate the title of 'master' in their employers." And he adds, "Neither is an American servant that same indolent, careless, besotted being as an European." He has another word of praise too for the American servants, "who work harder, and *quicker* than even in England." [2]

The absence of livery was a subject of constant comment. William Cobbett, in 1828, asserts that "the man (servant) will not wear a *livery*, any more than he will wear a halter round his neck. . . . Neither men nor women will allow you to call them *servants*, and they will take

---

[1] *Democracy in America*, II., 194.

[2] *The Americans in their Moral, Social, and Political Relations*, pp. 236–237.

Thomas Grattan also says, "The native Americans are the best servants in the country." —*Civilized America*, I., 260.

especial care not to call themselves by that name." He
explains the avoidance of the term "servant" by the fact
that slaves were called servants by the English, who having fled from tyranny at home were shy of calling others
slaves; free men therefore would not be called servants.[1]

But while the democratic spirit that prevailed during
this period found commendation in the eyes of those of
similar tendencies, it often evoked only mild surprise or
a half sneer. Mrs. Trollope found that "the greatest
difficulty in organizing a family established in Ohio, is
getting servants, or, as it is there called, 'getting help,'
for it is more than petty treason to the Republic to call a
free citizen a *servant*."[2] Chevalier asserted that "on
Sunday an American would not venture to receive his
friends ; his servants would not consent to it, and he can
hardly secure their services for himself, at their own hour,
on that day."[3] Samuel Breck considers that "in these
United States nothing would be wanting to make life
perfectly happy (humanly speaking) had we good servants."[4] Isabella Bird wrote of Canada in 1854, "The
great annoyance of which people complain in this pleasant land is the difficulty of obtaining domestic servants,
and the extraordinary specimens of humanity who go out
in this capacity." "The difficulty of procuring servants

[1] *A Year's Residence in the United States*, p. 201.

Charles Mackay also says that "service is called 'help,' to avoid
wounding the susceptibility of free citizens." — *Life and Liberty in
America*, I., 42.

[2] *Domestic Manners of the Americans*, I., 73.

[3] *Society, Manners, and Politics in the United States*, p. 284.

[4] He adds the interesting facts that cooks usually received $1.50
per week; chambermaids, $1.25 ; gardeners, $11 per month, and waiters
$10 per month. — *Recollections*, pp. 299–300.

is one of the great objections to this colony. The few there are know nothing of any individual department of work, — for instance, there are neither cooks nor house-maids, they are strictly ' *helps*,' — the mistress being expected to take more than her fair share of the work." [1] The conditions she found there were the same as in the United States.

Thomas Grattan wrote of the condition :

"One of the subjects on which the minds of men and women in the United States seem to be unanimously made up, is the admitted deficiency of *help*. . . . Disguise it as we may, under all the specious forms of reasoning, there is something in the mind of every man which tells him he is humiliated in doing personal service to another. . . . The servile nature of domestic duties in Europe, and more particularly in England, is much more likely to make servants liable to the discontent which mars their merits, than the common understanding in America, which makes the compact between 'employer' and 'help' a mere matter of business, entailing no mean submission on the one hand, and giving no right to any undue assumption of power on the other. . . . Domestic service is not considered so disgraceful in the United States, as it is felt to be in the United Kingdom." [2]

Grattan's observations lead him to believe that the democratic spirit is not always to be deplored.

"An American youth or 'young lady' will go to service willingly, if they can be better paid for it than for teaching in a village school, or working on a farm or in a factory. . . . They satisfy themselves that they are *helps*, not servants, — that they are going to work with (not for) Mr. so and so, not going to service, — they call him and his wife their *employers*, not their master and mistress." [3]

[1] *The Englishwoman in America*, pp. 43, 214.
[2] *Civilized America*, I., 256-258.
[3] *Ibid.*, I., 259.

But like all Europeans, he never ceases to be surprised by this spirit, particularly by those manifestations of it that led to active work on the part of the mistress of a home and to the use of the word "help." "There are no housekeepers," he writes, "or ladies' maids. The lady herself does all the duties of the former. . . . Servants are thus really justified in giving to themselves the favorite designation of 'helps.'" [1] But he closes a long and interesting chapter on the subject with the prophecy, "They (employers) will, by degrees, give up the employment of native servants who will be in future less likely than even now to submit to their pretensions, and confine themselves to the fast increasing tribes of Irish immigrants." [2]

Curiously enough nearly forty years earlier Madame d'Arusmont had written of friends who thought of coming to America and urged, "Let them by all means be advised against bringing servants with them. Foreign servants are here, without doubt, the worst; they neither understand the work which the climate renders necessary, nor are willing to do the work which they did elsewhere." [3] She, like all travellers, found that however subservient domestic servants might be when they left Europe, the first contact with the democratic atmosphere of America wrought a sudden change; subserviency disappeared, and the servant boasted of his equality with all. She explains that those educated in America perceive the difference placed between the gentleman and the laborer

[1] *Civilized America*, I., 264.
[2] *Ibid.*, I., 269.
[3] *Views of Society and Manners in America*, p. 338.

by education and conditions, but the foreigner taking a superficial view of the matter sees no difference.[1]

This second period in the history of domestic service continued from about the time of the Revolution until 1850. It was the product of the rapid growth of democratic ideas fostered by the Revolution and the widespread influence of the French philosophical ideas of the latter part of the eighteenth century. It was a period chiefly characterized by social and industrial democracy, as the political system was also in its spirit democratic. This democratic industrial spirit showed itself in the universal use at the North of the term " help," in the absence of liveries and all distinguishing marks of service, in the intolerance on the part of both employer and employee of servility and subserviency of manner, in the bridging of the social chasm between master and servant as long as the free employment of native born Americans continued, and in the hearty spirit of willingness with which service was performed. The results of this democratic régime were the difficulty of securing help, since new avenues of independent work were opening out to women and the class of indented servants had disappeared; the lack of all differentiation in household work, since the servant conferred a favor in "going out to work" and did what she knew how to do without troubling to learn new kinds of work; and, most important, the subtle change that the democratic atmosphere everywhere wrought in the servants who came from Europe.

This condition of free, democratic, native born white service at the North and compulsory slave service at the

[1] *Views of Society and Manners in America*, pp. 338–342.

South continued practically unchanged until about the middle of the century. Between 1850 and 1870 four important political changes occurred which revolutionized the personnel in domestic service and consequently its character. These changes brought about the third period in the history of the subject.

The first of these changes was due to the Irish famine of 1846. Previous to this time the immigration to this country from Ireland had been small, averaging not more than twenty thousand annually between 1820 and 1846. In the decade preceding the famine the average number of arrivals had been less than thirty-five thousand annually. In 1846 the number was 51,752, and this was more than doubled the following year, the report showing 105,536 arrivals in 1847. In 1851 the number of arrivals from Ireland had risen to 221,253. Since that time the number has fluctuated, but between fifty and seventy-five thousand annually come to this country from Ireland.[1] A large proportion of these immigrants — forty-nine per cent during the decade from 1870 to 1880 — have been women who were classed as "unskilled laborers." Two occupations were open to them. One was work in factories where as manufacturing processes became more simple unskilled labor could be utilized. The Irish immigrants, therefore, soon displaced in factories the New England women who had found, as has been seen,[2] new opportunities for work of a higher grade. The second occupation open to the

[1] *Arrivals of Alien Passengers and Immigrants in the United States from 1820 to 1890*, pp. 16, 23.

By the *Census of Massachusetts* for 1885 it is seen that forty-nine per cent of all women in that state of foreign birth are Irish. I., 574–575.

[2] *Ante*, p. 11.

Irish immigrants was household service. Here physical strength formed a partial compensation for lack of skill and ignorance of American ways, and the Irish soon came to form a most numerous and important class engaged in domestic employments.[1]

A second important European change, influencing the condition of domestic service, was the German Revolution of 1848 with the events preceding and resulting from it. Before this period the emigration from Germany had been insignificant, fewer than fifteen thousand having come to this country annually between 1830 and 1840. In 1840, owing to political reasons, the number had risen to 29,704. It soon became evident that the hopes raised by the accession of the new monarch were without foundation, and emigration rapidly increased until the number of emigrants coming to America reached 74,281 in 1847. During the year of the Revolution the number decreased, but the failure of the cause of the revolutionary party and the political apathy that followed again increased the movement towards America. This reached its climax in 1854, when the sympathies of the Court had been openly expressed during the Crimean War in favor of Russian despotism. During this year the number of Germans arriving in this country was 215,009 — a number equalled but once since that time, although the number has averaged nearly a hundred and fifty thousand annually during

[1] Lowell says of the Irish immigration, "It is really we who have been paying the rents over there [in Ireland], for we have to pay higher wages for domestic service to meet the drain." — *Letters*, II., 336.

A racy discussion of the influence of the Irish cook in the American household is given by Mr. E. L. Godkin under the title "The Morals and Manners of the Kitchen," in *Reflections and Comments*, p. 56.

the last decade.[1] A large number of these immigrants
have been women, the proportion of women emigrating
from Germany being greater than from any other foreign
country except Ireland.[2] The ranks of domestic service
have been recruited from their number also, the Germans
being second only to the Irish as regards the number and
proportion engaged in this occupation.[3]

A third political influence affecting the question was
the establishment of treaty relations between the United
States and China in 1844. This fact and the discovery
of gold in California in 1848, together with the building of
the Union Pacific railroad in 1867–1869, opened the doors
to the immigration of considerable numbers of Chinese.
Many of these found their way into domestic service, and
on the Pacific coast they became formidable competitors
of household servants of other nationalities.[4]

The political and economic conditions in Europe and
the breaking down of long-established customs in Asia
have thus since 1850 brought to this country large numbers of men and women who have performed the household service previously done by native born Americans.
The presence of the Irish in the East, of the Germans in
the West, of the Scandinavians in the Northwest, and of
the Chinese on the Pacific coast has thus introduced a

[1] *Arrivals of Alien Passengers and Immigrants in the United States
from 1820 to 1890*, pp. 15, 22.

[2] Women constituted 41.8 per cent of the total number of German
immigrants arriving here during the twenty-two years ending June 30,
1890 ; the Irish forming 48.5 per cent. — *Ibid.*, p. 11.

[3] The United States Census for 1890 gives the number of domestic servants born in Ireland as 168,993 ; the number born in Germany was
95,007.

[4] The number of Chinese in domestic service in 1890 was 16,439.

new social, as well as a new economic, element at the
North. It has led to a change in the relation of employer and employee; the class line which was only
faintly drawn in the early part of the century between
employer and "help" has been changed into a caste line
which many employers believe it to their interest to preserve. The native born American fears to lose social
position by entering into competition with foreign labor.

While this change, owing to political conditions in the
Old World, was taking place at the North in the character
of the service, a similar change was taking place at the
South growing out of the abolition of slavery in 1863.
The negroes who had previously performed all domestic
service for their personal expenses have since then received for the same service a small remuneration in
money. This fact prevents now as effectually as during
the slavery period any competition in domestic service
on the part of native born white employees. It does not
prevent all competition on the part of foreign born white
employees, since prejudice against the negro does not
exist in Europe owing to the fact that negro slavery has
not prevailed there. The effects of these great movements upon the nature and personnel of domestic service
will be discussed later in considering its present condition. They have had a direct and conspicuous influence
on the condition of domestic service and even in the use
of the term applied to those who engage in it.

But other political influences more subtle and possibly
more far-reaching in their effect have been at work.
Our loose naturalization laws, and the determining of
the qualifications for the right of suffrage by as many

F

standards as there are states, have made the enormous number of men coming to this country annually an easy prey to scheming politicians and demagogues. The labor vote, the Irish vote, the German vote, have been flattered and sought by party managers until the wage-earning man feels that "like Atlas of old he carries the world on his shoulders." If the laboring man feels the weight of the world, his wife and daughter believe that some share of the burden rests on them. The democratic tendencies of the country, the political practices of the day, have everywhere broken down the high wall of separation between employer and employee. They are subversive even in the household of that patriarchal relationship that has been driven from every stronghold but this.

While the political movements of the century have thus changed the personnel of domestic service in America, the development of the material resources of the country has affected its status. Before the present century employees of every kind were in a sense stationary. This was due partly to the influence of the English poor laws; partly to the system of indenture which bound a servant for seven, five, or four years, and to the system of slavery which bound the servant for life; partly to the system of apprenticeship which made the servant a member of the family of his master; partly to the custom prevailing in the country districts and small towns for unmarried workmen in all industries to board with their employers; and partly to the lack of facilities for cheap and easy means of communication between different sections of the country. There was no mobility of labor as regards either employment or place of employment — a fact true alike of domestic service and of other occupations. But this condition of affairs gradually changed. As has been seen, indented servants disappeared and every employee was free to break as well as to make an engagement for service. The establishment of the factory system of manufactures and the consequent substitution of mechanical for skilled processes of labor broke down the system of apprenticeship, and workmen of every occupation, except domestic service, ceased to be members of the families of their employers. A mobility of labor was made possible such as could not have been secured under the old system. At a later time the great era of railroad development and similar enterprises gave opportunity for a certain mobility as regards place of employment. The tide of western emigration due to the discovery of gold and the cheapness of western land caused much shifting of labor among the non-capitalist class, and this was increased as means of communication were rendered more easy. The establishment of companies to encourage foreign immigration with the object of developing the material resources of the country was another weight in the scale in favor of greater mobility of labor as regards both place and employment. The abolition of slavery removed the last important legal barrier against perfect mobility.

All of these industrial movements have been important factors in changing the condition and character of domestic service. It is true, in a general sense, that every great change in economic conditions affects all occupations. But domestic service has through these causes been affected in certain specific ways. The employee who

disliked housework, but to whom no other occupation
had been open, could go into a factory or a mill, since
no time was consumed in learning the simple processes
of mechanical work. Every invention formed the basis
for a new occupation. Domestic service had a hundred
competitors in a field where before the era of inventions
it had stood alone. Moreover, these new occupations
required little skill, no preparation, and possessed the
charm of novelty. Again, the rapid development of
railroad interests, with the increase of competition and
consequent lowering of passenger rates, often influenced
families emigrating to the West to take with them their
trusted employees. The same fact made it possible for
women seeking new employments to go from place to place
in ways unthought of in the early part of the century.

In view of these changed and changing economic conditions it may be said that the immobility of labor, which
has seemed to some economists so great an obstacle to
the industrial advancement of women,[1] has practically
ceased to exist in the case of domestic service. In fact,
industrial development has so far changed conditions that
the problem has now come to be how to make this form
of labor not more mobile, but more stable. One illustration of this is found in the fact that when seven hundred
domestic employees represented on the schedules were
asked how many of them had ever been engaged in any
other occupation, twenty-seven per cent replied that they
had. The mobility as to the place of labor was found
to be even greater. Twenty-seven per cent of the native
born employees did not reside in the same state in which

[1] Walker, *Wages*, pp. 376–377.

they were born, and adding to these the number of
foreign born, it was found that sixty-eight per cent did
not reside in their native country or state. Moreover,
this statement is below the truth as it does not take into
account the number of changes made within a single
year and refers to only one change from place of birth
to present residence.[1]

An indication of these various changes in the condition of domestic service during these different periods
is seen in the history of the word " servant." As used
in England and in law at the time of the settlement of
the American colonies it signified any employee, and no
odium was in any way attached to the word.[2] But five

[1] An illustration of these various changes is seen in the case of one
employee, who was born in Ireland, engaged in service in New York, and
afterwards drifted to Minnesota, where the report was made.

[2] This is indicated by the various definitions given in early dictionaries.
It is a curious fact that *The New World of Words or General English
Dictionary*, large quarto, third edition, London, 1671, does not contain
the word "servant." Phillips' *Universal English Dictionary*, London,
1720, has "*servant*, a man or woman who serves another." Bailey's
Dictionary, London, 1721, 1737, and 1770, defines *servant* as "one
who serves another." *The Royal Standard English Dictionary*, first
American edition, Worcester, Massachusetts, 1788, "being the first
work of the kind printed in America," defines *servant* as "one who
serves." The second edition, Brookfield, 1804, has "*servant*, one who
serves for wages."

Some interesting illustrations of this early use of the word are found
in colonial literature. Thus Thomas Morton in his *New English Canaan*,
p. 179, says, "In the month of June Anno Salutis, 1622, it was my
chance to arrive in the parts of New England with thirty servants and
provisions of all sorts fit for a plantation."

Governor Bradford in his *History of Plymouth*, pp. 235–236, speaks of
"Captaine Wolastone and with him 3. or 4. more of some eminencie,
who brought with them a great many servants, with provisions & other
implments fit for to begine a plantation."

A "Narrative concerning the settlement of New England," 1630, says,

things led to its temporary disuse : first, the reproach connected with the word through the character and social rank of the redemptioners ; second, the fact that when the redemptioners gave place at the South to negro slaves the word " servant " was transferred to this class,[1] and this alone was sufficient to prevent its application to whites ;[2] third, the levelling tendencies that always prevail in a new country ; fourth, the literal interpretation of the preamble of the Declaration of Independence ; and fifth, the new social and political theories resulting from the introduction of French philosophical ideas. At the North the word " help " as applied especially to women superseded the word " servant," while at the South the term " servant " was applied only to the negro. From the time of the Revolution, therefore, until about 1850 the word " servant " does not seem to

---

" This yeare there went hence 6 shippes with 1000 people in them to the Massachusetts having sent two yeares before betweene 3 & 400 servants to provide howses and Corne against theire coming, to the charge of (at least) 10,000*l*., these Servants through Idlenes & ill Government neglected both theire building & plantinge of Corne, soe that if those 6 Shippes had not arived the plantation had ben broke & dissolved." — *Mass. Hist. Soc. Proc.*, 1860–1862, pp. 130–131.

The same use of the word is found a number of times in the list of the Mayflower passengers.

[1] J. F. D. Smith says, London, 1784, " However, although I now call this man (a backwoodsman of the Alleghanies) my servant, yet he himself never would have submitted to such an appellation, although he most readily performed every menial office, and indeed every service I could desire." — *Tour in the United States*, I., 356.

[2] Fanny Kemble writes, " They have no idea, of course, of a white person performing any of the offices of a servant ; " then follows an amusing account of her white maid's being taken for the master's wife, and her almost unavailing efforts to correct the mistake. — *Journal of a Residence in Georgia*, pp. 44–46.

have been generally applied in either section to white persons of American birth.[1]

Since the introduction of foreign labor at the middle of the century, the word "servant" has again come into general use as applied to white employees, not, however, as a survival of the old colonial word, but as a reintroduction from Europe of a term signifying one who performs so-called menial labor, and it is restricted in its use, except in a legal sense, to persons who perform domestic service. The present use of the word has come not only from the almost exclusive employment of foreigners in domestic service, but also because of the increase of wealth and consequent luxury in this country, the growing class divisions, and the adoption of

---

[1] An illustration of this change is seen in the different definitions given to the word. In the *Royal Standard English Dictionary*, 1813, a servant is "one who attends and obeys another, one in a state of subjection."

Johnson's *Dictionary*, London, 1818, gives: "(1) One who attends another and acts at his command; the correlative of master. Used of man or woman. (2) One in a state of subjection."

Richardson's *New Dictionary of the English Language*, London, 1838, defines *servant* as the correlative of *master*.

The American usage was practically the same. The first edition of Webster, 1828, gives: "(1) Servant, a person, male or female, that attends another for the purpose of performing menial offices for him, or who is employed by another for such offices, or for other labor, and is subject to his command. *Servant* differs from *slave*, as the servant's subjection to a master is voluntary, the slave's is not. Every slave is a servant, but every servant is not a slave."

Worcester, 1860, says of *servant*: "(1) One who serves, whether male or female; correlative of *master*, *mistress*, or *employer*. (2) One in a state of subjection; a menial; a domestic; a drudge; a slave."

These various definitions all suggest the class association of the terms "servant" and "slave."

many European habits of living and thinking and speaking.[1]

These simple historical facts are one explanation of the unwillingness of American women to engage in work stigmatized by an offensive term applied to no other class of laborers.

In studying the question of domestic service, therefore, the fact cannot be overlooked that certain historical influences have affected its conditions; that political revolutions have changed its personnel, and industrial development its mobility. It is as impossible to dream of restoring the former condition of household service as

[1] A curious illustration of the social position of servants in Europe is seen in their lack of political privileges.

The French Constitution of 1791 was preceded by a bill of rights declaring the equality and brotherhood of men, but a disqualification for the right of suffrage, indeed, the only one, was "to be in a menial capacity, *viz.*, that of a servant receiving wages." Title III., chap. 1, sec. 2. The Constitution of 1795, after a similar preamble, states that the citizenship is suspended "by being a domestic on wages, attending on the person or serving the house." Title II., 13, 3. The Constitution of 1799 has a similar disqualification. Title I., art. 5. It is probable that these provisions were intended to punish men who would consent to serve the nobility or the wealthy classes when it was expected that all persons would be democratic enough to serve themselves, not to cast discredit on domestic service *per se*. — Tripier, pp. 20, 105, 168.

During the revolutionary movement in Austria, the Hungarian Diet at its session, in 1847-1848, passed an act providing that the qualification for electors should be "to have attained the age of twenty years; Hungarians by birth or naturalized; not under guardianship, nor in domestic service, nor convicted of fraud, theft, murder, etc." Act 5, sec. 2. — Stiles, II., 376.

The qualifications for suffrage in England also excluded domestic servants, but there was no discrimination against them as a class.

The Declaration of Independence, declaring all men free and equal in the presence of African slavery, thus has its counterpart in these free constitutions disfranchising domestic servants.

it is of restoring former household employments, and neither is to be desired. In each case the question is one of preparing for the next step in the process of evolution, not of retrograding toward a condition impossible to restore. Any attempt to secure a change for the better in the present condition of domestic service must be ineffective if it does not take into consideration these historic aspects of the subject.

CHAPTER V

ECONOMIC PHASES OF DOMESTIC SERVICE [1]

THE attempt has been made in the foregoing chapters to indicate the extent to which domestic employments and domestic service have been influenced by industrial and political events arising outside of the household, and apparently having little or no connection with it. That domestic service is amenable to some of the general economic laws and conditions which affect other occupations and that it is also governed by economic laws developed within itself will perhaps be evident from an examination of a few of these economic conditions and principles. These may be stated for the sake of brevity in the form of propositions.

The first group of propositions to be suggested concerns the number and distribution of persons of foreign birth engaged in domestic service.

(1) A large proportion of the domestic employees in the United States are of foreign birth. This is evident from the following table prepared from the schedules sent out : [2]

[1] Some of the figures given in this chapter have been taken from advance sheets kindly furnished by the Census Bureau, and hence it is impossible to give in every case page references.

[2] Preface, p. 1, and Appendix I.

74

TABLE I

PLACE OF BIRTH OF EMPLOYEES

PERSON REPORTING	NUMBER			PER CENT		
	Native born	Foreign born	Not given	Native born	Foreign born	Not given
Employer..........	922	1,212	411	36.23	47.62	16.15
Employee.........	324	395	....	45.06	54.94	....

The statement may be more fully illustrated from the Eleventh Census, which shows that the number of foreign born in domestic service is 30.86 per cent of the entire number.[1] The geographical distribution of the different classes of domestic employees is seen from Table II on the following page.

Another illustration of the same point is found by an examination of the relative number of native born and foreign born domestic employees in the individual states and territories. In nine states and territories the number of foreign born domestic employees exceeds the number of native born white employees,[2] in sixteen about one half of the white domestic employees are of foreign birth,[3] in twenty-four states and territories the number of native born white employees largely exceeds the foreign born,[4]

[1] The percentage of foreign born as given here differs slightly from that given on page 80, as it includes a small number of Chinese and Japanese.

[2] Arizona, California, Connecticut, Massachusetts, Minnesota, New Jersey, New York, North Dakota, Rhode Island.

[3] Colorado, District of Columbia, Illinois, Michigan, Montana, Nebraska, Nevada, New Hampshire, Oregon, Pennsylvania, South Dakota, Texas, Utah, Washington, Wisconsin, Wyoming.

[4] Alabama, Arkansas, Delaware, Florida, Georgia, Idaho, Indiana,

TABLE II

Domestic Employees in the United States, 1890

Geographical Section	Number				Per Cent		
	Total	Native white	Foreign white	Colored	Native white	Foreign white	Colored
Pacific Coast [1]....	78,700	29,576	28,198	20,926	37.58	35.83	26.59
Eastern [2].........	134,016	52,419	74,004	7,593	39.11	55.22	5.67
Middle [3]..........	394,062	176,194	175,819	42,049	44.71	44.62	10.67
Western [4]........	388,920	233,274	128,761	26,885	59.98	33.11	6.91
Border [5]	251,544	79,611	16,649	155,284	31.65	6.62	61.73
Southern [6]	207,549	34,812	6,432	166,305	16.77	3.10	80.13
United States..	1,454,791	605,886	429,863	419,042	41.65	29.55	28.80

while in fifteen states colored employees are in excess.[7] It will be seen that the states in which the number of native born white domestic employees exceeds the number of the foreign born are those states having relatively

Iowa, Kansas, Kentucky, Louisiana, Maine, Maryland, Mississippi, Missouri, New Mexico, North Carolina, Ohio, Oklahoma, South Carolina, Tennessee, Vermont, Virginia, West Virginia.

[1] Arizona, California, Colorado, Idaho, Montana, Nevada, New Mexico, Oregon, Utah, Washington, Wyoming.

[2] Connecticut, Maine, Massachusetts, New Hampshire, Rhode Island, Vermont.

[3] New York, New Jersey, Pennsylvania.

[4] Minnesota, Illinois, Indiana, Iowa, Kansas, Michigan, Nebraska, North Dakota, Ohio, Oklahoma, South Dakota, Wisconsin.

[5] Delaware, District of Columbia, Kentucky, Maryland, Missouri, Tennessee, Virginia, West Virginia.

[6] Alabama, Arkansas, Florida, Georgia, Louisiana, Mississippi, North Carolina, Texas.

This classification is made with reference to conditions apparently similar as regards domestic service.

[7] Alabama, Arkansas, Delaware, District of Columbia, Florida, Georgia, Kentucky, Louisiana, Maryland, Mississippi, North Carolina, South Carolina, Tennessee, Texas, Virginia.

a small number of foreign born residents.[1] A still more specific illustration is found in the experience of one state. In Massachusetts in 1885 the foreign born domestic servants formed 60.24 per cent of the entire number.[2]

These different illustrations seem to show the truth of the proposition stated.

(2) The converse of the preceding proposition is also true — the concentration of women of foreign birth engaged in remunerative occupations is on domestic service.

The Eleventh Census shows that, in 1890, 59.37 per cent of all foreign white women at work were engaged in domestic and personal service. This leaves only 40.63 per cent to be distributed among all other gainful occupations.[3] A specific illustration in the case of an individual state is seen in Massachusetts. Here the percentage of the foreign born in the entire population is 27.13, while, as stated above, the number of foreign born women in domestic service is 60.24 per cent.[4]

(3) The foreign born population as a class seek the large cities.

In 1890 the persons of foreign birth in the United

---

[1] *Eleventh Census*, Population, Part I., p. lxxxiii.

[2] *Census of Massachusetts*, 1885, Part II., p. 38.

[3] *Eleventh Census*, Occupations, p. 20. It is interesting to note the increasing proportion of women of foreign birth who go into domestic service. The Tenth Census shows that, in 1880, 49.31 per cent of all women of foreign birth employed for pay were engaged in domestic service ; thus in ten years an increase of 10.06 per cent was made.

[4] *Census of Massachusetts*, 1885, Part II., pp. xxxvi, xxxviii. In this statement only the number of women engaged in domestic service for remuneration is considered.

States formed 14.77 per cent of the entire population. But of the total foreign population, 44.13 per cent was found in the one hundred and twenty-four cities having a population of twenty-five thousand or more.[1]

(4) The foreign countries having the largest absolute representation in the largest cities are Ireland, Germany, Great Britain, Sweden, and Canada and Newfoundland. The following table shows the relative number of persons born in these countries who are found in the United States as a whole, and in the large cities:

TABLE III

PROPORTION OF PERSONS OF FOREIGN BIRTH IN THE UNITED STATES

COUNTRY OF BIRTH	United States	Number in principal cities	Per cent in principal cities
Ireland	1,871,509	1,047,432	55.97
Germany	2,784,894	1,328,675	47.71
Great Britain	909,092	369,979	40.70
Canada and Newfoundland	980,938	307,660	31.36
Sweden and Norway	800,706	219,112	27.36

(5) The foreign countries having the largest absolute and relative representation in domestic service are, in order, Ireland, Germany, Sweden and Norway, Great Britain, and Canada and Newfoundland. This will be evident from the following table, which indicates the place of birth of all persons of foreign birth engaged in domestic service and the per cent of each nationality so engaged:

[1] *Eleventh Census*, Population, Part I., p. lxxxix.

TABLE IV

PLACE OF BIRTH OF DOMESTIC EMPLOYEES

COUNTRY OF BIRTH	Number of foreign born persons, 10 years of age and over, in domestic service	Per cent of foreign born persons, 10 years of age and over, in domestic service
Ireland............................	168,993	37.64
Germany	95,007	21.16
Sweden and Norway...............	58,049	12.93
Great Britain.....................	34,537	7.69
Canada and Newfoundland.........	31,213	6.95
Other countries...................	61,195	13.63

Similar results were reached through individual schedules sent out. The returns as made by employers and employees show that the place of birth of foreign born employees and the relative percentages are as follows :

TABLE V

NUMBER OF FOREIGN BORN IN DOMESTIC SERVICE

PLACE OF BIRTH	PERSON REPORTING			
	EMPLOYER		EMPLOYEE	
	Number	Per cent	Number	Per cent
Ireland.......................	653	53.88	217	54.94
Sweden and Norway..........	147	12.13	50	12.66
Germany....................	128	10.56	37	9.37
Great Britain................	122	10.07	32	8.10
British America..............	104	8.58	42	10.63
Other countries..............	58	4.78	17	4.30
Total.....................	1,212	100.00	395	100.00

This group of five propositions in regard to the number and distribution of the foreign born engaged in domestic service seems to indicate that in this country, with the exception of the sections employing colored servants, domestic service is as a rule performed by persons of foreign birth belonging to a few well-defined classes as regards nationality, who prefer city to country life. The facts given are an understatement of the influence exerted on domestic service by persons of foreign extraction, since they do not take into consideration the factor of foreign parentage.

A second group of propositions may be suggested in regard to the general distribution of domestic employees.

(1) The number of domestic servants is absolutely and relatively small in agricultural and sparsely settled states.

This will be evident by the reference to the accompanying chart, which shows the number of persons to each domestic servant in each of the states. The states last in the list, where the smallest relative number of servants is employed, are all large in area, and as a rule have the smallest population in proportion to the area of settlement. This condition is probably due to the two facts that all housework is as a rule performed without remuneration by housewives, since they are more free from social and other interruptions than are women in cities, and also to the aversion of domestics as a class to country life.

(2) The number of domestic servants is absolutely and relatively large in those states containing a large urban population.

This is also made evident by the diagram. Forty-nine

CHART SHOWING THE NUMBER OF PERSONS TO EACH DOMESTIC EMPLOYEE IN
THE VARIOUS STATES AND TERRITORIES AND THE DISTRICT OF COLUMBIA

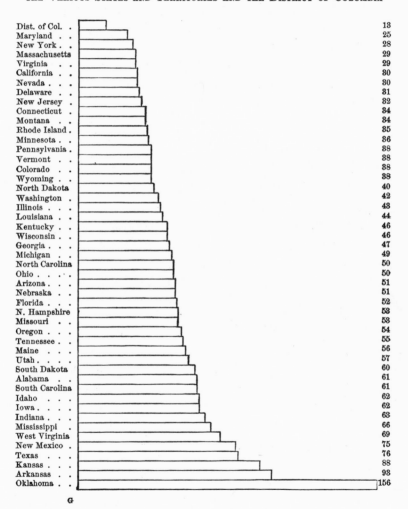

Dist. of Col. . .	13
Maryland . .	25
New York . .	28
Massachusetts	29
Virginia . .	29
California . .	30
Nevada . . .	30
Delaware . .	31
New Jersey .	32
Connecticut .	34
Montana . .	34
Rhode Island .	35
Minnesota . .	36
Pennsylvania .	38
Vermont . .	38
Colorado . .	38
Wyoming . .	38
North Dakota	40
Washington .	42
Illinois . . .	43
Louisiana . .	44
Kentucky . .	46
Wisconsin . .	46
Georgia . . .	47
Michigan . .	49
North Carolina	50
Ohio	50
Arizona . . .	51
Nebraska . .	51
Florida . . .	52
N. Hampshire	53
Missouri . .	53
Oregon . . .	54
Tennessee . .	55
Maine . . .	56
Utah	57
South Dakota	60
Alabama . .	61
South Carolina	61
Idaho . . .	62
Iowa	62
Indiana . . .	63
Mississippi .	66
West Virginia	69
New Mexico .	75
Texas . . .	76
Kansas . . .	88
Arkansas . .	93
Oklahoma . .	156

G

of the fifty largest cities in the United States are found in the first thirty-four states in the list ; only one of the fifty is found in the last fifteen states. The fact is apparently most clearly shown in the case of the District of Columbia, which has an almost exclusively urban population and ranks first with reference to the number of servants employed. The condition here, however, is due not so much to its urban character as to the employment of colored help and the fact that the city contains an abnormally large number of temporary residents requiring a disproportionate amount of service. The truth of the proposition is better indicated by the examples of New York, Massachusetts, and New Jersey, which stand nearly at the head of the list and contain seventeen of the fifty largest cities.

(3) The aggregate wealth of a state has little appreciable effect on the relative number of domestic servants employed.

This is evident from a study of the relative true and assessed valuation of real and personal property in the different states.[1] In more than one half the states it has no apparent connection whatever with the relative number of servants.

(4) The per capita wealth of a state has, with the exception of the Southern states as a class, a somewhat important bearing on the relative number of servants employed.

This will be seen from an examination of the per capita assessed valuations of real and personal property in the various states.[2] The rank of each state in the class of

---

[1] *Eleventh Census*, Wealth, Debt, and Taxation, Part II., p. 16, Chart.
[2] *Ibid.*, p. 59.

per capita wealth and in the relative number of domestic servants employed, with the exception named, does not vary materially. The variation in the Southern states is due to the presence of negro employees. The extremely low wages paid by employers enables them to command the services of a larger number of persons for the same expenditure of money than is possible at the North.

These facts may be considered as indicative in a general way of the truth of the current opinion that an increase in income generally shows itself first in the employment of additional service. They prove nothing absolutely on this point, however, as they are too general in character.

(5) Domestic employees are found in the largest numbers, relatively and absolutely, in the large cities. The fifty largest cities in the United States contain 18.04 per cent of the total population of the country. They have, however, 32.32 per cent of the total number of domestic servants. To put the same fact in another way, domestic servants constitute 2.32 per cent of the total population, but 4.07 per cent of the population of the fifty largest cities. The force of gravity exerted, therefore, by the large cities seems to act with nearly twice the power on the class of domestic employees that it does on the population as a whole.

The conclusion seems to follow that in general employers in large cities have less difficulty in securing servants than have persons living elsewhere, but that they are practically restricted in their choice to those of foreign birth. The conclusion does not follow that these employers have less difficulty than have others in dealing with the question of domestic service, since the facts given concern only the number of servants, not the quality of service.

(6) The proportion of persons engaged in domestic service varies with geographical location and prevailing industry.

This fact is indicated by the chart, which shows that in Southern cities, where the colored population is large, and in New York and Boston, which are ports of entry and therefore able to secure a large number of foreign born servants, the proportion of servants to the total population is large. In cities where the leading occupation is manufacturing, as Lowell, Paterson, and Fall River, the proportion of servants is small. In cities where the industrial conditions are similar the proportions are similar.

The same fact may be illustrated in two other ways. In Washington, Richmond, Atlanta, Memphis, and Nashville, — the five cities having the largest number of domestic employees in proportion to the population, — the domestic employees constitute in each city more than fourteen per cent of the entire number of persons engaged in all gainful occupations. In these five cities more than one third of all women engaged in remunerative occupations are in domestic service. On the other hand, in Camden, Trenton, Lowell, Paterson, and Fall River, — the five cities having the smallest number of domestic employees in proportion to the population, — the per cent of domestic employees with reference to the total number of persons engaged in all gainful occupations is less than seven, while in Lowell and Paterson only ten per cent and in Fall River only seven per cent of all women engaged in

CHART SHOWING THE NUMBER OF PERSONS TO EACH DOMESTIC EMPLOYEE
IN THE FIFTY LARGEST CITIES

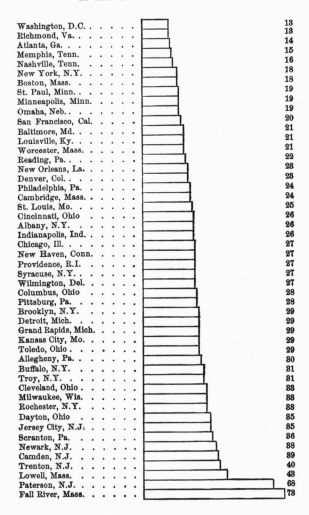

Washington, D.C.	13
Richmond, Va.	13
Atlanta, Ga.	14
Memphis, Tenn.	15
Nashville, Tenn.	16
New York, N.Y.	18
Boston, Mass.	18
St. Paul, Minn.	19
Minneapolis, Minn.	19
Omaha, Neb.	19
San Francisco, Cal.	20
Baltimore, Md.	21
Louisville, Ky.	21
Worcester, Mass.	21
Reading, Pa.	22
New Orleans, La.	23
Denver, Col.	23
Philadelphia, Pa.	24
Cambridge, Mass.	24
St. Louis, Mo.	25
Cincinnati, Ohio	26
Albany, N.Y.	26
Indianapolis, Ind.	26
Chicago, Ill.	27
New Haven, Conn.	27
Providence, R.I.	27
Syracuse, N.Y.	27
Wilmington, Del.	27
Columbus, Ohio	28
Pittsburg, Pa.	28
Brooklyn, N.Y.	29
Detroit, Mich.	29
Grand Rapids, Mich.	29
Kansas City, Mo.	29
Toledo, Ohio	29
Allegheny, Pa.	30
Buffalo, N.Y.	31
Troy, N.Y.	31
Cleveland, Ohio	33
Milwaukee, Wis.	33
Rochester, N.Y.	33
Dayton, Ohio	35
Jersey City, N.J.	35
Scranton, Pa.	36
Newark, N.J.	38
Camden, N.J.	39
Trenton, N.J.	40
Lowell, Mass.	43
Paterson, N.J.	68
Fall River, Mass.	73

remunerative occupations are in domestic service. The following table will show these contrasts:

TABLE VI

DOMESTIC SERVANTS AND WOMEN COMPARED WITH THOSE IN GAINFUL OCCUPATIONS

CITIES	Per cent of domestic servants as compared with the total number of persons in all gainful occupations	Per cent of women in domestic service as compared with the total number of women in all gainful occupations
Washington	17.10	40.46
Richmond	16.66	40.36
Atlanta......................	5.43	36.72
Memphis	5.21	39.07
Nashville	4.61	38.69
Camden	5.89	26.13
Trenton	6.13	26.07
Lowell	4.48	10.29
Paterson......................	3.34	10.84
Fall River	2.82	6.98

(7) Neither per capita wealth nor aggregate wealth has an appreciable influence in determining the number of servants in cities.

Three illustrations of this are seen : (1) Washington, Richmond, Atlanta, Memphis, and Nashville rank respectively as regards per capita wealth, 13, 27, 19, 24, and 41, although they are the five cities that head the list in the proportion of servants to the total population; (2) Lowell and Fall River are at the foot of the list as regards the proportion of servants, but rank 10 and 12 in per capita wealth ; (3) Nashville ranks fifth in the number of servants and Paterson forty-ninth, while both rank nearly the same in point of wealth.[1] There are indeed many instances where there is apparent connection between these two conditions, but they seem rather to be illustrations of the following point:

(8) The prevailing industry of a city, rather than its population or wealth, determines the number of domestic employees.

This conclusion seems to follow naturally as a result of the two previous propositions, but a few other facts in support of it may be mentioned. In eleven of the fifty principal cities the proportion of domestic servants to the total population is smaller than is the proportion in the states in which they are severally located.[2] The leading occupation in each of these cities is some form of manufacturing, and in each of them the proportion of persons engaged in manufacturing processes is larger than, with few exceptions, in the other cities. This fact explains the apparent contradiction between this statement and the one that domestic servants are found in the largest proportions in the largest cities.

That manufacturing industries tend to decrease the number of domestic employees in a city is both a cause and a result. The competition in industry draws women from domestic service, and at the same time a large part of the population in a manufacturing city is unable or does not care to employ large numbers of servants. It has been seen, however, that several of the manufacturing cities rank comparatively high in per capita wealth.

[1] *Eleventh Census*, Wealth, Debt, and Taxation, Part II., pp. 376–403.
[2] Brooklyn, Buffalo, Camden, Fall River, Jersey City, Lowell, Newark, Paterson, Rochester, Trenton, Troy.

It seems possible in view of the facts stated in this second group of propositions to draw these conclusions. In states containing a relatively high urban population it is possible for wealth to command the services of a large proportion of persons for work in domestic service. But in cities where wealth comes into competition with manufacturing industries the proportion of domestic servants is small. Where such competition does not exist the proportion is large. In other words, persons are willing to enter domestic service for a consideration in cities where no other avenues of work are open to them with the qualifications they possess. They are unwilling to do so where such openings do exist.

A third group of propositions remains to be considered concerning the subject of wages. They may be thus stated:

(1) Wages in domestic service vary in different sections according to the economic conditions of the several localities.

TABLE VII

AVERAGE WEEKLY WAGES BY GEOGRAPHICAL SECTION

GEOGRAPHICAL SECTION	AVERAGE WEEKLY WAGES	
	Men	Women
Pacific coast	$7.57	$4.57
Eastern section	8.68	3.60
Middle section	7.62	3.21
Western section	6.69	3.00
Border section	4.86	2.55
Southern section	3.95	2.22
United States	$7.18	$3.23

This principle is illustrated by Table VII on the preceding page based on a classification of the returns received through individual schedules relating to 2,545 employees.

The difference indicated apparently conforms to the general variation in wages in different sections indicated by the Fourth Annual Report of the Commissioner of Labor,[1] and by examination of a considerable number of reports of various state bureaus of labor. The slight exception in the case of the wages of men on the Pacific coast is accidental, owing to the small number of returns.

(2) Skilled labor commands higher wages than unskilled labor.

This will be evident from Table VIII on the following page based on the schedules received from employers and employees and the returns from a Boston employment bureau.

In every instance it is seen that it is the skilled laborer — the cook — who commands the highest wages. The general servant who is expected to unite in herself all the functions of all the other employees named in the list becomes, on account of this fact, an unskilled worker, and, therefore, receives the lowest wages. The same principle holds true in the case of the seamstress and the laundress, the gardener and the choreman. It is difficult to make a deduction in the case of men employed in household service, since no universal custom prevails, as with women employees, in regard to adding to the wages paid in money, board, lodging, and other personal expenses.

[1] P. 68.

DOMESTIC SERVICE

TABLE VIII

AVERAGE WEEKLY AND DAILY WAGES BY OCCUPATIONS

OCCUPATION	WEEKLY WAGES		
	General schedule of		Boston employment bureau
	Employer	Employee	
WOMEN			
Cooks	$3.80	$3.64	$4.45
Parlor maids	....	....	3.94
Cooks and laundresses..........	3.50	3.27	....
Chambermaids	3.31	3.47	3.86
Waitresses	3.23	3.15	3.76
Second girls	3.04	3.27	3.34
Chambermaids and waitresses...	2.99	3.21	....
General servants..............	2.94	2.88	3.16
MEN			
Coachmen.....................	7.84	....	....
Coachmen and gardeners	6.54	....	....
Butlers	6.11	....	....
Cooks........................	6.08	....	....
	DAILY WAGES		
WOMEN			
Seamstresses	$1.01	....	....
Laundresses..................	.82	....	....
MEN			
Gardeners.....................	1.33	....	....
Choremen	.87	....	....

A corollary to the proposition may be added. The skilled laborer is a better workman than the unskilled laborer. The question was asked of employers, "What is the nature of the service rendered? Is it 'excellent,'

'good,' 'fair,' or 'poor'?" The replies show that in proportion to the number of answers the largest percentage
of service characterized as "excellent" is rendered by
cooks, while the largest percentage characterized as
"poor" is given by the general servants. These are, it
is true, matters of opinion; and without a fixed standard,
which it is impossible to secure, such judgments can have
no absolute value. But the fact is of interest as showing
the opinion of a large number of housekeepers. The following table will show the results in regard to these two
classes of employees :

TABLE IX

NATURE OF SERVICE RENDERED

OCCUPATION	Total number of re- plies	Not an- swered	KIND OF SERVICE RENDERED							
			Excellent		Good		Fair		Poor	
			Num- ber	Per cent	Num- ber	Per cent	Num- ber	Per cent	Num- ber	Per cent
Cooks...........	262	30	83	32	113	43	58	22	8	3
General servants.	585	53	151	26	221	38	177	30	36	6

(3) The foreign born in domestic service receive
higher wages than the native born.

This was found to be true in every class of occupatīons,
in every section, in the case of both men and women, and
in the returns made by both employers and employees.
But two trifling exceptions were found, both accidental.
The principle cannot of course be stated absolutely as
the facts at command are far from exhaustive, but so
striking a uniformity cannot be considered purely acci-

dental.   An explanation is found in three facts : (1)
the preference of the foreign born for the large cities,
where wages in domestic service are higher than in the
country; (2) the large proportion of negroes among the
native born; (3) the relatively better class of foreign
born than of native born women who enter domestic
service.   This statement must be made somewhat dog-
matically here, since its proof demands a discussion of
the entire subject of the unwillingness of native born
women to enter domestic service.

(4) The wages of men engaged in domestic service are
higher than the wages of women.

This will be evident by reference to Table VII and to
Table VIII.   Two things, however, must be borne in
mind : first, that nearly all the men classified as cooks are
employed on the Pacific coast, where wages are relatively
high; second, that forty per cent of the men in domestic
service do not receive board and lodging in addition to
wages in money, while only two per cent of women so
employed, principally laundresses, do not receive board
and lodging.   But although these facts modify the discrepancy between the wages of men and women, they do
not wholly remove it.   Whether the difference is as great
as in other occupations cannot be stated.

(5) A tendency is found towards an increase in wages
paid by employers, as is seen in Table X on the following page.

An interesting historical illustration of the same fact
is given in a summary of wages and prices in Massachusetts from 1752 to 1860.   In 1815, the first time the
work of women is mentioned specifically, domestic ser-

vants received with board $.50 per week, while at the same time women were able to earn as papermakers $6.50 a week.[1]

TABLE X
COMPARISON OF WAGES PAID

WAGES PAID	NUMBER			PER CENT		
	Men	Women	Total	Men	Women	Total
Same as last year......	414	1638	2052	87.72	79.02	80.63
More than last year....	54	368	422	11.44	17.75	16.58
Less than last year.....	4	67	71	.84	3.23	2.79

(6) The wages received in domestic service are relatively and sometimes absolutely higher than the average wages received in other wage-earning occupations open to women.

A comparison may be made between the wages received by domestic employees and by two other classes — teachers in representative city schools and the wage-earning women included in the investigations made by the Commissioner of Labor. As illustrating the wages received in domestic service, the following tables are given, showing (1) the classified weekly and daily wages received and (2) the average weekly and daily wages with the percentages receiving more or less than the average. These facts are taken from the general schedules. Similar tables are given showing a somewhat higher rate of wages in all domestic occupations in the special city of Boston.

[1] *Report of the Bureau of Statistics of Labor, 1885*, pp. 196–312.

TABLE XI

Classified Daily and Weekly Wages by Occupations

Occupation / Schedule of Employers	Under $1	$1, but under $2	$2, but under $3	$3, but under $4	$4, but under $5	$5, but under $6	$6, but under $7	$7, but under $8	$8, but under $9	$9, but under $10	$10, but under $11	$11, but under $12	$12, but under $13	$13, but under $14	Over $14	Total
WOMEN																
General servants	1	33	251	276	39	5		1								606
Second girls		17	50	76	18	4	1	4								170
Cooks and laundresses		4	21	70	41	5										141
Cooks	4	6	38	104	86	31	7			3	1					280
Chambermaids and waitresses	2	9	44	69	7	2										133
Chambermaids	1	6	18	45	18	4										92
Waitresses		3	43	32	23	2										103
Nurses	1	11	30	46	18	9		6			4					125
Housekeepers				1	2				1							4
Total	9	89	495	619	252	62	8	11	1	3	5					1,654
MEN																
Butlers		3	2	5	3	8	6	4	3	6	2	1		1		44
Coachmen and gardeners		2	7	11	18	22	21	3	12	10	11	4	1	1		123
Coachmen		1	5	8	10	14	17	3	9	12	7	11	3	6	3	109
Cooks		1		1	3	2	3	3	1	3						17
Total		7	14	25	34	46	47	13	25	31	20	16	4	8	3	293

TABLE XI (Continued)

CLASSIFIED DAILY AND WEEKLY WAGES BY OCCUPATIONS

OCCUPATION — SCHEDULE OF EMPLOYERS	Under $1	$1, but under $2	$2, but under $3	$3, but under $4	$4, but under $5	$5, but under $6	$6, but under $7	$7, but under $8	$8, but under $9	$9, but under $10	$10, but under $11	$11, but under $12	$12, but under $13	$13, but under $14	Over $14	Total
EARNING DAILY																
WOMEN																
Laundresses	123	121														244
Seamstresses	48	51	6													105
Total	171	172	6													349
MEN																
Gardeners	26	87	8	1												
Choremen	24	14	1													
Total	50	101	9	1												161
EARNING WEEKLY																
SCHEDULE OF EMPLOYERS																
General servants	1	16	152	187	24	3										383
Second girls			11	18	10											39
Cooks and laundresses		4	6	22	13											45
Cooks	1	3	20	39	23	11	3	1								101
Chambermaids and waitresses		1	6	15		1										23
Chambermaids		2	7	9	6	1										25
Waitresses		1	14	16	2	2	1									36
Nurses			5	10	1				1	1						18
Housekeepers				2	1	1										4
Total	2	27	221	318	80	19	4	1	1	1						674

TABLE XII [1]

AVERAGE WEEKLY AND DAILY WAGES BY OCCUPATIONS

| OCCUPATION | PERSON REPLYING | | | | | |
| | EMPLOYER | | | EMPLOYEE | | |
	Average weekly wages	Per cent receiving more than the average	Per cent receiving the same or less than the average	Average weekly wages	Per cent receiving more than the average	Per cent receiving the same or less than the average
WOMEN						
General servants.............	$2.94	52.97	47.03.	$2.88	55.87	43.13
Second girls.................	3.04	40.00	60.00	3.27	53.85	46.15
Cooks and laundresses........	3.50	43.97	56.03	3.27	53.33	46.67
Cooks......................	3.80	45.71	54.29	3.64	43.56	56.44
Chambermaids and waitresses.	2.99	58.65	41.35	3.21	52.17	47.83
Chambermaids...............	3.31	47.83	52.17	3.47	32.00	68.00
Waitresses	3.23	43.69	56.31	3.15	44.44	55.56
Nurses	3.53	36.00	64.00	3.03	33.33	66.67
Housekeepers	5.15	25.00	75.00	5.15	25.00	75.00
Total......................	$3.23	47.88	52.12	$3.11	50.95	49.05
MEN						
Butlers.....................	$6.11	50.00	50.00	....	....	....
Coachmen and gardeners......	6.54	44.72	55.28	....	....	....
Coachmen...................	7.84	46.79	53.21	....	....	....
Cooks	6.09	47.06	52.94	....	....	....
Total......................	$6.93	46.42	53.58	....	....	....
	Average daily wages					
WOMEN						
Laundresses.................	$0.82	53.28	46.72	....	....	....
Seamstresses	1.01	39.05	60.95	....	....	....
Total......................	$0.90	49.00	51.00	....	....	....
MEN						
Gardeners...................	$1.33	56.56	43.44	....	....	....
Choremen	.87	43.59	56.41	....	....	....
Total......................	$1.29	53.42	46.58	....	....	....

[1] In the classification in these two tables the employees in several large boarding houses were omitted. All of those included under the term "nurses" are nurse-maids, with the exception of the few receiving the highest wages.

The following tables show the classified and average wages paid in the principal occupations as reported by a Boston employment bureau:

TABLE XIII
CLASSIFIED WEEKLY WAGES BY OCCUPATIONS

OCCUPATION	EARNING WEEKLY										Total
	$1, but under $2	$2, but under $3	$3, but under $4	$4, but under $5	$5, but under $6	$6, but under $7	$7, but under $8	$8, but under $9	$9, but under $10	$10, but under $11	
General servants..	8	183	577	143	3	....	....	....	....	....	914
Second girls........	2	41	363	69	....	....	....	....	....	....	475
Cooks	1	3	39	347	145	28	4	3	....	4	574
Chambermaids	....	3	40	37	2	....	....	....	....	....	82
Waitresses........	....	4	29	16	1	....	....	....	....	....	50
Parlor maids......	....	....	11	45	1	....	....	....	....	....	57
Nursery maids....	7	45	119	57	3	1	1	....	....	....	233
Laundresses	....	1	9	27	15	1	....	....	....	....	53
Total...........	18	280	1,187	741	170	30	5	3	....	4	2,438

TABLE XIV
AVERAGE WEEKLY WAGES BY OCCUPATIONS

OCCUPATION	Average weekly wages	Per cent receiving more than the average	Per cent receiving the same or less than the average	Highest wages received	Lowest wages received	Total number
General servants........	$3.16	40.5	59.5	$5.00	$1.50	914
Second girls............	3.34	62.2	37.3	4.50	1.50	475
Cooks..................	4.45	50.0	50.0	10.50	1.00	574
Chambermaids..........	3.86	57.4	42.6	5.00	3.00	82
Waitresses.............	3.76	48.4	51.6	5.00	2.50	50
Parlor maids	3.94	80.4	19.6	5.00	3.50	57
Nursery maids	3.26	51.3	48.7	7.00	1.00	233
Laundresses............	4.44	44.4	55.6	6.00	2.00	53
Total................						2,438

H

It is seen from Table XII that the average weekly wages in domestic service are $3.23 — a fair average in this case, since forty-eight per cent receive more than the average and fifty-two per cent the same or less than the average. The average domestic employee, therefore, is able to earn in money during the year $167.96 — a fair estimate, since in seventy-five cases out of every hundred the vacation granted women employees during the year is given without loss of wages.[1] This forms, however, but a part of the annual earnings. To this sum must be added board and lodging, fuel and light. For the equivalent in quality and quantity to that furnished by the employer the employee would in general be obliged to pay for board, lodging, and other incidental expenses at a reasonable estimate five dollars per week, or $250 annually, deducting board for two weeks' vacation. The total annual earnings of a domestic employee, therefore, amount to nearly $420. To this the negative facts must be added that there is no expense for laundry work, and that the work involves few personal expenses in the way of clothing, and that these necessary expenses are often partially met through gifts from the employer. Again, the position entails no expenditures for car fares in going to and from work, or other demands such as are made in a business way by other occupations, and it involves no outlay for appliances for work, as a sewing-machine, type-writer, text-books, etc. Moreover, no investment of capital is necessary in learning the principles of the work, since employers have thus far been willing to make of their own homes training-schools for employees. The domestic

[1] *Post,* p. 136.

employee is therefore never obliged to pay back either the capital invested in preparing for her work or the interest on that amount. It thus seems possible for the average household employee to save annually nearly $150 in an occupation involving no outlay or investment of capital in any way, and few personal expenses.

TABLE XV
CLASSIFIED ANNUAL SALARIES OF WOMEN TEACHERS

CITY	EARNING ANNUALLY											
	Under $300	$300, but under $400	$400, but under $500	$500, but under $600	$600, but under $700	$700, but under $800	$800, but under $900	$900, but under $1,000	$1,000, but under $1,200	$1,200, but under $1,500	More than $1,500	Total
Albany, N.Y.	1	26	34	153	22	11	6	....	....	1	....	254
Atlanta, Ga.	7	1	32	31	3	4	1	....	....	2	....	81
Baltimore, Md.	....	....	628	246	101	1	1	40	3	....	....	1,020
Cambridge, Mass.	....	1	22	19	146	10	3	11	2	....	....	214
Cincinnati, Ohio	....	....	26	50	59	359	98	1	5	19	2	619
Cleveland, Ohio	....	....	119	124	269	89	16	8	14	10	4	653
Detroit, Mich.	....	54	63	111	20	121	35	5	3	14	1	427
Lawrence, Mass.	....	....	43	49	6	....	2	1	1	1	....	103
Lowell, Mass.	....	....	8	5	155	9	1	....	....	1	1	180
Milwaukee, Wis.	....	2	76	72	197	19	7	15	9	2	....	399
New Haven, Conn.	....	54	73	38	107	14	11	....	1	2	1	301
New Orleans, La.	2	172	174	3	18	7	....	5	1	....	....	382
Paterson, N.J.	....	55	97	26	8	9	2	....	....	....	....	197
Rochester, N.Y.	45	57	287	3	7	14	6	....	1	2	....	422
St. Louis, Mo.	61	36	182	362	122	133	42	20	12	13	13	996
Syracuse, N.Y.	....	35	52	139	21	3	13	1	....	....	....	264
Total	116	493	1,916	1,431	1,261	803	244	107	52	67	22	6,512

A comparison may be made between these wages and the annual salaries received in sixteen representative cities by the women teachers in the public schools. Tables XV and XVI show the annual classified and average salaries received. [1]

[1] The figures are taken from the annual reports of city superintendents.

TABLE XVI

Average Annual Salaries of Women Teachers

City	Average salary	Per cent receiving more than the average	Per cent receiving the same or less than the average
Albany, N.Y............	$505.73	27.70	72.30
Atlanta, Ga.............	459.05	48.12	51.88
Baltimore, Md..........	500.92	37.12	62.88
Cambridge, Mass.......	628.35	22.32	77.68
Cincinnati, Ohio........	702.87	20.60	79.40
Cleveland, Ohio........	625.60	43.20	56.80
Detroit, Mich..........	607.96	96.02	3.98
Lawrence, Mass........	511.16	26.22	73.78
Lowell, Mass...........	608.66	6.71	93.29
Milwaukee, Wis........	588.00	63.59	34.41
New Haven, Conn......	536.41	52.96	47.04
New Orleans, La.......	429.78	28.08	71.92
Paterson, N.J..........	455.20	22.84	77.16
Rochester, N.Y........	431.63	57.34	42.66
St. Louis, Mo..........	574.68	34.89	65.11
Syracuse, N.Y..........	494.98	67.04	32.96

The concentration of salaries is seen to be on those between $400 and $500, the average salary being $545. This sum represents the full amount of wages received. To ascertain the amount it is possible to save annually there must be deducted at least $260 for board and

The attempt was made to find the average salaries in the fifty largest cities, but many cities do not publish in detail the salaries paid. The reports used were those for the year ending in 1889, — the year for which reports were made through the schedules, — with the exception of Paterson, where the report for 1890 was used. Half-day teachers are omitted as far as known. In cities having separate schools for colored and for white children, the teachers in colored schools are included where the salaries paid are the same as those paid in white schools of the same grade, — otherwise they are omitted.

lodging, and $25 for laundry expenses, leaving a cash balance of $260. Out of this sum, however, must come other necessary expenses, as the outfit for work, — books, stationery, etc., — travelling expenses, car fares, society fees, etc., and a large item for clothing. There should also be deducted the interest on the capital invested in securing the education demanded in preparation for the work. If all of these items are considered, and the greater social demands entailed by the position, it seems possible for the average domestic employee to save at least as much money as the average teacher in the city schools. This comparison is probably relatively higher in favor of the teacher than it should be, since in the average wages for domestic employees are included the wages received in agricultural districts, where wages are lower than in cities. It is also a comparison between skilled workers on the one hand, and on the other hand an occupation in some of the subdivisions of which the laborers are unskilled.

It has, unfortunately, not been possible to compare the wages received in the same city by teachers and domestic employees. A comparison, however, can be made between the wages received in Boston for domestic service and by the teachers in the public schools in the neighboring city of Cambridge.

The average wages received by a cook in a private family in Boston are, as has been seen by Table XIV, $4.45. This judgment is based on five hundred and seventy-four returns, and is an exact average, since fifty per cent receive more than that amount, and fifty per cent the same or less than that. She therefore earns annually $231.40 plus $275 for board, lodging, fuel, light, and laundry expenses, or $506.40.

Fifty-six per cent of the teachers in the city schools in Cambridge earn annually $620, or, deducting $285 for board, etc., for fifty-two weeks, $335 in money. This is $103 more than is received by the Boston cook, but out of this must come numerous expenses entailed by the position, from which the domestic employee is exempt. The cash annual savings in the two cases cannot vary materially.

It will also be seen by reference to Tables XV and XVI that the Boston cook earns absolutely more than does the average city teacher in Albany, Atlanta, Baltimore, New Orleans, Paterson, Rochester, and Syracuse.

A second comparison is suggested by the investigations conducted by the Department of Labor. Through these it was found that the annual cash earnings of the working-women in twenty-two typical cities are $272.45.[1] This average takes into consideration time lost — a factor which does not enter into domestic employments except in a casual way. The annual earnings, therefore, of the class of women represented by the Report are much less than those of the domestic employee. The same point is also illustrated by a comparison of the amounts saved in the two occupations. In eleven cities investigated by the Department of Labor the average amount saved was less than $50; in nine cities it was $50, but under $100, while in only two cities was it more than $100, the highest average amount being $111.[2] As has been suggested, the

[1] *Fourth Annual Report*, pp. 520–529.
[2] *Ibid.*, p. 625.

highest of these averages is small in comparison with the amount it is possible to save in domestic service.

No question in regard to earnings saved was asked on the schedule sent to employees, but many statements on this point were voluntarily made by employees.[1] The question as to comparative amounts saved has also been asked the cashiers of banks in small cities and towns where factories are found and the personnel of depositors is known by the officials of the banks. No records are of course kept, but the opinion has been several times expressed that the factory employees do not save as much, as a class, as do domestic employees. In one place, where about two thousand factory employees are found, it was stated that no woman employee had a sum to her credit as large as had been deposited by a domestic.

A corollary follows from this proposition. High wages alone are not sufficient to counterbalance the inducements offered in other occupations where wages are relatively or absolutely lower but whose special advantages are deemed more desirable.

(7) The wages paid in domestic service are on the average high, but the occupation offers few opportunities for advancement in this direction.

An examination of Table XI shows but one instance, with the exception of nurses, where the weekly cash wages reach $10.00 per week, and only nine others where they rise above $7.00. In the two occupations the wages in which have been compared with those in domestic service, while the general average wages are low, it is possible to reach through promotion a comparatively high

[1] *Post*, p. 132.

point.   The fact that the wage plane is a high one is one
inducement for women of average ability to enter the
occupation.   On the other hand, the fact that the wage
limit, high as it is, is soon reached must act as a barrier
in the case of others.

(8) The amount of time unemployed is less in domestic
service than in nearly every other occupation.

The element of time unemployed is an important factor
in determining annual earnings.   While in nearly every
occupation there is a limit to the demand, in domestic
service there is no limit and hence few persons are
necessarily without employment.   The most important
illustration of this point is derived from the report of
the Massachusetts Bureau of Statistics of Labor on the
unemployed in that state in 1885.[1]   Of the total number of
women in the state engaged in remunerative occupations
at the time, thirty per cent were unemployed.   These
were distributed as regards occupations as follows:

Manufacturing industries 78.22
Government and professional services . . . 9.08
Domestic service 6.33
Personal service 3.99
Trade 1.98
Minor occupations 40

But if the number of unemployed is compared with the
total number employed in each industry, a still lower percentage of unemployed is found in domestic service.   A
comparison with other wage earners will make clear this
point.   The percentage of the unemployed in the leading
industries in which women are engaged was as follows:

[1] *Report of the Bureau, 1887*, pp. 216–219, 225.

Straw-workers 93.74
Boot and shoe makers 71.08
Teachers 49.58
Woollen mill operatives 45.02
Cotton mill operatives 43.59
Hosiery mill operatives 40.56
Tailoresses 32.98
Milliners 27.46
Seamstresses 27.08
Dressmakers 23.99
Paper-mill operatives 21.26
Saleswomen 11.73
Book-keepers and clerks 9.19
Servants in families 6.78
Housekeepers 3.65

The demand for domestic servants varies in the different states, but the condition of the unemployed in this occupation in Massachusetts may perhaps be considered fairly typical of that in other localities.

(9) High wages are maintained without the aid of strikes or combinations on the part of the employees.

In but five states are strikes reported among domestic employees;[1] they number but twenty-two and involve less than seven hundred persons, all of them being connected with hotels or restaurants, and nine tenths of them men. Only two instances of permanent organization among this class have come to notice, and neither of these has had as its object the increase of wages. The strike in domestic service assumes the form of a "notice," is individual in character, and is able to accomplish its object without the organized effort considered necessary in other occupations where the supply of laborers is greater than the demand.

[1] *United States Bureau of Labor, 1887*, pp. 794-797.

This group of nine propositions concerning wages it is believed will suggest three conclusions: the conformity of wages in domestic service to certain general economic laws, the fact that the wage factor alone does not determine the number of persons in the occupation, and the existence of a few conditions which affect, perhaps unconsciously, the willingness of the women to engage in this work.

The three groups of propositions stated it is believed will suggest the conclusions that the general economic condition of the country has an appreciable influence on the condition of domestic service, both as regards the character and number of persons engaged and the compensation given for service required. It must follow therefore that many questions must arise connected with the employment, which the individual employer cannot settle from an exclusively personal point of view.

CHAPTER VI

DIFFICULTIES IN DOMESTIC SERVICE FROM THE STAND-POINT OF THE EMPLOYER

THE understanding of domestic service has been seen to involve the consideration of many historical changes both industrial and political, and an examination of the general economic laws to which it is amenable. It involves also a study of the economic conditions that surround the average family, and the problems that confront it when undertaking to deal with the question of domestic service.

The average family reached through the schedules was found to consist of about five persons,[1] exclusive of servants. Its members have kept house eighteen years,[2] they have boarded two years and a half,[3] and at some time during their housekeeping experience they have been without servants. They employ at the present time two servants and a half, or rather, they command

[1] More definitely, it numbered 4.85 persons.

[2] Forty-six per cent had kept house longer than this, averaging nearly thirty years; while forty-four per cent had kept house for a shorter period, averaging about eight years and a half. Seventeen reports came from housekeepers of fifty years or more experience.

[3] Seventy per cent reported that they had boarded since marriage; about one third of these had boarded less than the average time, and one half had boarded from one to five years.

the full time of two persons and half the time of the
third, to whom they pay weekly for service rendered, on
the basis indicated in the schedule of average wages,
$10,[1] exclusive of board and lodging, or $500 annually, the expense of service exclusive also of waste,
breakage, and general wear and tear of household
furniture and appliances. In about one third of all the
families with servants men are employed in some capacity
about the house; in one family in every seven the number of servants is the same as the number of persons in
the family or exceeds it, while in the average family one
servant renders service to every two persons.

When the average family undertakes the task of dealing with domestic servants the difficulties that confront it
are many and serious.

It has first the task of assimilating into its domestic
life those who are of a different nationality and who consequently hold different industrial, social, religious, and
political beliefs. More than one half of all domestic employees are of foreign birth or belong to another race,[2]
who come not only from the prominent European countries but also from the remote corners of the globe,[3]
where all conditions are totally unlike those of America.

---

[1] This estimate is based on the supposition that a cook is employed at
$3.80 per week, a second girl at $3.04, and a man half a week at the
rate of 87 cents a day.

[2] Table II, p. 76.

[3] The place of birth of the employees represented by the schedules in-
cluded the following countries : Australia, Austria, the Azores, Canada,
China, Denmark, England, Finland, France, Germany, Holland, Iceland,
Ireland, Japan, New Brunswick, Norway, Nova Scotia, Ontario, Poland,
Prince Edward's Island, Russia, Scotland, Spain, Switzerland, Sweden,
Wales, the West Indies.

Moreover this number does not include the very large percentage of those who are themselves native born, but who are the children of foreign born parents and have inherited to a certain extent un-American characteristics; 4.02 per cent of the domestic employees in this country do not speak the English language.[1] Those who come to this country, often with preconceived and erroneous ideas as to the independence prevailing here, expecting high wages in return for inexperienced and unskilled labor,[2] must be trained in all the ways not only of American life, but of the family of the individual employer. It has been found difficult to assimilate into our political system the large foreign element coming here, though this system is simple and lends itself readily to such assimilation, as our history has thus far proved. It is far more difficult to assimilate this mass into the infinitely more complex and delicate organism — the modern household. It is not strange that congestion and inflammation so often result from the attempt. The question is one also that becomes more difficult as the proportion of foreign employees increases.

A second difficulty is that of the spirit of restlessness which everywhere prevails among the working classes, though not confined to them, and the consequent brief tenure of service. The average length of service of a

---

[1] *Eleventh Census*, Occupations, p. 122.

[2] An employer in a large city where there is much complaint of the inferior character of the foreign population writes : " A general impression prevails in most foreign families that any girl, no matter how stupid, dishonest, or untidy, can apply for and rightfully accept a position as general servant or housemaid at current prices." A similar complaint comes from many other employers.

domestic servant is found to be less than a year and a half, and this, in many cases and in some localities, is a high average. In the East, in the vicinity of the great lakes, on the Pacific coast, and in some sections of the South, proximity to popular summer or winter resorts lessens the average duration of service. In the South, the cotton-picking season draws many women from household work, as they are able at that time to earn enough money to enable them to live for some months in idleness. In other localities, the hop-picking season, the berry-picking season, and the grape-picking season all offer temporary inducements for girls to leave domestic service. In still other places the canning factory, the pickle factory, and the fruit-drying establishment successfully offer temporary competition. To the question asked of employees, "Have you ever had any other occupation besides domestic service?" twenty-eight per cent answered "Yes." This at first might seem to indicate a decided preference for domestic service, but a closer examination shows that more often it means that housework is taken up when the berry-picking and the fruit-canning season is over, when the mill or the factory has closed in a dull time, or when the hurry of plantation work is ended at the South. A similar indication of this restlessness is found in the replies given by employers to the question, "How many servants have you employed since you have been house-keeping?" Twenty-five per cent did not answer the question definitely and of these one half state as their reason the fact that the number was too great to remember. "Their name is legion," answer fifteen house-keepers, a series of exclamation points tells the story for others, "infinity-minus," writes one, and still another bids the compiler "read her answer in the stars."

This condition of affairs is not to be wondered at. That spirit of restlessness, nervous discontent, and craving for excitement which foreigners find characteristic of all who breathe American air is not confined to business men and society women — it permeates the kitchen, the nursery, the laundry, and every part of the household. Among employers the mode of life tends more and more towards a winter in California, a summer in Europe, an autumn in the mountains, and a spring in Florida. On both sides of the Hudson there are magnificent country houses deserted because their owners prefer the excitement of city life, the attractions of Bar Harbor, or the society at Newport. The towns on the Hudson are nearly stationary as regards population, though possessing every natural advantage, while the large cities are powerful magnets drawing from every direction. Domestic service cannot remain unaffected by these characteristics of the age. A new situation is often like a voyage to Europe so desired by others — it gives change, excitement, new experiences, and it is often the only way in which these can be secured. A summer engagement at the sea-shore, among the mountains, or at the springs is often as eagerly sought as is the height of the season at Saratoga or among the Berkshires by persons whose opportunities for change are far less restricted. The occupations temporarily open at the time of the hop-picking season, or the fruit-canning season, offer the attraction of large numbers of fellow-workers in the company of whom "a good time" is expected.

The tenure of service also apparently varies somewhat with the size of the place, the average duration being longer in cities of from ten thousand to eighty thousand inhabitants than in smaller towns or larger cities. In small towns the desire for city life shortens the terms of service. In the largest cities, as New York, Brooklyn, Boston, Philadelphia, the average time is shortened by the fact that employers are often obliged to engage as a temporary expedient persons who have just arrived in this country; while it is also seen to be true that there is greater difficulty than in small cities in obtaining reliable testimonials.

It is not strange, therefore, that reasonable, intelligent, and competent employers have difficulties to meet that lie entirely without the domain of their own households, and that many persons who twenty-five years ago experienced no difficulty whatever find to-day serious trouble in retaining their employees.

A third difficulty is the fact that employers are so often obliged to engage for skilled labor the assistance of unskilled laborers. Many who seek employment as servants do not know even the names of the household tools they are obliged to use — still less are they acquainted with their uses. A part of this ignorance and lack of skill is due to the prevalence of the old idea that anybody can do everything — a theory abandoned in most occupations but still dominating the household. Household employments and service are still generally considered occupations that any one can "pick up," but the picking-up process has resulted in the household, as elsewhere, in unscientific, haphazard work and has seldom produced expert workmen. The Superintendent of the Census wrote in 1880, " The organization of domestic service in the United States is so crude that no distinction whatever can be successfully maintained (between the different parts of the service)."[1] In confirmation of this statement is the testimony of a large number of employees to the effect that they have become domestic servants because they had not education enough to do anything else.[2] From this general conception of the nature of household service several things result : first, few opportunities exist for learning household duties in a systematic way ; second, if the opportunities were created, few would avail themselves of them so long as this low estimate of the occupation prevails ; third, many housekeepers are obliged to conduct in their own households a training-school on a limited scale ; fourth, the expense is far greater than it should be, since unskilled labor is always improvident of time and materials ;[3] fifth, the hygienic results of "instinctive cookery " and "picked up " knowledge are often seen in ill health and a derangement of household affairs erroneously attributed to other causes.

[1] *Tenth Census*, I., 708.

[2] " I went into housework because I was not educated enough for other work."

" I haven't education enough to do anything else."

" I would change my occupation if I knew enough to do anything else."

[3] This is illustrated by the experience of one housekeeper who frequently does her own work. At these times her ordinary kitchen expenses come within $50 per month. This sum is exclusive of fuel, rent, and water. When employing a servant, the same expenses amount to $80 per month, while if fuel, light, and water were included (rent not being affected) the difference would be still greater.

I

A fourth difficulty arises when the seemingly inevitable annual change of employees comes. Four courses are open to the housekeeper: (1) she may employ a new servant without asking for a recommendation, (2) she may take the recommendation of previous employers, (3) she may consult an employment bureau, (4) she may advertise.

Few persons are willing to adopt the first expedient and take a stranger into their service, not to speak of their family life, without some recommendation.[1]

But the second course open — taking the recommendation of others — is scarcely more practicable. There must always be a difference in standards, and "excellent" to one may mean "fair" or even "poor" to another. It is also true that an employee may succeed in one place and be ill adapted to meet the requirements of another. Again, it is a common complaint that the recommendation does not always carry with it implicit confidence in its contents. Daniel DeFoe wrote nearly two hundred years ago:

"One of the great Evils, which lies heavily upon Families now, in this particular Case of taking Servants, is the going about from House to House, to take Characters and Reports of Servants, or by Word of Mouth; and especially among the Ladies this Usage prevails, in which the good Nature and Charity of the Ladies to ungrateful Servants, goes so far beyond their Justice to one another, that an ill Servant is very seldom detected, and the Ladies yet excuse themselves by this, *namely*, that they are loth to take away a poor Servant's Good Name, which is starving them; and that they may

---

[1] Yet so great is the demand for help that this is apparently sometimes done. In Milwaukee it is a common thing to see affixed to houses, or standing upright in the dooryard, well-painted signs looking as if ready for frequent use, reading "Girl wanted."

perhaps mend, when they come to another Family, what was amiss before, which indeed seldom happens. . . . The Ladies are cheating and abusing one another, in Charity to their *Servants*. It is Time to put an End to this unreasonable Good nature." [1]

These words are as true a description of this phase of the subject in America to-day as they were in England at the beginning of the last century. It seems impossible to devise any system of personal recommendations that will convey the truth, the whole truth, and nothing but the truth.

The third expedient — the employment bureau — is apparently coming into general use, especially in the large cities where some means of communication is necessary between those desiring employees and employment. But it is in the large city, where the greatest need for it exists, that the employment bureau is most unsatisfactory. The bureau lives by the fees paid to it by those desiring help and those seeking employment. Every expedient, therefore, is used to extort fees from both classes, and it is difficult to tell which suffers more from this extortion. Even when numberless fees have been paid, the employer too often finds himself without the service to which his fee presumably entitles him. The first department abandoned by a large philanthropic institution in Boston, was the intelligence office, " because it was found impossible to supply well-trained servants while there was no demand for any other." [2] But the greatest objection to the intelligence

---

[1] *Behaviour of Servants*, p. 298.

[2] A lady recently went to an employment bureau, and in answer to her application for " a good cook," received the reply, " Madam, good cooks are an extinct race."

office is that it is often a breeding place for vice and
crime. An investigation recently made of the intelligence offices in a large city showed that it supported
one hundred and twenty, two thirds of them controlled
by foreigners, many of them managed by minor ward
politicians, and four of them under police supervision.
The employees that can be found through such agencies
are not those willingly received into a respectable family.[1]
Employment bureaus in small cities are apparently more
satisfactory than those in large ones, while those offices
are to be commended which use printed forms for obtaining statements from previous employers as to the
qualifications of applicants.[2] Those agencies patronized

One large bureau in Philadelphia reports that the demand for good
servants is twenty per cent greater than the supply.

[1] The character of some of the intelligence offices in another city is
described by F. Hunt, in *The American Kitchen Magazine*, November,
1895.

[2] An excellent blank is used by the employment bureau connected with
the Boston Young Women's Christian Association. Seven questions are
asked the persons to whom the employee has referred :

    "(1) How long have you known her ?
    (2) Is she temperate, honest, and respectable ?
    (3) Is she neat in her person, and about her work ?
    (4) Is she of good disposition ?
    (5) Is she faithful to her work, and is she trustworthy ?
    (6) In what capacity did she serve you, and how long ?
    (7) Was she capable and efficient in that capacity ? "

The bureau states its aim to be "the recommendation of worthy persons only." The detailed form of the questions asked is more successful in preventing an evasion of disqualifications, than is the personal
recommendation of a general character, which often tells the truth, but
not the whole truth.

One large bureau states that it formerly used blank forms, which it
sent out with each employee. Employers were asked to fill out these
blanks and return them at the end of service, and these were kept on
file as recommendations. It was soon found that employers grew lax

by an inferior class of employers and employees, especially those that are at no pains to secure recommendation of employees from respectable persons, are worse than useless.

Employers who adopt the fourth policy and advertise for help are forced to open an intelligence office on a small scale in their own homes.

All of these difficulties are so great, especially that of securing reliable testimony from responsible employers, that many persons tolerate incompetent service rather than incur the risk of a change for the worse.

A fifth difficulty encountered by the employers of domestic service, and probably the most serious of all, is the prevailing indifference among housekeepers to the action of economic law — a failure to realize that in domestic service, as in other occupations, the course followed by one employer has an appreciable effect on the condition of service as a whole. This can be best explained by a few concrete illustrations " drawn from life."

Mr. A, an employer, leaves his city home during the summer, retaining in it two servants to care for the house and paying them their usual wages, $16 a month. No special service is required of them, but wages are paid in consideration of the tacit understanding that they are to remain in his employ. On the return of Mr. A, Mr. X, who has discharged his servants during the summer, offers the employees of Mr. A $18 a month. This price he can afford to pay since he has been at no expense for service during the summer. Mr. A, rather

and would not take the pains to fill them out, and the practice was abandoned.

than lose his trusted employees, pays them the advance offered by Mr. X, although the services of neither employee are worth more than three months previous.

Mrs. B, an employer of limited means, with a natural gift for cooking considered as a fine art, takes an inexperienced girl from Castle Garden and teaches her after long training something of her own skill. She pays fair wages, which are considered entirely satisfactory by the employee in view of the instruction she has received. Mrs. Y, who ignores Mrs. B socially and is indifferent to the matter of wages, calls on Mrs. B's cook and offers her $5 per week. This is much above the current rate of wages in the place and moreover Mrs. B cannot afford to pay it. She therefore loses her trained cook.

Mr. C, an employer in haste to reach his distant home and anxious to secure a servant, engages in the afternoon a Swedish girl who has that morning landed in America and of whom he knows nothing. She is to accompany his family, which includes five children, to their Western home, have all of her expenses of travel paid by her employers, and receive $4.00 a week for her services as a nurse-maid.

Mrs. D, a housekeeper with a large family, moderate income, and ambitious tastes, employs one general servant and requires, in addition to the ordinary duties of such a servant, dining-room and chamber service.

Mrs. E, her nearest neighbor, a housekeeper with a small family, simple tastes, and free from numerous social demands, makes all of the desserts herself, requires no table service of her employee, and expects her daughter to assume the care of the chambers.

Mrs. F pays full wages to her inexperienced "help," fifteen years old, because the latter has an invalid mother dependent on her.

Mr. G, with a family of two, prides himself on paying the highest wages in the place to his cook, second girl, and coachman.

Mrs. H, who has inherited a large family homestead, which she occupies with her sister, provides her three employees each with a separate bedroom, a special dining-room, a sitting-room well furnished, and grants many personal privileges, as the use of the horse and carriage for early church. She does not understand how any housekeeper can have trouble in securing and retaining competent employees. She often quotes to her nearest neighbor, "A good mistress makes a good servant," her neighbor being obliged to use her back parlor with a mantel bed as a guest-room and therefore to limit somewhat the accommodations granted her employees.

Mrs. I gives each of her employees a key to the side door and makes no inquiries as to the hours they keep.

Mrs. J gives her servants her discarded evening dresses because "it keeps them in good humor."

Mrs. K, the wife of a millionaire, "burns all of her old finery," and makes it a special point to teach all of her twelve employees how to dress well and economically within the wages they receive.

Mrs. L does not permit her employee to wear frizzes or bangs, disapproves of her having company, and will not tolerate a young man caller under any circumstances.

Mrs. M, a lifelong invalid whose physician has prescribed absolute rest two hours every afternoon, reasons that her employee who rises two hours earlier than herself must need the same rest and therefore sends her every afternoon to take a nap. The latter thus never works afternoons and is able to attend more evening entertainments than other employees in the neighborhood.[1]

Mrs. N assists her husband in his business six hours each day and gives her employee full control of the house during her absence.

Mrs. O requires all her employees to perform their work according to minute directions laid down by herself and is constantly present to see that these are not deviated from in the slightest degree.

Mrs. P discharges her nursery maid for untruthfulness and gives her a recommendation testifying to her neatness, quickness, pleasant disposition, and fondness for children.

Mr. Q discharges his butler for incapacity, but in view of the fact that the latter has a widowed mother and an invalid sister dependent on him gives him an excellent recommendation.

Mr. R discharges his housekeeper "for infirmity of temper," as he subsequently testifies in court, but gives her so excellent a recommendation that she believes she has been discharged for physical disability, and gives her testimony to this effect in the same lawsuit.

---

[1] DeFoe says, "To be a good Master is to be a Master that will do his Servant Justice, and that will make his Servant do him Justice; he may be kind to a Servant, that will let him sleep when he shou'd work, but then he is not just to himself, or a good Governour to his Family." — *Behaviour of Servants*, p. 293.

Mrs. S has a cook who drinks to excess one fourth of the time, but the latter has no fear of dismissal because three fourths of the time she cooks in a superior manner.

Mrs. T dislikes manual labor of every kind. Her servants therefore know that she will tolerate inefficient and incompetent service rather than be left for a single day without help.

Mr. U, the father of three young sons, has a coachman who swears like a trooper, but he retains him because Mrs. U considers him the most stylish coachman in the city.

Mrs. V applies to an employment bureau for a domestic and refuses six applicants because they are not " pretty " and "refined." After finding one whose appearances are satisfactory, she parts with her because she is unwilling to black the gentlemen's boots.

Mrs. W engages a woman to go out of town for service, the latter to wait a week before going and meantime to pay her own board. At the time agreed upon she reaches the employer's house, to learn that the former "help" has decided to remain. She has thus lost a week's board and wages and more than two dollars in going and returning to the city, and all of "her set" refuse to make engagements in the country.

The different economic, social, and moral questions connected with these various conditions, the illustrations of which could be multiplied indefinitely, may be, generally are, decided by each individual without reference to society at large. Wages are too often regulated by the employer's bank account, hours of service by his caprice, and moral questions by his personal convenience. The employer is too often the autocrat in his own home. He considers that neither his neighbor nor the general public has any more concern in the business relations existing between himself and his domestic employees than it has in the price he pays for a dinner service or in the color and cut of his coat.

Yet domestic service is the only employment in which economic laws are so openly defied and all questions connected with it settled on the personal basis. No manufacturer can from charitable motives double the wages ordinarily paid to unskilled labor without being called to account for it by competing manufacturers, nor can he reduce unduly the wages of his employees without being held responsible for his course by the employees of other establishments, nor can he prolong by one fourth of an hour the daily period of labor without overstepping his legal privileges. Within certain narrow limits he has freedom, but competition, labor organizations, and the arm of the law combine to keep him within these limits. Before domestic service is freed from all the difficulties that attend it there must be a more widespread recognition of the responsibility of the individual employer to those outside his own household.[1]

Five general classes of perplexing conditions have been suggested. All of them are independent of the personal characteristics and habits of employer and employee and of the personal relationship that exists between them.

---

[1] Repeated statements like the following are made by employers : " A few wealthy families keep a large number of servants at high wages, which wholly unfits them for general service and moderate wages, and establishes customs and rates which cannot be met by the mass of people with moderate incomes."

They do not take into account the fact that throughout the South and wherever negroes are employed in the household the housekeeper must be ever on the alert to guard against dishonesty and immorality on the part of these employees, that intemperance has been found a besetting sin of cooks and coachmen irrespective of race and nationality, that many agree with Mr. Joseph Jefferson when he says, " I am satisfied that domestic melancholy sets in with the butler. He is the melodramatic villain of society." They do not consider the tendencies encountered here as elsewhere towards indifference, idleness, laziness, low ideals and standards, insubordination, and a desire to obtain much for nothing.[1] They do not include lack of harmony in the personal relations between employees in the same household,[2] the constant friction that necessarily arises from the presence of a stranger in the family, the question of compatibility of disposition between the mistress and the maid, the feeling between employees and the children of the household. They are as prone to trouble a good mistress as a poor one, they are independent of knowledge of household affairs, of housekeeping experience, of good or ill treatment of employees, of any personal element whatever in employer or em-

---

[1] An employer recently engaged a cook at high wages with sufficient recommendations it was supposed. The first dinner (an hour delayed) showed her incapacity, and when questioned more closely it was found that the only domestic work she had ever done was preparing vegetables in a boarding house. When asked why she had engaged as a cook, the reply was, " They told me I could get higher wages if I called myself a cook." The experience does not seem to be exceptional.

[2] An employer writes: " I find no place on the schedule for stating that my cook and coachman have to-day each given notice of leaving unless the other is discharged."

ployee. They are difficulties apparently inherent in the
present system of domestic service.

It is of interest to note the opinion of housekeepers on
this point. The question, "Have you found it difficult
to secure good domestic servants?" was answered with
the following result :

Difficult		545
Yes	290	
Very difficult	148	
At times	72	
Rather difficult	20	
Generally	15	
Not difficult		418
No	328	
Not especially	34	
Not generally	29	
Not lately	13	
Very little difficulty	8	
Very seldom	6	
Not answered		42
Total		1005

Fifty-seven per cent therefore of the housekeepers represented by the schedules have found more or less difficulty in securing good servants. This is, probably, an
underestimate of the true condition. Many housekeepers
who see only the personal element involved in the employment of service consider an acknowledgment of difficulty a confession of weakness and inability on their own
part to cope with the question and are therefore silent.
Others have had the experience of one who writes, "I
have had no difficulty, my cook having been with me
eighteen years, and my second girl, her daughter, ten
years. But if they should leave I should not know where

to turn." Again, the replies do not represent the experiences of a class not represented on the schedules — the many in the large cities who are able to employ servants only occasionally and find them through the lowest grade of intelligence offices.

These difficulties are certainly not decreasing,[1] and the demand for competent servants is in most places evidently greater than the supply.[2] These difficulties are, at times,

[1] " When I began housekeeping in 1870 I had one 'general housework girl' who stayed with me nine years. Now I consider myself fortunate to retain a cook or a second girl as many weeks."

"Thirty years ago I had no difficulty whatever. I do not think my character has changed meantime, or my method of treating servants, or our style of living, yet now it is almost impossible to secure servants."

"The question is very different now from what it was forty years ago."

" The problem in this place grows more perplexing every year."

" Many housekeepers here are between the Scylla and Charybdis of trying to tolerate wretched, inefficient servants, and the impossibility of getting along with them."

[2] " In advertising recently for a general housework girl twelve answered the advertisement. Advertising the same week for my former servant, twenty-two ladies applied personally and twelve others wrote that a girl was wanted. Although I told each of the twenty-two that if the girl were even fair I would keep her myself, only two hesitated on that account to try to secure her."

The report of a large employment bureau for the year 1889 is as follows :

Number of employers registered	1,512
Number of employees registered	1,541
Number of employers supplied with servants	1,366
Number of employees supplied with situations	1,375

The number of employees registered exceeds the number of employers, but many register who are incompetent to fill the position they seek, and therefore many employers are without servants. The bureau regrets " its inability at times to supply with competent help the large number of patrons."

Another bureau reports 2,659 applications from employers, only 2,099 of which could be filled.

somewhat modified by the conditions in which the employer is placed. They are apparently less in large cities that are ports of entry or the termini of leading railroad lines, and have comparatively few manufacturing industries in which women are employed ; they are less in small families employing a large number of servants and paying high wages. But even all of these favorable conditions only modify — they do not change — the nature of the question.[1] A careful study of the returned schedules with reference to the location, population, and prevailing industry of the towns, the number of servants employed, size of family, and wages paid leads to this conclusion. Of the five hundred and forty-five employers who re-

Still another bureau filling about three thousand positions annually reports that at times it has had six hundred applications from employers in excess of the number that could be filled with competent applicants for work.

The domestic employment bureau connected with the Boston Young Women's Christian Association reports for the year ending 1890 :

Orders registered	2,120
Orders filled	1,753

[1] "Our committee have been greatly puzzled to know how to supply the constantly increasing demand for good and efficient workers in small households, where fair compensation is offered for moderate requirements. This demand is great in the city, but more so in the suburbs and country. It is very difficult to find a woman willing to take service in a family living out of sight of Boston Common. It is still more difficult to find any one who will go twenty miles into the country." — *Report of the Women's Educational and Industrial Union*, Boston, 1888, p. 29.

One employer in an inland city of twenty-five thousand inhabitants, who has a family of eight, and employs sixteen servants, writes : "It is impossible here to secure competent servants."

Another employer, employing thirteen servants, in a city of twelve thousand, writes : "It is very difficult to secure servants, since women here prefer to work in the factories."

One employer with seven servants and a family of two, in a large manufacturing city, says : "It is impossible to find well-trained employees."

ported that they had difficulty in securing competent servants, only twenty-six gave in explanation a reason that would not have been applicable in any city, town, or village in the country, and those twenty-six had reference to the negroes at the South and the Chinese at the West. One half of the employees reporting state that they would go into another occupation provided it would pay them as well,[1] although the number is very small of those who are dissatisfied except with the disadvantages of the position. If these difficulties are found in every place irrespective of its size, its geographical location, its prevailing industry, the character of its inhabitants, and the personal relations of mistress and maid, something more is involved for the employer than "kind treatment" and personal consideration.

The belief has apparently been general that these perplexities are confined to our own country and that the adoption of English or German or French methods of dealing with the subject would remove them all. The question is undoubtedly a less difficult one in England than it is in this country, since it is not complicated by

[1] "This is the first time this question has been put to me directly, and I frankly answer, Yes — to-morrow, if an opportunity were offered me. For years it has been my wish to find employment of some kind which would keep me from being a servant. Mrs. X has been very kind to me, and tried to find me other work ; but, of course, a girl who has been in a kitchen for so long (thirteen years) is inexperienced in different work. Nevertheless, I have met girls who had no better education than I, and now hold high and respectable positions and make a fair living."

A colored man, who has been a cook for forty years, replies with some caution : " I don't know, unless the other work was in sight. Can't say, unless somebody had done offered me another job, and I could look into it."

differences of race, religion, interests, and traditions, by foreign immigration, and possibly not by the same ease with which labor is transferred from one employment to another, while tradition and social custom have favored country rather than city life and have thus eliminated one of our difficulties. But with all these obstacles removed, DeFoe's *Behaviour of Servants* shows that even in England the question is an old one, and current literature indicates that it is far from settled.[1]

If the question is asked in Germany, "Is it easy to secure good domestic servants here?" the almost invariable answer is, "It is very difficult, almost impossible." The reasons for the difficulty are precisely the same as in America — the attractions of city life, the competition of shops and factories, the growth of democratic ideas, the difficulty of securing, in spite of the system of service books, unimpeachable recommendations, and the spirit of restlessness that everywhere prevails among the working classes. In some of the higher classes, where something of the old patriarchal relationship between mistress and maid still exists, there is apparently no difficulty; but each year these classes become more and more under-

---

[1] See articles by Mrs. Ellen W. Darwin, *The Nineteenth Century*, August, 1890 ; Miss Amy Bulley, *Westminster Review*, February, 1891 ; Miss Emily Faithful, *North American Review*, July, 1891 ; C. J. Rowe, *Westminster Review*, November, 1890, on the question in the Australian colonies.

"If things go on much longer in the present state, we shall have to introduce the American fashion, and live in huge human menageries." — *M. E. Braddon.*

An admirable scientific presentation of the subject of domestic service in London is given by Charles Booth and Jesse Argyle in *Life and Labour of the People in London*, Vol. VIII.

mined by the social democratic spirit, and must in time be affected by the same conditions that bring perplexity to other classes. Yet it is true in Germany as in America that servants seeking places are always to be found, that intelligence offices are crowded with applicants for work, and that an army of incompetents is always at hand.

In France the problem is the same. It varies in details; the proportion of men employed in housework is far greater than in America, England, or Germany, servility of manner is not expected as in England, and waste of material is less common than in America. But fundamentally the conditions are the same as elsewhere.

The difficulties that meet the employer of domestic labor both in America and in Europe are the difficulties that arise from the attempt to harmonize an ancient, patriarchal industrial system with the conditions of modern life. Everywhere the employer closes his eyes to the incongruities of the attempt and lays the blame of failure, not to a defective system, but to the natural weaknesses in the character of the unfortunate persons obliged to carry it out. The difficulties in the path of both employer and employee will not only never be removed but will increase until the subject of domestic service is regarded as a part of the great labor question of the day and given the same serious consideration.

K

CHAPTER VII

ADVANTAGES IN DOMESTIC SERVICE

THE question as to who constitute the class of domestic employees has been partially answered. One fourth are of foreign birth or belong to a different race from that of their employers, the majority are of foreign birth, of foreign parentage, or of a different race. Nearly one third of the number represented on the schedules have been engaged in other occupations besides domestic service — a fact indicating three things : first, the spirit of restlessness that characterizes the class, though not peculiar to it; second, the industrial independence of a considerable number of domestic employees, since they can at any time change not only employers but employment; [1] third, the fact that many do not enter domestic service with the thought of making it a permanent occupation.[2] About two thirds of those who have had other

---

[1] It is of interest to notice some of these occupations. The list includes apparently nearly every form of work in every kind of mill and factory, farm work, cigar-making, sewing, dressmaking, millinery, tailoring, crocheting, lace-making, carpet-making, copying ; places as cash girls, saleswomen, nurses, post-office clerks, compositors, office attendants ; six have been teachers ; others, ladies' companions, governesses, and matrons. It is of interest, also, to note that the per cent of native born who have been engaged in other occupations is slightly higher than the per cent of foreign born (thirty-one to twenty-five).

[2] One employee writes, " I wanted to see for myself what it was to be a hired girl."

130

work report that they received higher wages in these occupations than in domestic service. In nearly every case, however, these represented the cash weekly or monthly wages received, not the yearly earnings, nor did they include the factor of personal expenses as in domestic service.

The reasons why women have entered domestic service are many and various. The following classification has been made of the reasons assigned by the employees returning the schedules :

It was most available	239
Preference for it	202
Health grounds	100
Most profitable employment	37
To earn a living	17
Prefer it to work in mills	17
To have a home	17
Gives steady employment	12
To learn how	11
More leisure time than in other work . . .	5
No capital necessary	2
To earn money to finish education	2
Greater variety in the work	1
Total	662

These reasons and others demand a more detailed examination. It is true in domestic service, as in other occupations, that many drift into it because it is apparently the only course open to them, but there are certain advantages and disadvantages which a person who is free to choose always weighs before deciding for or against the occupation.

The most obvious advantage is that of high remuneration,[1] including not only wages and expenses, but as has been seen, the factors of steady employment, certainty of position, and the fact that no capital is required at any stage of the work or in preparation for it.

A second advantage is that the occupation is conducive to good health, including as it does regularity and variety of work, and involving no personal inconvenience or discomfort.[2] In one third of the families considered men servants are employed in some capacity, and this means that much of the hard work is done by them.

---

[1] An employee in Colorado, who receives $35 a month, writes : "I choose housework in preference to any other, principally because for that I receive better pay. The average pay for store and factory girls is eight and nine dollars a week. After paying board and room rent, washing, etc., very little is left, and what is left must be spent for dress — nothing saved."

"It pays better than other kinds of work."

"My expenses are less than in any other kind of work."

"I can make more. I have put $100 in the savings bank in a year and a half. I had first $10 a month, but now I have $12."

"I can save more."

"I can earn more without constant change."

"I can earn more than in anything else ($15 a month), but do not save anything as I support my mother."

"Any one that is industrious and saving can save a great deal by working at housework."

"I began to live out when I was thirteen years old, and I am now twenty-seven. I have saved $1600 in that time. At first I had $.50 a week ; now I have $3.00. One summer I earned $3.00 a day in the hop-picking season."

[2] "We are not as closely confined as girls who work in stores, and are usually more healthy."

"I chose it because I thought it was healthy work."

"There is no healthier work for women."

"It is healthier than most other kinds of work I could do."

"You can have better-cooked food and a better room than most shop-girls."

A third advantage is the fact that it gives at least the externals of a home. This consideration weighs especially with the foreign born and those who have no homes of their own.[1] How varied and numerous these home privileges are is best illustrated by the replies given by employers to the question, " Do you grant any special privileges ? " Thirty answered " No," and one hundred and seventy-five gave no answer. Eight hundred enumerated special privileges, and these formed sixty-eight different classes. The most important of these are single rooms, medical care and attendance when sick, use of daily papers, books, and magazines, evening instruction, sitting-room for visitors, no restrictions as to visitors, use of bath-room and sewing-machine, use of horse and carriage when distant from church, seat at table except when guests are present, seat in church, and concert and theatre tickets (in the families of newspaper reporters). Many other privileges are mentioned, — these are the most frequently granted. Seventy per cent of the employers state that they give a single room, but about one

[1] " I came to a strange city and chose housework, because it afforded me a home."

" I am well treated by the family I am with, feel at home and under their protection."

" Housework fell to my lot and I have followed it up because it has secured me a home."

" Housework gives me a better home than I could make for myself in any other way."

" I have more comforts than in other work."

" I like a quiet home in a good family better than work in a public place, like a shop."

" When I came to —— and saw the looks of the girls in the large stores and the familiarity of the young men, I preferred to go into a respectable family where I could have a home."

half of this number employ only one domestic. In many cases a large room is given for every two domestics, with separate furniture for each. One hundred and forty-six specify the use of the dining-room, and ninety-four families give the use of a special sitting-room. All of these privileges show that even if the employee is not a member of the family, her life is as much a part of it, with the single exception of a seat at the family table, as is that of the average boarder.

This enumeration of privileges does not include two other classes which have in a sense ceased to be regarded as such, but rather as prerogatives of the position. These are freedom from work at specified times each week and a stated vacation during the year with or without wages.

The matter of free hours at stated times each week is apparently a simple one — there is at first thought more uniformity here among housekeepers than in regard to any other thing ; but while only three per cent of the employers do not give some specified time during the week, there are one hundred and twenty-three classes of combinations which housekeepers have found it possible to make out of the seven afternoons and seven evenings of the week, thus apparently disproving the common belief that the custom is universal of granting Thursday afternoon and Sunday evening. In sixty-eight of these classes one or more afternoons are included and in fifteen others some portion of Sunday. In the case of more than one thousand employees at least one afternoon each week is given, while more than four hundred employers give a part of Sunday.[1]

[1] *The New York Evening Post*, January 11, 1896, cites from *London*

The question in regard to vacation granted during the year was answered with reference to nearly a thousand employees, and in only one case was a vacation not given, the time varying from the legal holidays, which perhaps can hardly be called a vacation, to three months. Sixty-five per cent of employers give a vacation of from one week to three months, twenty per cent one of two weeks, fifteen per cent less than a week, and twenty per cent give a vacation but do not specify the length of time. These facts apply to women employees. In the case of men the conditions are not materially different, the facts given indicating apparently a smaller per cent among women receiving a vacation of more than two weeks and a larger per cent receiving less than a week. In the great majority of cases this vacation is given without loss of wages. Tables XVII and XVIII illustrate these facts.

A short vacation granted during the year without loss of wages has in many localities come to be regarded by employees as one of the prerogatives of the occupation, and not, as formerly, a special privilege given. All things considered, it is a matter of surprise that so much rather than that so little time is given. In other occupations a vacation can be granted employees during a dull season without loss to the employer. But the household machinery cannot stop action without disaster. A vacation given

Truth an account of a bill under consideration in the New Zealand Parliament providing that every domestic servant in the colony is to have a half-holiday every Wednesday, and that the employer is to be fined £5 if the domestic is deprived of this privilege. The "half-holiday" practically means that the servant will be entitled to leave of absence from two until ten. Inspectors are to be appointed to enforce the provisions of this measure, if it becomes a law.

household employees means that the employer must perform a double amount of domestic work, or provide for special assistance — often a difficult and even impossible task.

TABLE XVII
VACATION GRANTED DURING THE YEAR

REPORTED BY EMPLOYEES	WOMEN		MEN	
	Number	Per cent	Number	Per cent
Total number of employees.......	2073	....	472	....
Not reported	898	....	267	....
Not applicable (laundresses, etc.)..	203	....	50	....
Reported and applicable..........	972	....	155	....
Vacation granted	971	....	153	....
Time not specified	202	20.78	34	21.94
Less than one week..............	127	13.07	42	27.10
One week	150	15.43	18	11.61
More than one week, less than two.	25	2.57	5	3.22
Two weeks.....................	210	21.61	33	21.29
More than two weeks	257	26.44	21	13.55
No vacation	1	.10	2	1.29

TABLE XVIII
VACATION GRANTED WITH OR WITHOUT LOSS OF WAGES

REPORTED BY EMPLOYERS	WOMEN		MEN	
	Number	Per cent	Number	Per cent
With loss of wages..............	210	21.63	20	13.07
Without loss of wages...........	723	74.46	133	86.93
Half wages.....................	37	3.81	....	....
Cost of board added.............	1	.10	....	....
Total	971		153	

A fourth advantage that domestic service has as an occupation is the knowledge it gives of household affairs and the training in them — knowledge of which every woman, whatever her station in life and whether married or unmarried, has at times most pressing need.[1]

A fifth consideration is that it offers congenial employment to many whose tastes lie specially in this direction.[2] It is undoubtedly true that many persons in other occupations would honestly prefer housework if some of its present disadvantages could be eliminated.[3]

[1] "I choose housework as my regular employment for the simple reason that young women look forward to the time when they will have housework of their own to do. I consider that I or any one in domestic employment will make a better housekeeper than any young woman who works in a factory."

"I think you can learn more in doing housework."

"It requires both care and study and so keeps our mind in constant thought and care, and ought to be respected."

[2] "At home I was my mother's help even when we had a girl of our own, and from childhood had always loved to cook, and learned to do all kinds."

"My mother was a housekeeper and did most of her own work and taught me how to help her. When my father and mother died, and it became necessary for me to earn my own living, the question was, ' What can I do ? ' The answer was plain — housework."

"I have a natural love for cooking, and would rather do it than anything else in the world."

"I like it best, was used to it at home, and it seems more natural-like."

"I enjoy housework more than anything else."

"I was a dressmaker several years because my mother thought dressmaking more respectable than going out to work. But I always liked housework better, and when my health broke down I was glad to get a place as parlor maid."

[3] A successful teacher says : "I have never liked teaching particularly, and would much rather be a good cook."

A sewing woman says : "I should prefer to do housework, but do not wish to leave my home."

A teacher says : "I am fond of children, and should like nothing better than to be a nurse-girl, but I will not wear livery."

Still another advantage is the legal protection offered
domestic employees, although as Mr. James Schouler well
says, the relation of master and servant is in theory hostile
to the genius of free institutions, since it bears the marks
of social caste. "It may be pronounced as a relation of
more general importance in ancient than in modern times
and better applicable at this day to English than to
American society."[1] But technically, the relation according to Chancellor Kent is a legal status resting entirely
on contract. One agrees to work and the other to pay,
but both are on an equality as far as rights are concerned.[2] The legal rights accorded a servant are freedom
from physical punishment,[3] proper food and support in
illness or disability during the time of employment,[4]
the right to the enjoyment of a good character — provided she has one — and the law presumes she has it
until the contrary appears,[5] wages, if the servant has performed his part of the contract,[6] and damages in case of
discharge before the expiration of the contract.[7]

These advantages which domestic service as an occupation has over most other employments are patent. They
would be recognized by all, whether domestic employees
or not, as the accompaniments of the service as it exists
under reasonably favorable conditions. They are advan-

[1] *Law of the Domestic Relations*, p. 599.
[2] *Commentaries*, II., 258.
[3] Kent, II., 260–261.
[4] Story, *On Contracts*, II., §§ 1297–1298.
[5] Starkie, *On Slander and Libel*, p. 19.
[6] Story, *On Contracts*, II., § 1304.
[7] Daly, IV., 401.
A good discussion of "The Legal Status of Servant Girls" is given by
Oliver E. Lyman, *Popular Science Monthly*, XXII., 803.

tages which, with the exception of the home privileges, are independent of the personal character and disposition of employers. They are apparently inherent in the occupation, as much to be expected as are free Sundays and evenings after six o'clock in mills and factories. They are the inducements which, when a choice has been possible, have led intelligent women to become household employees. They are the advantages that have been repeatedly set forth by the press and the pulpit to sewing-women and shop-girls working at the starvation limit of wages in large cities to induce them to better their condition. Unquestionably many such women would be far better off than they are now if they were in comfortable domestic service. It has been said by the head of one of our great labor bureaus that all questions concerning wage-earning women resolve themselves into those of "wages, hours, health, and morals," and domestic service conforms to all the requirements that could be demanded under these four heads, with the possible exception of hours under unfavorable conditions. But, notwithstanding these advantages, women in cities still prefer sewing, country girls drift into mills and factories, teachers' agencies are crowded with applicants who can never secure a position and could not fill one if obtained ; there must be something else involved in the question besides the matter of "wages, hours, health, and morals."

CHAPTER VIII

THE INDUSTRIAL DISADVANTAGES OF DOMESTIC SERVICE

No one occupation includes every advantage and no disadvantages. There must always be a balancing of the pros and cons, and domestic service has its industrial disadvantages, which are as patent as its advantages, and like them are independent of the personal relationship existing between the employer and the employee.

The question was asked of employees, " What reasons can you give why more women do not choose housework as a regular employment? " The reasons assigned may be classified as follows :

Pride, social condition, and unwillingness to be called servants	157
Confinement evenings and Sundays	75
More independence in other occupations	60
Too hard and confining	42
Other work pays better	42
Lack of consideration by mistresses	38
Hours too long	38
Do not like housework	19
Do not know how to do housework	12
Can live at home by working in shops	11
Girls are too lazy	8
Health considerations	8
Girls are too restless	6
Too few privileges	6
Hard work, little pay	5

Other occupations easier	4
Different tastes	4
Bad character of some reflects on others	3
Receive no encouragement	3
Too lonely and meals alone	3
Constant change in work	3
Shop work cleaner	2
No chance for promotion	2
Miscellaneous reasons, one each	11
Total	562

Some of these and other reasons demand a more detailed explanation.

The first industrial disadvantage is the fact that there is little or no opportunity for promotion in the service nor are there opening out from it kindred occupations. An ambitious and capable seamstress becomes a dress-maker and mistress of a shop, a successful clerk sets up a small fancy store, the trained nurse by further study develops into a physician, the teacher becomes the head of a school; but there are no similar openings in household employments. Success means a slight increase in wages, possibly an easier place, or service in a more aristocratic neighborhood, but the differences are only slight ones of degree, never those of kind. "Once a cook, always a cook" may be applied in principle to every branch of the service. The only place where promotion is in any way possible is in hotel service.[1] Those women who would become the most efficient domestics are the ones who see most clearly this drawback to the occupation.[2]

[1] An article on the last point is found in the *Boston Herald*, November 23, 1890.

[2] "Housework soon unfits one for any other kind of work. I did not realize what I was doing until too late."

The second disadvantage is the paradoxical one that it is possible for a capable woman to reach in this employment comparative perfection in a reasonably short time. Table service is a fine art which many waitresses never learn, but it is easily mastered by one who "mixes it with brains." One illustration of this is the superior service given at summer resorts by college students without special training. The proper care of a room is understood by few maids, but the comprehension of a few simple principles enables an intelligent woman soon to become an expert. The work of a cook involves much more, but because many persons cook for years without learning how to provide a single palatable and nourishing dish, it does not follow that the art cannot be readily acquired. This fact taken in connection with the previous one unconsciously operates to prevent a large number of ambitious women from becoming domestics.

A third disadvantage is the fact that "housework is never done." In no other occupation involving the same amount of intelligent work do the results seem so literally ephemeral. This indeed is not the true statement of the case — mistresses are learning slowly that cooking is a moral and scientific question, that neatness in caring for a room is a matter of hygiene, and that table service has æsthetic possibilities. But if it has taken long for the

"I should prefer to housework a clerkship in a store or a place like that of sewing-girl in a tailor-shop, because there would be a possibility of learning the trade and then going into business for myself, or at least rising to some responsible place under an employer."

"I would give up housework if I could find another position that would enable me to advance instead of remaining in the same rut day after day."

most intelligent part of society to understand that the results of housework are not transient, but as far-reaching in their effects as are the products of any other form of labor, it cannot be deemed strange that domestics as a class and those in other occupations complain "in housework there's nothing to show for your work."

A fourth disadvantage is the lack of organization in domestic work. The verdict from the standpoint of the statistician has been quoted.[1] A domestic employee sums up the question from her point of view when she says, "Most women like to follow one particular branch of industry, such as cooking, or chamber work, or laundry work, because it enables one to be thorough and experienced; but when these are combined, as a general thing the work is hard and never done."

A fifth disadvantage is the irregularity of working hours. This is a most serious one, since the question is complicated not only by the irregularity that exists in every family, but also by the varying customs in different families. The actual working hours of a general servant may vary from one instance of five hours in Kansas to another of eighteen hours in Georgia. They sometimes vary in the same city from seven to seventeen hours. It is a difficult matter to ascertain with the utmost definiteness, but a careful examination of all statements made seems to show that the actual working hours are ten in the case of thirty-eight per cent of women employees, thirty-seven per cent averaging more than ten hours, and twenty-five per cent less than this. The working hours for men average somewhat longer than the hours for

[1] *Ante*, p. 113.

TABLE XIX
Actual Daily Working Hours

Occupation	Number working							Per cent working				
	10 hours	11 hours	12 hours	Less than 10 hours	More than 12 hours	Not answered	Total	10 hours	11 hours	12 hours	Less than 10 hours	More than 12 hours
WOMEN												
General servants	149	28	91	142	45	188	638	32.75	6.15	20.00	31.21	9.89
Second girls	29	6	26	40	21	52	174	28.77	4.92	21.31	32.79	17.21
Cooks and laundresses	25	7	21	21	26	42	142	25.00	7.00	21.00	21.00	26.00
Cooks	58	9	41	45	43	92	288	29.59	4.59	20.92	22.97	21.94
Laundresses	94	11	16	86	3	91	251	58.75	6.88	10.00	22.50	1.87
Chambermaids and waitresses	34	4	20	21	20	36	185	34.34	4.04	20.20	21.21	20.20
Chambermaids	23	8	10	17	6	37	96	38.98	5.09	16.95	28.81	10.17
Waitresses	46	8	2	7	10	89	107	67.65	4.41	2.94	10.29	14.71
Nurses	25	8	25	8	19	45	180	29.41	9.41	29.41	9.41	22.85
Seamstresses	57	2	4	26	...	18	107	64.04	2.25	4.50	29.21	...
Housekeepers	...	...	...	1	...	4	5	...	...	...	...	...
Total	540	81	256	864	198	639	2078	37.66	5.65	17.86	25.88	18.45
MEN												
Butlers	11	...	10	5	7	13	46	88.84	...	30.30	15.15	21.21
Coachmen and gardeners	31	8	26	20	10	85	180	32.68	8.42	27.37	21.05	10.58
Coachmen	27	4	18	5	10	48	112	42.19	6.25	28.18	7.81	15.62
Gardeners	52	6	12	28	8	25	126	51.49	5.94	11.88	22.27	7.92
Choremen	7	1	2	11	8	17	41	29.17	4.17	8.88	45.83	12.50
Cooks	7	...	3	3	1	8	17	50.00	...	21.43	21.43	7.14
Total	185	19	71	67	39	141	472	40.79	5.74	21.45	20.24	11.78

Per cent working	Women	Men
Ten hours	87.66	40.79
Less than ten hours	25.88	20.24
More than ten hours	86.96	88.97

women, while there are slight differences in the various classes of servants ; but they are of too indefinite a character to be specially noted. Table XIX will illustrate these points.

Many of these differences are inherent in the composition of the family, and can never be removed ; many of them are accidental and their number could be lessened were employers so inclined ; many of them grow out of necessarily differing standards of living. This is seen where one family of ten employs one general servant and another family of ten employs eleven servants ; one family of four employs nine servants, while seventy-eight other families of the same size each employ only one servant ; one family of eight has sixteen servants, while each one of eight other families consisting of eight persons employs one servant ; twenty-three families numbering seven each have one general servant, while another family of seven has thirteen employees ; in another instance, three employees serve a family of one. These contrasts could be multiplied indefinitely. They simply indicate in one way the hopeless confusion that must exist at present in the matter of hours of service required. The irregularities in even a well-regulated family are always great. Many of these are apparently necessary, and the employee must expect to meet them — they are often not so great as those that perplex the mistress of the house in her share of the household duties, but the fact cannot be ignored that they exist and have weight. The one afternoon each week with generally one or more evenings after work is done is not sufficient compensation.[1] It is the

----

[1] " You are mistress of no time of your own ; other occupations have

L

irregularity in the distribution of working time rather than the amount of time demanded that causes dissatisfaction on the part of employees. No complaint is more often made than this, and the results of the investigation seem to justify the complaint. To a young woman therefore seeking employment the question of working hours assumes the aspect of a lottery — she may draw a prize of seven working hours or she may draw a blank of fourteen working hours; she cannot be blamed for making definite inquiries of a prospective employer regarding the size of the family and the number of other servants employed.

A sixth disadvantage closely connected with the preceding is the matter of free time evenings and Sundays. This objection to housework is frequently made ;[1] it is one that can never be wholly obviated, since the household machinery cannot stop at six o'clock and must be kept in order seven days in the week, but were society so inclined the objection could be lessened.

A seventh difficulty is presented to the American born

well-defined hours, after which one can do as she pleases without asking any one."

[1] " Women want the free use of their time evenings and Sundays."

" If I could bear the confinement I would go into a mill where I could have evenings and Sundays."

"Sunday in a private family is usually anything but a day of rest to the domestic, for on that day there are usually guests to dinner or tea or both, which means extra work."

" I wouldn't mind working Sundays if it wasn't for the extra work."

" I suppose the reason why more women choose other work is, they would rather work all day and be done with it, and have evenings for themselves."

" Some families have dinner at three o'clock Sundays and lunch at eight or nine, and that makes it very hard for girls."

girl when she realizes that she must come into competition with the foreign born and colored element.[1] Although much of this feeling is undoubtedly unreasonable, it is not peculiar to domestic service. The fact must be accepted, with or without excuse for it.

Another disadvantage that weighs with many is the feeling that in other occupations there is more personal independence. This includes not only the matter of time evenings and Sundays, which they can seldom call unconditionally their own, but there is a dislike of interference on the part of the employer, either with their work or with their personal habits and tastes. This interference is often hard to bear when the employer is an experienced housekeeper — it is intolerable in the case of an inexperienced one. The "boss" carpenter who himself knew nothing about the carpenter's trade would soon have all his workmen arrayed against him; in every occupation an employee is unwilling to be directed except by his superior in knowledge and ability.[2] It seems unreason-

[1] "A great many very ignorant girls can get housework to do, and a girl who has been used to neatness and the refinement of a good home does not like to room with a girl who has just come from Ireland and does not know what neatness means."

"In —— they have much colored help and do not have white help, so the white girls think any other work is better than housework."

"In California self-respecting girls do not like to work with Chinamen — they do not know how to treat women."

"Before the introduction of Chinese labor a young girl never lost social caste by doing housework; but since this element came, household service as an occupation has fallen in the social scale."— *Employer.*

"When a native American girl goes out to housework she loses caste at once, and can hardly find pleasure in the foreign immigrants that form the majority of servants, and who make most of the trouble from their ignorance and preconceived notions of America."— *Employer.*

[2] "The reason for dislike of housework is the want of liberty, and

able to expect domestic service to be an exception to this universal rule. But even experienced housekeepers often do not realize how difficult it is for one person to work in the harness of another, and by insisting on having work done in their own way, even by competent servants, they sometimes unconsciously hinder the accomplishment of their own ends.[1] There is also connected with this the preference for serving a company or a corporation rather

the submission which girls have to submit to when they have to comply with whatever rules a mistress may deem necessary. Therefore many girls go into mechanical pursuits, that some of their life may be their own."

"Girls in housework are bossed too much."

"There are too many mistresses in the house when the mother and grown-up daughters are all at home."

"Most of us would like a little more independence, and to do our work as we please."

"In housework you receive orders from half a dozen persons, in a shop or factory from but one."

"A man doesn't let his wife and daughters and sons interfere in the management of his mill or factory — why does a housekeeper let everybody in the house boss?"

[1] A description of domestic service in Japan is of value on this point. "From the steward of your household, to your *jinrikisha* man or groom, every servant in your establishment does what is right in his own eyes, and after the manner he thinks best. Mere blind obedience to orders is not regarded as a virtue in a Japanese servant; he must do his own thinking, and, if he cannot grasp the reason for your order, that order will not be carried out." "Even in the treaty ports [Japanese attendants] have not resigned their right of private judgment, but, if faithful and honest, seek the best good of their employer, even if his best good involves disobedience of his orders." — Alice M. Bacon, *Japanese Girls and Women*, pp. 299, 301.

F. R. Feudge, in *How I Kept House by Proxy*, quotes from her Chinese cook, who said that he could boast of forty years "of study and practice in his profession." "I am always willing to be told *what* to do, but never *how* to execute the order — especially when in that department I happen to know far more than my teachers." — *Scribner's Monthly*, September, 1881.

than a private individual. It is hard to explain this feeling except on general grounds of prejudice, but the belief undoubtedly exists that there is more personal independence connected with work in a large establishment than there is in serving an individual. There is often a similar feeling of independence in working in families employing a large number of servants, or in those occupying a high station in life.[1]

The industrial disadvantages of the occupation are best summed up by a young factory operative who was for a time in domestic service. In answer to the question, " Why do girls dislike domestic service ? " she writes :

"In the first place, I don't like the idea of only one evening a week and every other Sunday. I like to feel that I have just so many hours' work to do and do them, and come home and dress up and go out or sit down and sew if I feel like it, and when a girl is in service she has very little time for herself, she is a servant. In the second place, a shop or factory girl knows just what she has to do and can go ahead and do it. I also think going out makes a girl stupid in time. She gets out of style, so to speak. She never reads and does not know what is going on in the world. I don't mean to say they all get stupid, but it makes gossips of girls that if they worked in shops or factories would be smart girls. Then I think shop or factory girls make the best wives. Now I don't mean all, but the biggest part of them, and the cleanest housekeepers. The domestic after she gets married gets careless. She don't take the pride in her home that the shop-girl does. She has lived in such fine houses that her small tenement has no beauty for her after the first glow of married life is over. She don't try either to make her home attractive or herself, and gets discouraged, and is apt to make a man disheartened with her, and then

[1] A shrewd young colored woman gives her version, verbally, of the servant question. She lays great stress on her own " bringin' up," as "she wa'n't brung up by trash," and thinks the average colored girl " only a nigger." She prefers to live " at service," but insists upon " high-toned " employers, and " can't abide common folks."

I think she is extravagant. She has so much to do with before she is married and so little to do with after she don't know how to manage. She can't have tenderloin steak for her breakfast and rump roast for her dinner, and pay the rent and all other bills out of $12 a week — and that is the average man's pay, the kind of man we girls that work for a living get. Of course I don't mean to say the domestics don't have a good time, they do; some of them have lovely places and lay up money, but after all, what is life if a body is always trying to see just how much money he or she can save?"

The industrial disadvantages of the occupation certainly are many, including as they do the lack of all opportunity for promotion, the great amount of mere mechanical repetition involved, the lack of organization in the service, irregularity in working hours, the limitation of free time evenings and Sundays, competition with the foreign born and the negro element that seems objectionable to the American born, and the interference with work often by those less skilled than the workers themselves. The industrial disadvantages, however, form but one class of the two that weigh most seriously against the occupation. The social disadvantages will be discussed in the following chapter.

CHAPTER IX

THE SOCIAL DISADVANTAGES OF DOMESTIC SERVICE

THE most serious disadvantage in domestic service that remains to be considered is the low social position the employment entails at the present time on those who enter it. This shows itself in various ways. The most noticeable is the lack of home privileges. It is true that the domestic employee receives board, lodging, protection, and many incidental privileges in the home of her employer; that these are as a rule better than she could provide for herself elsewhere, and much superior to those which can be secured by women working in shops and factories. But board and lodging do not constitute a home, and the domestic can never be a part of the family whose external life she shares. The case is well stated by an employee who writes:

"Ladies wonder how their girls can complain of loneliness in a house full of people, but oh ! it is the worst kind of loneliness — their share is but the work of the house, they do not share in the pleasures and delights of a home. One must remember that there is a difference between a *house*, a place of shelter, and a *home*, a place where all your affections are centred. Real love exists between my employer and myself, yet at times I grow almost desperate from the sense of being cut off from those pleasures to which I had always been accustomed. I belong to the same church as my employer, yet have no share in the social life of the church."

151

This appreciation of the difference between being in a family and being a part of it is in direct ratio to the delicacy and sensitiveness of the organization of the employee. An American who can be considered one of the family is the very one who most appreciates the difference between being one of the family and like one of the family. The differences which are most keenly felt are three. The first is the fact that a certain amount of regulation must always be exercised by the employer in regard to the number and character of visitors received by the employee. It is a matter of self-protection, and is sometimes due to the employee as well. It often does not differ in kind or in degree from the care exercised for the other members of the household. The necessity for it is recognized by the better class of employees.[1] Nevertheless the restraint is irksome, the desire for independence not always unreasonable, and the wish for a place in which to receive visitors not surprising.

Another deprivation is the lack of opportunity for receiving or showing in even a slight degree that hospitality which can be accepted and exercised in every other employment involving equal intelligence.[2] The domestic

[1] " In some families no acquaintance can call on the servant; she may have one or two friends, but the number is always limited, because, says the lady of the house, not without truth, ' Who wants a dozen strange girls running in and out of one's back door ? ' "

[2] " There are reasons why I sometimes feel dissatisfied with doing housework for other people. I would prefer to do work where people would say, supposing they were to give a company, ' There is Miss So and So, let us invite her.' " This is from an unusually intelligent employee who says she does housework because she likes to do it best, and because a domestic can have better-cooked food and a better-ventilated room than most shop-girls, and who also writes, " Intelligence, brains, and good judgment are essential in getting up a dinner for six or eight."

employee can neither accept nor give an invitation to sup-
per ; she cannot offer a cup of tea to a caller ; she does not
ask a friend to remain to dinner, except perhaps at rare
intervals a mother or a sister. She has the privilege of
using without limit for her own necessities the food purchased by her employer, but she cannot share it without
transgressing this privilege. She cannot invite her
friends for an afternoon tea to meet a friend from another
place, or give a small dinner party or a chafing-dish sup-
per. She can do none of these things the desire for which
is so natural and which can be gratified in a small way
in almost every other occupation. Even more than this,
she is never a sharer in the general social life of the community.[1] She is precluded not by her character but by
her condition from exercising those social privileges which
are instinctive in all persons.

Another social barrier is the failure of society to recognize the need on the part of the employee of those opportunities for personal improvement so freely accorded to
those in other occupations. If she has a taste for music
or art she can cultivate it only at the expense of ridicule,[2]

[1] One illustration of this social barrier was found in a small manufacturing city. The factory employees, all men and skilled workmen,
arranged one winter a series of evening entertainments. Invitations were
sent to the self-supporting women in the city, the list including dressmakers, milliners, stenographers, saleswomen, and others, but the social
line was drawn at cooks.

[2] A lady was recently about to complete the engagement of a cook, a
German girl, when the head of the employment bureau said : " I fear
after all that A B will not suit you. You live in a flat, and as she wishes
to take violin lessons her practising might annoy you." The incident was
narrated to a company of friends, and created much amusement, until
one said, " This shows how unregenerate we are ; why should she not
take violin lessons ? " It is not easy to find an answer.

while her need of intellectual advantages in a similar way meets with no recognition.[1] If she is refined and cultivated, she must often associate with those who are coarse and ignorant.[2]

But the question of social standing goes farther than this. Not only are social advantages of every kind denied the domestic employee, but the badge of social inferiority is put upon her in characters as unchangeable

A gentleman, whose family includes only himself and his wife, writes : "Our maid-of-all-work is a young Swedish girl of eighteen, who recently came to America. Three months ago she said, 'If I had a musical instrument and a place to practise, I would get a music teacher and stay with you always.' A few days later my married daughter sent us an organ of sweet tone, which was placed in a small room little used. We gave our maid permission to use it, and she at once secured a teacher. This morning she said : ''My father writes me if I am on the street much. I write him, No, I enjoy myself better — I practise my music.' We seem to have solved the domestic question — at least for a time."

[1] "I should like work where I could come in contact with more people who would be of help to me."

"A young woman doing housework is shut out from all society, nor can she make any plans for pleasure or study, for her time is not her own."

"No one seems to think a girl who works out good enough to associate with, except those who are in domestic service themselves."

"Domestics never have a chance to go to school or study."

A domestic employee recently went to a public library for a book. The attendant was about to give it to her, thinking from her manner and appearance that she was a teacher in a neighboring school ; but when the question was asked and the answer given, "not a teacher, but a housemaid," the book was withheld, as servants were required to bring recommendations.

[2] "Domestics are not admitted into any society, and are often for want of a little pleasure driven to seek it in company that is often coarse and vulgar."

"It is very hard for a young, refined woman to give up a pleasant home, and live constantly with ignorant and ill-bred people, as is very often the case where more than one servant is kept."

as are the spots of a leopard. This badge assumes several different forms. The first is the use of the word "servant." [1] We may prove from etymology that every person who confers a favor on another is his servant. We may present a lawyer's brief showing to the satisfaction of every local and national court that every employee in the eye of the law is a servant. We may argue from the biblical standpoint and show without a flaw in our chain of reasoning that we are all servants of one another. We may point to the classification of occupations made by the national census bureau and show that clergymen, doctors, lawyers, teachers, and domestic servants are placed together. We may quote to every employee the proudly humble motto of the Prince of Wales, "Ich dien," and the example of the Pope, who calls himself "the servant of the servants of the Lord." We may by a social fiction subscribe ourselves a score of times each day, "Your most humble and obedient servant." We may do all of these things, but just as long as common phraseology restricts the ordinary use of the word to those persons engaged in domestic employments for which they receive a fixed compensation, just so long will arguments prove of no avail and the word "servant"

[1] "I fairly hate the word 'servant.'"
"I don't like to be called a 'menial.'"
"The girls in shops call us 'livers-out.'"
"No woman likes to be called a 'hired girl.'"
"American girls don't like the name 'servants.'"
"I know many nice girls who would do housework, but they prefer doing almost anything else rather than be called 'servants.'"
"Some people call us 'kitchen mechanics.'"
"I don't know why we should be called 'servants' any more than other people."

continue to be a mark of social degradation. The efforts of domestic employees to substitute the terms "maid" or "working housekeeper" have as yet in many quarters excited little more than ridicule.

A second mark of social inferiority is the use of the Christian name in address. It may seem a very trifling matter, yet the fact again remains that domestic employees are the only class of workers, except day laborers, who are thus addressed. The weight that is attached to the matter in other walks of life is seen in the policy of more than one well-known newspaper; a strong weapon of attack in encounter with opponents has been the reference by Christian name to those whom the writers wish to consign to political obscurity. In no way does advancement in age and dignity show itself sooner than in the substitution of the surname for the Christian name. The boy shows his sense of growing importance by dropping the Christian name in addressing his companions. In the eyes of the débutante the first card bearing the name "Miss Brown" throws into insignificance many other advantages of the new position. Probably few persons would choose to go through life addressed by even their most intimate friends, aside from kith and kin, as are the class of domestic employees. The use of the Christian name in address undoubtedly grew out of the close family relationship that existed between the employer and the employee, but it has become a badge of social inferiority since it is used alike by strangers and friends. Any person considers himself privileged to use the familiar address towards any employee simply by virtue of the employee's position. Even more objectionable is the

English custom, sometimes affected in America, of dropping the Christian name and using the surname without
a title, since it implies social inferiority even more than
the familiar address.[1]

A third badge of the position sometimes insisted on is
the cap and apron. These are not worn, as are the cap
and sleeves of the trained nurse, to indicate the completion of a regular course of scientific training; they are
not the uniform of the postman or the policeman, which
shows the recognition by national or municipal authorities
of superior fitness for the position filled and carries with
it somewhat of the prestige of the power the wearer
serves; they represent necessarily no attainment on the
part of the person wearing them, nor are they, as worn,
always the object of laudable ambition. The cap and
apron sometimes indicate the rise of the employer in the
social scale rather than the professional advance of the
employee. The wider the separation in any community
between employer and employee, the greater is the tendency to insist on the cap and apron. The same principle
is involved when coachmen are not permitted to wear

---

[1] A woman who had been for years a domestic employee left her place
on account of sickness, and ultimately opened a small bakeshop. Her
former employer called on her one day, and said, "Well, Sarah, how do
you like your work?" She replied, "I never thought of it before, but
now that you speak, I think the reason I like it so well is because everybody calls me 'Miss Clark.'"

An employer invited her Sunday-school class to her home to spend an
evening. One of the members went into the kitchen to render some assistance, and found there the housemaid, an unusually attractive young
woman. The employer said, "Miss M, this is Kate." The maid, who
never before had showed the slightest consciousness of occupying an inferior position, said, under her breath, "I am Miss, too."

beards and hotel and club waiters are required to sacrifice the moustache.

A fourth badge is the fact that domestic servants are made not only to feel but to acknowledge their social inferiority. Not only deference but even servility of manner is demanded as of no other class, and this in an age when social and family relationships are everywhere becoming more democratic, when reverence and respect for authority are sometimes considered old-fashioned virtues, when even undue freedom of speech and manner are permitted to other classes. The domestic employee receives and gives no word or look of recognition on the street except in meeting those of her own class; she is seldom introduced to the guests of the house, whom she may faithfully serve during a prolonged visit ; the common daily courtesies exchanged between the members of the household are not always shown her ; she takes no part in the general conversation around her ; she speaks only when addressed, obeys without murmur orders which her judgment tells her are absurd, " is not expected to smile under any circumstances," and ministers without protest to the whims and obeys implicitly the commands of children from whom deference to parents is never expected.

A fifth mark of social inferiority is the fact that domestic employees, especially those connected with boarding houses, restaurants, and hotels, are generally given a fee for every service rendered.

A self-respecting man or woman in any other occupation is insulted by the offer of a fee. The person who through mistake offers a fee to a person belonging to his own station brings upon himself only ridicule and embarrassment. The shop-girl who works for $7 a week spends half an hour in a vain attempt to match for a customer a bit of ribbon; but she would be justly indignant, as would be her employer, if she were offered a fee. In hotels and restaurants, the larger the establishment and the more the price of every article should warrant exemption from such outside dues, the greater is felt to be the pressure for their payment. Nowhere else is the democratic principle "first come first served" so flagrantly violated, and nowhere else would its violation be tolerated. Feeing is a system of begging that cannot be reached by charity organization societies, a species of blackmail levied on all who wish good service, for which there is no legal redress, a European and American form of backsheesh that carries with it the taint of the soil from which it has sprung. It has its origin in snobbishness and it results in toadyism and flunkeyism. It is objectionable because it makes the giver feel as humiliated in giving as the recipient ought to feel in receiving. It puts a price on that kindness and consideration which ought to be the "royal bounty" in connection with every paid service, it destroys genuine sympathy and unselfishness, it creates an eye service and introduces into every branch of domestic service an element of demoralization and degradation that is incalculable. It takes from the person receiving it the option of placing a value on the service rendered by him, and it is the only occupation where fees are given that does not carry with it this privilege. A lawyer or a physician must be the best judge of the value of his services, but the domestic servant takes "what you please."

One of the results of the system is indicated by a jesting paragraph that recently went the rounds of the daily press to the effect that the porter of the Grand Pacific Hotel, in Chicago, had retired with a fortune of $100,000 accumulated from tips given him by guests of the house,[1] while the men who contributed it were still struggling to keep the wolf from the door. In tipping, as in bribery, the social odium falls on the one who takes the tip or the bribe, not on the one who offers it. The fortune of $100,000, more or less, would not give social position to one who had acquired it through fees. But the fee is at bottom a bribe offered for service for which payment is presumably made by the employer; it is a bribe because it is an additional sum offered for quick service or good service which a waiter will not give without this extra compensation from the person served. As long as this form of bribery prevails, every person who accepts the bribe is socially tainted and no amount of financial success resulting from it can eradicate the taint.

Not only is the fee objectionable in itself, but the manner of giving it is equally so. It is bestowed surreptitiously, as if the giver appreciated the fact that he was doing an insulting thing and was ashamed of it; or it is offered openly with the patronizing manner of one who says, " I have no use for such a trifle ; take it, if you wish it." It is folded in a napkin, tucked under a plate,

[1] That this jest has a basis of fact in England is evident from the testimony of the footman of the Earl of Northbrook, who some time since stated under oath, in a court of law, that although his regular wages amounted to but $300 annually, yet he received from $2,000 to $2,500 more each year in the shape of tips from the Earl's guests. " Her Majesty's Servants," in the *New York Tribune*, August 23, 1896.

slipped into the hand of a waiter with a vain attempt to appear unconscious, left ostentatiously on a tray, or contemptuously flung at an attendant. It can be neither given nor received with the self-respect that accompanies any reputable business transaction.

Two excuses for feeing are given. One, "because every one else does it and one feels contemptible if he doesn't do it," an easy, good-natured way of disposing of a serious problem. Comparatively few persons are controlled by general principles; each acts according to what seems most convenient at the time being. The second excuse is that employees in hotels and restaurants and porters in drawing-room and sleeping cars are underpaid. This is undoubtedly true, and *it will remain true as long as the general public frees the class of hotel, restaurant, and boarding-house proprietors, and palace and sleeping car companies, from the responsibility of paying their own assistants.* But the general public also knows that the saleswomen in many large stores work for almost nothing, that street-car conductors and motor men are overworked and underpaid, that school teachers receive but a pittance. The public, however, pursues here a different policy; it puts on "the white list" employers who pay their saleswomen well, it allows street-railway employees to fight out the matter of low wages by strikes or in such other ways as they deem fit, it permits the school teacher to struggle on with a salary of $400 or $500 a year and patronizes a fair held for the benefit of a pension fund. It is difficult to see why this reason for feeing a domestic employee should not hold good in all underpaid employments; that it

M

does not is one reason why those in other occupations do not fall in the social scale. That the public continues to pay directly the employees in this occupation as it does in no other is one explanation of the ill repute it bears among self-respecting wage-earning men and women. Every person has a contempt for another who accepts a fee, and the reproach extends from the individual to every branch of the occupation he represents. No other thing has done more to lower domestic service in the eyes of the public than this most pernicious custom, and every person who fees a domestic employee has by that act done something to degrade what should be an honorable occupation into a menial service.[1]

Another phase of the social question is presented by an employer who writes, " There is something wrong when a young girl servant is sent out in the evening to accompany the daughter or perhaps the mistress and return alone." If protection is the thought, the maid needs it as much as the mistress; if it is in deference to a social custom, the maid must bitterly resent any custom which demands this distinction between herself and those whom she serves. Another aspect of the same question is suggested when it is realized what veritable dens of iniquity are some of the intelligence offices in large cities, and how difficult it often is for a domestic employee to come in contact with them without becoming contaminated by

---

[1] Mr. W. D. Howells has an excellent discussion of the feeing system in *Harper's Weekly*, May 16, 1896 ; also, Julia R. Tutwiler in the *American Kitchen Magazine*, April, 1896 ; still a third is found in the *Outlook*, August 8, 1896.

the touch. These are the things that lead many to believe that "the kitchen has become very like a social Botany Bay."[1]

It is this social position with its accompanying marks of social inferiority that, more than any other one thing, turns the scale against domestic service as an occupation in the thoughts of many intelligent and ambitious women whose tastes naturally incline them to domestic employments. Professor Arthur T. Hadley has well said in a discussion of comparative wages, "One thing which counts for more and costs more than anything else is social standing."[2] The social standing maintained by a cash girl on $3 a week which she fears to lose by going into domestic service ought not to be vastly superior to what is within the reach of intelligent cooks earning $10 a week; yet undoubtedly it is; and while this is true the number of intelligent women in domestic service will not increase.[3]

[1] One illustration of the fact that domestic service is never judged by the same social canons as are other occupations, is seen in the unwillingness shown by a young woman to enter the service of a family having a questionable reputation. Her "squeamishness," as it was called, excited only laughter in a circle of women, no one of whom would have exchanged calls with the family in question.

[2] *First Annual Report of the Bureau of Labor Statistics of Connecticut,* 1885, p. 12.

[3] An employer writes: "I recently advertised for a young woman to help me with the children, and be received as one of the family. The forty answers received formed the most pathetic reading I have ever seen. My selection was the daughter of a poor clergyman, and this was the class from which the majority of the answers came. All desired domestic service if unaccompanied with social degradation."

How conscious many are of this inferior position is seen from a single illustration. An employer recently invited her housemaid to take a boat-ride with her. The maid replied, "I should love to go if you wouldn't be ashamed to be seen with me."

Other objections to domestic service in addition to those enumerated are sometimes made. Some of them arise from misconceptions,[1] others are trivial and do not demand consideration, while others are individual rather than general. These are the disadvantages that tell most strongly against the occupation. They do not include the element of ill-treatment by mistresses or their lack of consideration; or the fact that there is sometimes much in the tone and manner of an employer that is most irritating to a self-respecting person; or that there are occasionally employers who feel that they rise in the social scale in the same proportion that they make employees sensible of inferiority or dependence; or that many mistresses demand more than can be performed; or that some employers are unreasonable, others disagreeable, and still others petulant and fault-finding; or that some "expect perfection at twelve dollars a month and positive genius at thirteen." These conditions are found, but they are not peculiar to domestic service; the disadvantages discussed are all independent of good or bad personal treatment, they may be modified by the character of the family to whom the service is rendered, but they cannot be removed by any individual employer acting alone, however much he has at heart the interests of his own employee or of domestic employees as a class.

[1] This is especially true in the matter of wages where wages and annual earnings are confused, the element of time lost never being considered. The fact is also often overlooked that when a young woman lives at home without paying her board, her family in effect pay a part of her wages and thus enable the employer to pay her low wages, though nominally more than paid in housework. Thus one employee writes: "If girls have homes where their board is given them, they can earn more money on other kinds of work than in housework."

In comparing the advantages and disadvantages of domestic service as an occupation it will be obvious that the advantages are numerous, substantial, and easily recognized; the disadvantages are many, but they are far more subtile, intangible, and far reaching. The advantages are those which the economic woman always sees and which take her from unhealthy tenement houses into country air and sunshine; from overcrowded occupations into one where the demand for workers is and always must be unlimited; from starvation wages to peace and plenty; from long hours of dreary mechanical toil to intelligent work; from failure in an uncongenial occupation to success and prosperity in this; from a life whose sufferings and privations, as yet but half told, have roused the sympathies of all social reformers, to a life of freedom from the sweater, the floor-walker, the officious and vulgar superintendent, the industrial Shylocks of every occupation, to a life of comparative ease and comfort. But while the economic woman, like the economic man, always sees these things, the actual woman looks at another side. She does not understand why work that society calls the most honorable a woman can do when done in her own home without remuneration, becomes demeaning when done in the house of another for a fixed compensation, but she recognizes the fact; she sees that discredit comes not from the work itself but from the conditions under which it is performed, and she does not willingly place herself in these conditions; she sees that a class line is always drawn as in no other occupation; she is willing and glad to pay her life for what seems to her *life* — excitement, city ways, society of home friends, personal independence which another might call slavery. She does not care for those advantages which another person points out; to her they count as nothing in comparison with the price she must pay for them. Of five hundred and forty employees of whom the question was asked, "Would you give up housework if you could find another occupation that would pay you as well?" one-half answered, "Yes." Yet the number is very small of those who complain of ill-treatment or lack of consideration on the part of the employer. There is, indeed, often much ground for complaint on this score, but it must be seen that other relationships besides the personal ones are entered into when the relation of employer and employee is established. That which decides the question is not always the economic advantage, not always the personal treatment, but that subtile thing the woman calls *life*. "Wages, hours, health, and morals" may all weigh in the scale in favor of domestic service, but *life* outweighs them all. The advantages are such as lead many people to urge domestic service for the daughters of others, the disadvantages are such as incline them to choose any occupation but this for their own daughters.[1]

[1] Domestic service, as seen by the employee, cannot be dismissed without suggesting the fact that as many tragedies in life are found here as elsewhere. One employee had planned to be a teacher, but sudden deafness prevented, and domestic service was all she could do. Another hoped to become a physician, but loss of property prevented her from completing her education. A similar reason prevented another from becoming a trained nurse. One had hoped to be a dressmaker, but it became necessary to earn money at once without serving an apprenticeship. Could the struggles and disappointments in thousands of such lives be known, the household employee would cease to be the butt of jest and ridicule that she sometimes is.

CHAPTER X

DOUBTFUL REMEDIES

The difficulties attending domestic service are so many and so pressing that a large number of measures intended to meet them have been proposed, all of them as varied as the personalities of those dealing with the problem. This difference of opinion in regard to the best methods of meeting the question is largely due to the fact that, not domestic service as an occupation, but domestic servants as individuals have been considered. It has also come from the fact that while the feudal castle of the Middle Ages has shrunk to the city apartment, the attempt is made to preserve intact the customs that had their origin in mediævalism and ought to have died with it, overlooking the fact that every other occupation has made at least some slight concession to economic progress. Moreover, it must be said that the purely ethical phases of the subject have been the ones most often kept in mind in discussing measures of relief. This ethical side of the question is indeed important, but it is largely based on the assumption that the relation between employer and employee is a purely personal one. Since the discussion of the question up to this point has been based on a different theory, namely, that other relations besides the personal ones are established when that of employer and employee is assumed, and that domestic service has been and is affected by political, economic, industrial, social, and educational questions, the present discussion of possible and impossible remedies in domestic service cannot take into consideration the purely ethical questions involved in the subject, but must deal with its other aspects.

Before attempting to answer the question of what can and what cannot be done, a few general principles deduced from the consideration of the subject up to this point must be indicated. First, since the evils are many and complicated no panacea can be found. The patent medicine that cures every physical ailment from consumption to chilblains is disappearing before the scientific studies of the day; it is quite as little to be recommended for economic and social maladies. Second, the remedy applied must have some relation to the nature of the disease. A sprained wrist will not yield to the treatment for dyspepsia, nor can rheumatism and deafness be cured by the same brown pills. The principle does not differ if moral remedies are administered for educational diseases and economic maladies are expected to succumb to social tonics. Third, reform in domestic service must be accomplished along the same general economic lines as are reforms in other great departments of labor — not at right angles to general industrial progress. Fourth, reform in domestic service must be the result of evolution from present conditions and tendencies — not a special creation. Fifth, no reform can be instituted which will remove to-morrow all difficulties that exist to-day. Domestic service cannot reach at a bound the goal towards which other forms of labor have been moving with halting steps.

These principles are simple and will perhaps be generally accepted. A few of the measures often suggested as affording means of relief may be tested by them.

It is the opinion of a very large class that all difficulties can be removed by the application of the golden rule. No belief is more widespread than this. But it rests wholly on the assumption that the relation between employer and employee is a personal one, and presupposes that if this personal relationship could be made an ideal one the question would settle itself. In so far as the connection between mistress and maid is a personal one, the golden rule is sufficient, but other factors are involved in the problem. The golden rule may be ever so perfectly observed, but that fact does not eliminate the competition of other industries where the golden rule may be observed with equal conscientiousness, nor does it remove the distasteful competition of American born employees with foreigners and negroes; it does not overcome the preference for city life or the love of personal independence; it is not always able to substitute intelligence, capability, interest, and economy for ignorance, inefficiency, indifference, and waste; the observance of the golden rule by the employer is not a guarantee that it will always be followed by the employee. For moral difficulties, moral remedies must be applied, but they will not always operate where the maladies are in their nature economic, social, and educational. The golden rule is a poultice that will relieve an inflammation but will not remove the cause of the evil — a tonic that will invigorate the system but which cannot be substituted for surgical treatment.

Another class of persons believes that the application of intelligence as well as of ethical principles is what is required of the employer. This position is best expressed by the correspondent of a leading journal who says : " The capable housekeeper is quite satisfied with the performance of her own domestic duties. If a true woman performs her whole duty, that which lies within her sphere of action, this everlasting cry of reform in domestic service would cease and in its place there would rise a more satisfied race of human beings." But intelligence, capability, and the observance of all ethical principles must, like the golden rule, encounter the question of free Sundays and evenings after six o'clock, as well as that of the regularity of working hours and the possibility of promotion found in other occupations. No system ever has been or ever can be found that will enable a housekeeper to conduct a household satisfactorily on the instinct or the inspiration theory, to substitute sentiment for educated intelligence and for a knowledge of economic conditions outside of the individual home. The ostrich is said to cover its head in the sand and imagine that it is safe from capture ; as well may the individual employer say, "I have settled the question for myself; it is sufficient and I am satisfied."

A third suggestion in harmony with the two preceding is to receive the employee into the family of the employer, giving her all of the family privileges, including a seat at the table. This plan finds many advocates among intelligent, conscientious employers who are earnestly trying to

DOUBTFUL REMEDIES   171

find a way out of present troubles. But there are several objections to it. One is the fact that such a policy is a distinct deviation from all economic tendencies of the century. A hundred years ago under the domestic system of manufactures the masterworkman received his apprentices into his family, and no other arrangement seemed possible. The factory system has revolutionized this manner of life, and a return to it in manufacturing industries would be as impossible as a restoration of the feudal system itself. The attempt to return to what was once a common custom in many parts of the North is an attempt to restore the patriarchal relationship between employer and employee in a generation which looks with disfavor on paternalism in other forms of labor. Another objection to the plan is its inherent impossibility. John Stuart Mill could conceive of another world where two and two do not make four, but it must in this world be at present an impossibility to conceive of a family in which the idea of unity is not an essential feature. The very foundation of a family is its integrity. Four plus one half can never equal five, and no one can ever be more than a fraction in any family into which he has not been born, married, or legally adopted. The family circle cannot be squared, and if it could be, the curve of beauty would be lost. Moreover, even if the plan could be carried out, it would not meet the needs of the majority of employees or of those who would become such if the conditions of service were more favorable. *What domestics as a class desire is the opportunity of living their own lives in their own way.* This is what other occupations offer to a greater degree than does domestic service, and it is one reason for the preference for them. The desire is not always on the part of the employees for the same friends, the same amusements, the same privileges, the same opportunities, the same interests, as those of their employers, but it is to have such friends, such amusements, such privileges, such opportunities, such interests, as they personally crave. Even what would be in themselves the greatest advantages often cease to be such when the element of personal choice in regard to them is removed. Still another objection is the failure of the plan to subserve the best interests of the employer, even granting that it is best. for the employee. It grows out of the nature of the family, as previously suggested. Comparatively few persons are willing, except as a business necessity, to open their homes even temporarily to those compelled to board. The privacy of home life is destroyed to even a greater extent by the attempt to make household employees permanently a part of it, not because those admitted within the family circle are of this particular class, but because they are not of the family. Marriage has been called a process of naturalization — a difficult one when all the conditions are most favorable. The process is infinitely more difficult when an extraneous element is introduced into a family, not as a result of mutual choice, but of a business agreement.

A fourth proposition for lessening the difficulties in domestic service is to increase the number of employees by bringing to the North negroes from the South. So seriously has this plan been contemplated that companies have in some places already been formed, and through them colored servants have been sent to different parts of

the Eastern states. But this plan assumes that no perplexities exist where colored servants are found, and also
that there are no difficulties which a greater supply of
domestic employees will not remove. That the former
assumption cannot rightly be made is evident from many
facts. The anomalous condition is found in at least one
Southern city of an organization to assist Northern housekeepers to secure colored servants, and of another to aid
Southern housekeepers in obtaining white employees from
the North.[1] The examination of a large number of advertisements for "help wanted" shows apparently a preference in many parts of the South for white servants,[2]

[1] An employer in South Carolina writes: "The difficulty here can only
be removed by the importation of competent servants."
[2] The following table will indicate the preference:

CITY OR STATE	NUMBER EXAMINED	No PREFERENCE	WHITE HELP PREFERRED	NEGROES PREFERRED
Charleston	259	143	65	51
Louisville	200	104	80	16
New Orleans	145	103	35	7
Savannah	106	66	26	14
Texas	67	31	35	1
Washington, D.C.	135	61	54	20
Total	912	508	295	109

The Charleston Employment Bureau advertises, "White help especially in demand." In Texas the proportion of the foreign born population is larger than in any other of the Southern states, and advertisements
from all the leading cities in the state show a decided preference for German or Swedish domestics. One from the *Fort Worth Gazette* reads,
"Wanted — A white woman (German or Swede preferred) as cook in a
private family." This illustrates a large number of "wants." An em-

while the testimony of many employers seems to show that service is at present in a transitional state — the older generation is disappearing, while in the younger generation the same tendencies are found as in other classes of employees.[1] The second assumption, that the question is settled wherever the supply is greater than the demand, also seems unwarranted in the judgment of many.[2] These

ployer writes from Austin, "In Texas cities domestic service is furnished by Germans and Swedes to a large extent, and the tendency to employ them is growing."

[1] "The older generation of negroes who were trained for service have nearly all died, and the survivors are too old to be efficient. The younger negroes are too lazy to be of much use."—*Brenham, Texas.*

"Old colored servants that were trained before the war are now inefficient; the younger ones will not submit to training." — *Austin, Texas.*

"Old trained colored servants are no longer to be had, — younger ones are not well trained, and consequently cannot do first class work. White servants are better trained, but scarce, and therefore independent." — *Austin, Texas.*

"We have 80,000 colored people in the city. The old trained servants of slavery times are mostly passed away, and the younger ones have not been properly trained." — *Washington, D.C.*

"The servants who were trained before 'freedom' are too old to do good work, and they are not training their children to be efficient." — *Anderson, South Carolina.*

"The majority of those now seeking domestic service are ignorant, uneducated, untrustworthy." — *Biloxi, Mississippi.*

"Servants have no training." — *Edgefield, South Carolina.*

[2] "One difficulty here is the indifference of our colored servants to what the morrow may bring forth. They are capable of living on a very small amount, and they assist each other during the time unoccupied." — *Charleston, South Carolina.*

"The negroes do not know how to render good service as a rule, and they do not understand the term 'thorough.'" — *Charleston, South Carolina.*

"Colored help have to be very patiently and charitably dealt with." — *Washington, D.C.*

"The difficulty here is the general shiftlessness and liking for changed conditions that is characteristic of the colored race." — *Austin, Texas.*

facts are in no sense to be regarded as an exhaustive presentation of the condition of domestic service at the South; they only indicate that in the opinion of many intelligent employers "the question of negro help is as broad as the negro question itself." If it has proved such to those who know the negro best, there is little hope that Northern employers would gain more than new and perplexing complications by introducing as domestic servants large numbers of negroes from the South.[1]

"There is special difficulty here during the cotton-picking season." — *Austin, Texas.*

"The majority of our servants, who are negroes, are not willing to do steady, faithful work for reasonable wages. Their idea of freedom is to come and go at will, and they expect full wages for light work." — *Austin, Texas.*

"The ease with which subsistence can be obtained in this productive climate and the high wages earned during the cotton-picking season make the labor supply unstable." — *Austin, Texas.*

"The negroes need training, but rarely remain in one place long enough to repay one for the trouble of teaching them." — *Brenham, Texas.*

"The negroes will do well enough if one is willing to overlook carelessness." — *Johnston, South Carolina.*

"The colored servants do not like to be kept at steady employment." — *Trenton, South Carolina.*

"The majority work only as a make-shift, with no idea of remaining." — *Biloxi, Mississippi.*

"The whole colored race is in a transitional period which is full of evils." — *Marion, Alabama.*

"Negroes are very stubborn under harsh treatment, but respond quickly to kind treatment." — *Crescent City, Florida.*

"Most of the negroes are indifferent to improving in any way as long as they have enough to eat, a place to sleep, and clothes to wear." — *Tallahassee, Florida.*

[1] A southern gentleman well known as a student of social science writes in regard to the importation of negroes to the North : "There is nothing to hope from it. I have been reared in the South, and I know the negro well. Speaking as one with no sectional prejudice and with the

Another suggestion of the same character is the importation of Chinese servants. While much has been said of the superiority of the Chinese as household employees,[1] and not a few housekeepers would be glad to see the restriction act repealed,[2] difficulties other than the present legislative and political ones stand in the way of adopting this policy. The Chinese, as well as the negroes, occupy in this country a social position inferior to that of Americans or Europeans. Gresham's law may perhaps be applied to domestic service and the principle

broadest sympathy for blacks as well as whites, I must tell you that in general negroes will not serve you as well as the Irish, Germans, or Swedes. Personal attachment alone will secure good service from colored people."

[1] "I must say from my own experience and observation that well-trained Chinese are the very best servants to be had here." — *San Francisco, California.*

"I have grown up with Chinamen in the house, and it seems to me quite revolting and unnatural to have in the heart of the house an alien woman who speaks your language, knows your affairs, is even in a way dependent on your companionship, yet is nothing to you as a friend, and would never be asked even as a guest into the house if it rested on her personal qualities." — *San Francisco, California.*

"Our Chinese cook is an admirable servant, invariably respectful, and does his work beautifully ; he has the self-respect to fill every requirement of respectful and obedient behavior that the occasion calls for." — *San Francisco, California.*

"Three Chinese were the most satisfactory servants we ever employed. In a housekeeping experience of nearly fifty years we have employed negro, Norwegian, and Irish servants." — *San Francisco, California.*

[2] "The difficulty can only be removed by repealing the restriction act." — *Centerville, California.*

"The Chinese have become very independent since the new restriction act." — *San Francisco, California.*

"The restriction act made the Chinese very independent. They thought the stopping of the supply would make those already here able to command higher wages." — *San Francisco, California.*

"One difficulty is the exclusion act." — *San Francisco, California.*

stated that superior and inferior labor cannot exist side by side — the inferior must drive out the superior. Unless employees of the lower social grade can be imported in such numbers as to meet every call for domestic servants, there must exist, as now, the discrepancy between supply and demand. The old struggle between free labor and slave labor must be repeated in miniature wherever the social chasm exists between two classes of laborers. The introduction to any considerable extent of Chinese servants would drive out European labor as that has in a measure driven out native born American service.

As a means of promoting a better adjustment of the business relations between employer and employee, it is sometimes proposed that licenses should be granted domestic employees by municipal corporations. This plan, however, would be a violation of the principles underlying the granting of such licenses. A municipal body is not justified in granting a license to any employment or industry unless such occupation is objectionable in itself as entailing expense, or danger of expense on the part of the taxpayers, as the sale of intoxicating liquors; or unless it involves special use by non-taxpayers of city improvements made at the expense of the taxpayers, as in the case of cabmen; or unless it brings into competition with tax-paying industries trades which contribute nothing to the general treasury, as is true of travelling peddlers; or unless it brings special danger, as of fire in the case of theatrical companies. The license is a tax imposed in return for special risks incurred or privileges granted. Domestic service comes under none of these

N

principles, and to place it under the care of municipal authorities as is not done with other occupations of its class would be to degrade it in an unjustifiable way. The license, when granted in accordance with a principle, is not more objectionable than an ordinary tax; if granted without principle, it becomes an obnoxious and tyrannical measure.

The system of German service books has been widely advocated as an efficient means of securing reliable testimony as to the character and capabilities of employees, thus removing one of the most serious of present difficulties. But even in Germany, where obedience is man's first law, as order is heaven's first law in other parts of the world, it is impossible to obtain service books that do not need to be supplemented by personal inquiries. The service book is of value in weeding out the most inefficient employees, but it can do little more. As in any other form of recommendation, the employer wishes to say the best possible thing for a servant that he may not injure his prospects of obtaining another place. Moreover, the law compels every employer to believe an employee innocent until he is proved guilty. The employer must state that the servant is honest unless he has proof positive to the contrary. He is not permitted to say that he is suspicious, or even to leave out the word "honest." The policy is a necessary protection to the weaker class, but it must vitiate somewhat the absolute reliability of the testimonials given. The German service book has a place where all occupations are permeated by government control, but it cannot be introduced into America. We must work out our own system of improvement in household service as we have worked out our own political system.

Other measures have been suggested that call for only a passing notice. It is often proposed to call together a convention of housekeepers to discuss the subject. But the mass must be disintegrated before anything can be accomplished, and moreover the difficulty of calling together such a convention and of securing through it any permanent results is the same, as is found in political circles in attempting to organize a citizens' party.

Other housekeepers seriously advocate abolishing the public schools above the primary grade on the ground that girls are educated above their station, and they follow the plan of one who says, " I do not engage women who have been beyond the third reader and the multiplication table." The quality of service obtained by such a policy is indicated by the remark of the father of a remarkably stupid girl, "She ain't good for much; I guess she'll have to live out." No statement can be more fallacious than that girls are educated above their station. There can be no so-called "station" in a democratic country. We have given the reins to our democratic views politically, and we must abide by the industrial and social results.

Still other housekeepers advocate the introduction of housework into all the public schools, and thus securing well-informed "help." But both this proposition and its converse overlook the fact that it is the function of the public school *to educate*, not to supply information on technical subjects.

In one large city a "Servant Reform Association" has been organized, with an office on a prominent street-corner, and its name conspicuously posted over the door and painted on all the window shades. Its clientele is very large and embraces some of the best-known residents of the city. Among other measures of reforming servants it plans for the establishment of schools to be equipped with every household appliance, and " to have for instructors women who are thoroughly schooled in the various branches of household duties and domestic economy," but it does not state where such instructors are to be obtained. Nothing shows so clearly how the times are out of joint as does the name of such an association.

The plan most widely advocated and believed to contain the greatest possibilities for improvement in domestic service, is that of establishing training-schools for servants, such schools to have a regular course of study and to grant a diploma on the satisfactory completion of the work. Much can be said in favor of the theory of such schools. If universally established, they would greatly lessen the ignorance and inexperience of the employees — one of the greatest stumbling-blocks in the way of improvement in the service. The diploma would be in effect a license without the objectionable features of the latter, and it would be a testimonial of capability and moral character more reliable than the personal recommendation of previous unknown employers. It would render possible a better gradation of wages, a more perfect organization of domestic work, and more satisfactory business relations between employer and employee. In no occupation is there greater need for systematic training. The army of incompetents in domestic service is not greater than in other occupations, but incompetency here is far more productive than elsewhere of inconvenience and positive suffering. Without such public and regular training every housekeeper is compelled to make a training-school of her own house, and too often she herself lacks the necessary information she ought to impart. But two test questions must be applied to the theory. First, as far as it has been carried out, has it accomplished what was expected of it? Second, is the training-school for servants in harmony with the educational, industrial, and social tendencies of the day?

The demand for such training-schools has been almost universal, and reports of their immediate establishment on a large scale have been repeatedly circulated through the press. One of the most widely spread rumors concerned a movement to be set on foot in connection with the World's Fair in 1893 for the organization of a national body with branches throughout every state and county in the country, each of these branches to establish a training-school for servants wherever practicable, and another concerned a scarcely less extended work to be begun in Washington. As far as can be learned, however, the number of such schools actually established has been extremely limited, and most of these have been discontinued for lack of success. As far as the results have been concerned, it must be said that, while not a failure, they have been far from commensurate with the efforts expended. In one training-school with accommodations for twenty, where neither labor nor expense had been spared to make it a success, there were when visited but five persons in attendance, and these five were the most unpromising material that could be brought together to train for such service, one being a partial cripple, another very deaf, a third too young to take the responsibility of a general servant, a fourth was deficient in mental capacity, and the fifth was a Swedish girl who attended to learn English. Another school also having accommodations for twenty reported that the number had never been full. The most successful of them all had had, a year or two since, total attendance of about four hundred during its ten years' existence.

The practical difficulties in the way of all these schools have been many. The minimum age of admission has been fixed at sixteen, but there has been constant pressure to make exceptions to the rule and take girls under that age. The course has been usually one of three months, but this time is insufficient for the thorough training of immature girls in household duties; yet to extend the course is to decrease the attendance. Those who enter such schools do so, not because those who have attended them have been unusually successful in securing work and retaining good positions, but because sent there by friends, guardians, pastors, or city missionaries. In no instance, so far as known, has a person entered a training-school because she found herself incompetent to fill the position she had taken, or from a desire to perfect herself in any branch of her work. Much has been accomplished through these schools for the individuals attending them; personal habits have been improved, better motives in life given, — everything that has been most admirable in a philanthropic way. But it must be said that they have done little or nothing towards accomplishing the object for which they were established;

the effect in elevating domestic service, in increasing the
supply of trained servants, in lessening the prevailing
ignorance of household affairs, has been infinitesimal. *The
training-school for servants is and must be a failure as long
as the class for whom it was founded will not voluntarily
attend it in any considerable numbers for the sake of the
instruction it is primarily intended to give.* They will
not attend it because while there is a theoretical demand
for such schools on the part of employers there is no
practical demand for them. Young women will not
spend three months in learning the details of such work
when they can receive high wages for doing it without
such instruction; not until domestic service loses its dis-
tinctive marks of drudgery, menial servitude, and social
degradation will the ,training-school receive any large
accession to its numbers. Moreover, public opinion has
not yet demanded that every housekeeper should have
both a general and a technical knowledge of domestic
affairs before she assumes the care of a household. The
stream cannot rise higher than its source, and the training-school for employees cannot succeed so long as
employers are content with unscientific methods in their
own share of the household duties. It is often said that
by the establishment of training-schools for nurses what
was formerly a trade, held in little repute, has become a
profession second only in importance to that of the physician, and that in a similar way the training-school for
domestic servants would elevate domestic service. But
a vital difference exists in the two cases. Until scarcely
more than a generation ago the medical profession could
lay little or no claim to being an exact science. Most

medical schools were poorly equipped and had a short
course of study, while all their processes were largely
experimental. But the Civil War and the scientific
studies resulting from it have made of surgery an exact
science, while rapid strides in biological investigation
have gone far towards making other branches of medicine also exact sciences. It has been well said that " educational forces pull from the top, they do not push from
the bottom." It has been the educational forces pulling
from the top as a result of increased scientific knowledge
among the leaders of the medical profession that have
made the training-school for nurses a necessity. Not until
similar forces pull from the top in the household through
the scientific and economic investigation of the processes
carried on there, will a permanent, successful training-
school for employees be even a remote possibility.

It must be said also that the training-school for domestic servants must be a failure as long as it is out of harmony with the tendencies in all other fields of education
and industry. Technical schools are everywhere springing up, and the demand for them is constantly increasing.
But the technical school teaches general and fundamental
principles, the wood carver learns drawing, the plumber
chemistry, the architect mathematics, and the engineer
mechanics. In each trade or profession the first step is
the principle underlying it, and the second the practical
application of the principle. In the training-school for
servants with a three months' course, the educational idea
is and must be totally different. Those attending it are
taken without examination, often they have had no previous education whatever, they may be of varying grades of

intelligence and capability, and any attempt at classification according to these grades is impossible. Its members must learn how to cook without a knowledge of chemistry and physiology, to care for a room without knowing the principles of ventilation and sanitation, and to arrange a table in ignorance of form and color. The work must be learned by simple mechanical repetition — a method fast disappearing from every department of education.

Again, such a plan is in opposition to present political and social tendencies. A training-school for servants is an anomaly in a democratic country. No father or mother born under the Declaration of Independence will ever send a child to be trained as a servant. A striking illustration of this is found in recent accounts of a new building about to be erected in a large city for the use of a woman's organization. Those in charge of the organization established a few years since a kitchen garden for the children of the poor. Families recommended by the Charity Organization Society were visited and the attendance of the young daughters of the family solicited. " At first not a few mothers objected on the ground that they did not wish to have their daughters trained to be servants, even if they were poor, but when it was explained that the object of the kitchen garden was to make the children more tidy and useful in their own homes the objection usually disappeared." Yet in the face of this experience — a common one wherever kitchen gardens have been started — the managers of the organization have provided for the establishment of a training-school for servants.

The opposition to such schools on social grounds is not
strange. No recognized industrial aristocracy is possible
in America. There are no training-schools for masons,
carpenters, day-laborers, or clerks. In the technical
school the boy learns masonry, carpentry, and brick-lay-
ing, but in these schools there is no division of those attending into "classes for gentlemen" and "classes for
laborers." American men will never recognize one kind
of training for a superior social class, and another for an
inferior. The training-school for servants means the
introduction of a caste system utterly at variance with
democratic ideas. It has not been possible at any time
since the abolition of slavery to educate any class in
society to be servants; it will never again be possible in
America. Democracy among men and aristocracy among
women cannot exist side by side; friction is as inevitable as it was between free labor and slave labor in the
ante-bellum days. Opportunity for scientific training in
all household employments must ultimately be given in
such a form that any and all persons can obtain it, but it
can never be given in a school distinctively intended for
the training of servants and called by that name.

Another plan, perhaps less widely but even more earnestly advocated by its supporters, is that of co-operative
housekeeping. There has been much looseness of phraseology in referring to this plan, and many experiments
have been called co-operative housekeeping which are
such in no sense of the word. Co-operative housekeeping, pure and simple, as described by the pioneer in the
movement, Mrs. Melusina Fay Peirce,[1] means the associa-

[1] *Co-operative Housekeeping.* The book is now out of print, but the

tion in a stock company of not fewer than twelve or
fifteen families. The first step is the opening of a co-
operative grocery on the plan adopted by the Rochdale
Pioneers, and this to be followed by the opening of a
bakery, and later by a kitchen for cooking soups, meats,
and vegetables. The next department to be organized is
that of sewing, beginning with the establishment of a
small dry-goods store, and developing from this the making of underclothes, dresses, cloaks, and bonnets. The
last step is to organize a co-operative laundry. The
main industries pursued in every house — cooking, sewing,
and laundering — are thus to be taken out of the house
and carried on at a central point, while the profits on all
the retail purchases are ultimately to accrue to the
purchasers.

The advantages in the scheme are in the saving of
expense in buying, economy in the preparation of all the
materials consumed, a division of labor on the part of the
co-operators which enables each to follow her own tastes
in work, and a removal of all difficulties with the subject
of service by making the servants responsible to a corporation, not to individuals. The essential point in the
whole plan, and that which justifies the name, is that each
housekeeper is to take an active part not only in the
management, but also in the actual work of the association, since co-operation ceases to be such if one individual
or "manager" is paid for assuming the responsibility of
the business.

The Cambridge, Massachusetts, Co-operative House-

original articles on which it is based can be found in the *Atlantic
Monthly*, November, 1868, to March, 1869.

keeping Association was organized in 1870 with forty
shareholders and continued about one year. It ap-
proached more nearly than any other experiment that
has been made to the ideal of its chief promoter, Mrs.
Peirce, but failed in the opinion of its founder for three
reasons : because all the shareholders did not patronize
the co-operative store; because three departments of
work — a bakery, kitchen, and laundry — were begun at
the same time instead of being allowed to develop as
experience should dictate; and because the whole was
given over to the charge of a board of seven directors,
one of whom was to be a paid officer and the manager
of the entire business. The theory in its realization,
therefore, lacked some of the essentials of a true co-
operative enterprise, but even in this form it is believed to have been the only experiment that can in
any real sense of the word be called co-operative
housekeeping.

The plan of co-operative housekeeping would, if carried out successfully, undoubtedly remove many of the
difficulties of the question of service. But it presents
others, some of which are inherent in human nature
and therefore not easily or speedily removed. It presupposes that all persons are equally endowed by nature
with business instinct, which by cultivation will develop
into business success; it overlooks the fact that ninety-five
per cent of men do not succeed in business when conduct-
ing it independently, and that these are in the employ of
the few gifted with executive talent, " one of the rarest
of human endowments." Again, the same difficulty
exists as was presented to Louis XVIII. when he at-

tempted to create a new order of nobility after the restoration of the Bourbon line; history tells us that he
could find many willing to be dukes and earls but none
willing to be anything less. Most persons are willing
to co-operate in the management of an association, but
modern industry, Nicholas Payne Gilman has well said,
"takes on more and more the character of a civilized
warfare in which regiments of brigadier-generals are
quite out of place."

Co-operation also requires for its success certain
positive characteristics. It implies an ability to sub-
ordinate the individual to the general welfare, to sacrifice present comfort to future good, to decide whether
an act is right or wrong by making it general, to put
all questions on an impersonal basis. The principles on
which the family is organized and the conditions surrounding the housekeeper make these necessary qualifications peculiarly hard to attain. Ideal co-operative
housekeeping implies ideal co-operators, and these it
will be difficult to find before the majority of the employers have more business training and more unsel-
fishness than are now found.

All the arguments that prevail against co-operation
in ordinary business enterprises must prevail against
the system in household management. "All that is
needed is the proper person to take the charge," it is
often explained. But it is at this very point that the
theory breaks down. If the competent manager is secured, the plan ceases to be co-operative housekeeping.
But the competent manager is the most difficult person
in the world to find. "The man we want to manage our

farm has a farm of his own," said a city lawyer of the old family homestead ; the same principle holds in the household. It must be said too that neither productive nor distributive co-operation has yet proved an unqualified success in other industries where the difficulties to be encountered are far less than in the case of that most complicated of organisms — the modern household. A larger number of successful experiments in co-operation must have been tried in this country in other and simpler fields before co-operative housekeeping can prove a panacea for all the troubles attending domestic service.

Certain practical difficulties have also been found. In all experiments in pure or partial co-operative housekeeping it has been found impossible to deliver cooked food hot and invariable in quality at the same hour to all the members of the association. In one city a company was organized as a business enterprise to furnish hot lunches to business men at their offices and also to supply family tables. The prices charged were double those of ordinary table-board, but the expenses were very heavy, no dividends were ever declared, and the object was ultimately changed to that of supplying clubs and private entertainments. That clock-like regularity in the serving of meals, demanded alike by health and business hours, is impossible, unless co-operation is universal, where families in the association reside from five to twenty blocks apart.

But the most insuperable objection to co-operative housekeeping as a remedy for the troubles with servants is the fact that the majority of persons do not wish it. The proposition suggests to many the homely adage of curing the disease by killing the patient. When its friends say in its favor, "Every time an apartment house is built having one common dining-room and one kitchen a blow is aimed at the isolated home," the great majority of Americans rise up in protest. The semi-co-operative system of living is apparently rendered necessary in New York City by reason of the enormous value of land, but wherever the detached house having light on four sides is possible, as it is everywhere else, the American home-lover will rally to its support. Unless the desire for co-operative housekeeping and co-operative living becomes more general than it is at present, some other means of relief must be sought.

Much, however, of the so-called co-operative housekeeping is in reality co-operative boarding. This is true of "The Roby" experiment tried successfully for a time at Decatur, Illinois.[1] Fifty-four of the leading persons in the city formed a club, adopted a constitution and by-laws, elected officers, and found that through this organization they could "live off the fat of the land for $2.75 per week." The plan in its essence is an old one ; it has been followed for years by college students in institutions that do not provide dormitories. In many college towns it is rendered almost necessary by virtue of the residence there of many persons owning houses who wish to take lodgers but not boarders and of many women without capital who wish to act as housekeepers. But probably few college students consider it an ideal way of living, it

[1] A full account of the plan is given in *Good Housekeeping*, July 19, 1890. It was also described in nearly all of the daily papers during May and June, 1890.

is tolerable only at a time of life when new experiences are always welcome, and few have ever been known to continue it beyond college days.

Undoubtedly by a system of co-operative boarding many families could live better, at much less expense, and at a saving of time and certain kinds of friction. But co-operative boarding is to the employer what high wages are to the employee—he is willing to sacrifice something for what seems to him *life*, that is, in this case, the unity, privacy, quiet, and independence of family life. The friction with servants is obviated since the plan includes a housekeeper who is to stand between the co-operators and the employees, but the common interest of desiring freedom from the care of servants and of securing the best board at the lowest rates is not a tie strong enough to bind together those whose interests in other directions are most diverse. Co-operative boarding will do much for the vast army of persons obliged to board, but all such plans should receive their proper designation and not be called co-operative housekeeping. For the great majority of housekeepers who do not care to give up their individual homes, the system proposed will bring no relief.

Still a third scheme called co-operative housekeeping is that proposed by Mr. Bellamy.[1] This is a union of co-operative housekeeping and co-operative boarding, with the application to both of certain business principles already recognized in the housekeeping of to-day. In so

---

[1] A more complete and possibly more serious account of Mr. Bellamy's views than that found in *Looking Backward* is given by him in *Good Housekeeping*, December 21, 1889.

far as it is a combination of the two plans already discussed, it is open to the same criticisms as are its component parts, while the business principles suggested are the result of the same unconscious, not conscious, co-operation that governs all industries.

It must be said, therefore, that all of these various measures of relief proposed to meet the difficulty fail, because, like the golden rule and the admission of the employee into the family life of the employer, they do not touch the economic, educational, and industrial difficulties; or because, like the license, the importation of negro and Chinese labor, the training-school for servants and co-operative housekeeping, they run at right angles to general economic, educational, and industrial progress. The question how to improve the present condition of domestic service is, however, not a hopeless one, but the answer to it must be based on an examination of the historical and economic principles underlying the subject.

o

CHAPTER XI

POSSIBLE REMEDIES — GENERAL PRINCIPLES

IT has been seen that any measure looking towards a lessening of the difficulties that stand in the way of securing at all times and in all places competent domestic employees, must fail of its object if it does not take into consideration economic history, economic conditions, and economic tendencies. Economic history has shown the remarkable effect of inventive genius and business activity on all household employments, and through them on domestic service; a study of economic conditions has shown the nature of the perplexities surrounding both employer and employee. What are the social and economic tendencies in accordance with which relief from present difficulties must be sought?

The first industrial tendency to be noted is that toward the concentration of capital and labor in large industrial enterprises. Not only have the factory and the mill superseded the individual system of manufactures, but the growth of "bonanza farms" and the increasing number of tenant farms show the same tendency in agriculture; the trust is the resort of wholesale business houses; the department stores of the day are driving out of the retail business circles the smaller houses of a generation ago; the pool may be considered an illustration of the same tendency at work in transportation industries.

A second tendency, forming the converse of the preceding one, is towards specialization in every department of labor. Adam Smith's famous illustration of this principle — that he found ten persons able to make nearly five thousand pins in a day, while each person working alone could make but one pin — can be seen in every department of work except in the household. Everywhere the field of labor has been narrowed in order to secure the largest and best results.

A third tendency, growing out of these two, is towards the association and combination for mutual benefit of persons interested in special lines of work. Nearly every class of employers has its own special organization; the associated press, associated charities, local, state, and national educational associations, and associations of learned societies, show the influence of organization in other departments; nearly every class of employees also has its trade union or mutual benefit association; everywhere, except in the household, mutual interests are drawing together for protection, for consultation, for economy of forces and resources, for a score of reasons, those engaged in the same activities.

A fourth tendency is the result of the specialization of labor in its higher forms. As all industries become more highly organized, greater preparation for work is required wherever labor ceases to be purely mechanical. Trade schools, technical schools, and schools for training in special work are everywhere demanded, and the demand must in time be fully met. While specialization is the end, special training must be the means to accomplish it.

A fifth tendency is towards a realization of the fact that all who share in industrial processes should participate in the benefits resulting from their work, that "perpendicular" rather than "horizontal divisions" in labor should be the aim in all industry. This is seen in the various efforts made to introduce productive and distributive co-operation, profit sharing, and other measures intended to give employees a share in the results of their labors, and thus to take a personal interest in their work.

A sixth tendency is towards greater industrial independence on the part of women. This is an inevitable result of the substitution of the factory for the domestic system of manufactures, and of the entrance of women into all industrial pursuits at the time of the Civil War, as well as of the inherent demand in every person for some opportunity for honorable work. A comparison of the different census reports shows that the percentage of women engaged in remunerative occupations increases faster than the percentage of men so engaged. Massachusetts shows a larger percentage than any other state of women occupied in business industry, while the investigations of the Massachusetts Bureau of Statistics of Labor show that the marriage rate and the birth rate in that state are both increasing. The facts and conditions do not seem to show that the tendency is incompatible with home life.

One other semi-social and industrial tendency must be noted. It is the result of that systematic study of social conditions seen in the evolution of the principles that the best way to help a person is to help him to help himself, and that reasonable measures aim at the amelioration of some of the conditions under which work is performed, not at the cessation of the work itself. The application of these principles has led to wiser charities, to the Chautauqua movement, to university extension, to working-girls' clubs, to enlarged opportunities everywhere for every class. These movements springing up in every locality mean that every individual is to have the opportunity of making the most of himself possible, and that the responsibility of so doing is to rest with him, not with society; they mean that ultimately the position in society of every person is to depend not on his occupation, but on the use he has made of these increasing opportunities for self-help and self-improvement; they mean that in time all social stigma will be removed from every occupation and work judged by its quality rather than by its nature; that in time, for example, a first-class cook will receive more honor than a second-class china decorator, or a third-rate teacher.

One general tendency in all business circles must also be mentioned — that towards increasing publicity in all business matters. It is coming to be recognized that society has the right to know certain general and even specific facts in regard to the conduct of affairs formerly guarded in jealous privacy by the individual. The National Census Bureau requires, for the benefit of society, an answer to a large number of personal questions, and the requirement is resisted only by the most ignorant. The state bureaus of labor have legal authority to obtain information in regard to the management of business enterprises which they wish to investigate. The salaries of all public employees are officially published, and legal inquiry is instituted when the expenses of such employees largely exceed the salary received. The number of joint-stock companies is increasing, and these companies are legally bound to render full and exact accounts of all receipts and expenditures. The Chinese wall of absolute privacy is practically retained only with reference to household occupations.

If then the question in domestic service is this: How can the supply of domestic servants be increased, or how can the demand for them be lessened? the only answer must be, by bringing household employments and household service into the current of these and other industrial and social tendencies. To state the case in detail, the problem is not so much how to improve the personal relationship between the employer and the employee as it is to decrease this relationship; not how to increase the number of household drudges, but to decrease the amount of household drudgery; not how to do more for domestics, but how to enable them to do more for themselves; not how to merge the individual home into the co-operative home or boarding house, but how to keep it still more intact by taking out of it as far as possible that extraneous element — the domestic employee; not how to restore the old household system, but how to bring about adaptation to present conditions; not so much how to persuade more persons to go into domestic service, as to use to better advantage the time and strength of those already engaged in it; not how to induce sewing women in the tenement houses of New York City to engage in work for which they have neither the physical nor the intellectual qualifications,[1] but how to utilize the idle labor in boarding houses and in the homes of the so-called middle and upper classes.

The statement cannot be made with too great emphasis that no plan can be suggested that will enable a housekeeper whose inefficient employee leaves to-day to secure a better one to-morrow; a complicated social malady of long standing demands time and patience to work a cure or even a relief. Two classes of measures, however, looking towards an improvement in the character of the service can be suggested, the first general, the second specific. It is believed that both classes will conform to the general industrial and social tendencies enumerated.

In the first place there must be a truer conception on the part of both men and women of the important place that household employments occupy in the economy of the world. The utter neglect of the subject by economic students and writers must give place to a scientific investigation of an employment which is at least wealth-consuming if not wealth-producing. A very large part of the wealth produced in the world is consumed in the household, yet neither those who produce nor those who consume know on what principles it is done. Time-saving and labor-saving devices are made at enormous cost for uses in production, while time and strength incalculable are wasted through consumption. In no other occupa-

[1] *The New York Tribune* says of the sewing women in that city: "They are a product of city life; a sort of vitalized machines, fitted only to do a certain mechanical work and disabled for any other industry mainly because they have been fastened to a sewing-machine all their lives."

tion is there so much waste of labor and capital; in no other would a fraction of this waste be overlooked. It is idle to complain of poor servants and of poor mistresses so long as domestic service is divorced from general labor questions, and employers everywhere are ignorant of the economic laws, principles, and conditions underlying the household. Men and women might better give to the study of domestic service as an occupation the time and energy that now are absorbed in considering the vices and virtues of individual employees.

This truer conception of the place of household economics considered from the theoretical standpoint will give rise to a more just estimate of their place in a practical way. Those employers who "despise housekeeping," who "cannot endure cooking," who "hate the kitchen," who "will not do menial work," will come to regard household work in a different light. Indeed, until the members of this class, far too large in numbers, change either their opinion or their occupation, it is hopeless to look for a reform in domestic service. That "dignity of labor" so often prescribed as a panacea for the troubles in the kitchen must first be maintained in the parlor if reform is to come. The simple prescription of the remedy will not effect a cure. "To know the workman," wrote Leclaire in 1865, "one must have been a workman himself, and above all *remember it.*" In a similar way the housekeeper must have not only a knowledge of household affairs, but a respect for them, and being presumably better educated and equipped, she must be the one to prove that the interests of employer and employee are the same.

Again, more systematic study of the subject in a general way must remove much of the ignorance, as well as of the aversion, that undoubtedly exists in regard to this occupation. Public sentiment has not yet demanded that when a woman assumes the care of a household she shall possess at least a theoretical knowledge of household affairs; it is deemed sufficient if she acquire it afterward. at an enormous cost of time, patience, energy, sometimes even of domestic happiness. But public sentiment will make such demand when the economic functions of housekeeping are understood. Until a larger number of housekeepers understand at least the rudiments of the profession they have adopted, it is to be expected that ignorant and inexperienced employees will waste the substance of their employers, and fail to become skilled laborers, and that able, intelligent, and ambitious girls will be unwilling to enter an occupation in which the employers are as untrained in a scientific way as are the employees. Water cannot rise higher than its source. As long as inefficient service is accepted inefficient service will be rendered; as long as mistresses are ignorant of the difference between rights and extraordinary privileges, employees, like children, will continue to be spoiled by careless indulgence; "as long as women hate kitchen and household cares, and servants know that they know more than their employers, just so long will employers everywhere have eye-servants."

A different conception must also come in regard to the work of woman, especially where the factor of remuneration is involved. An explanation is still needed for the fact that idleness is practically regarded as a vice in men

and a virtue in women ;[1] that a young man is condemned
by society for saying "the world owes me a living," while a
young woman is praised for her womanliness when she
says it by her life; that a wealthy woman must not
receive remuneration for services for which compensation
would be accepted by a wealthy man or by a poor woman.
This does not mean that all women should engage in
business enterprises, but that it should be honorable for
them to do so, dishonorable for them to be ignorant of
all means of self-support, and that they should receive
adequate remuneration for all public services performed
when men would be paid under the same circumstances.
Household employments are too often in effect, though
less often than in theory, belittled by both men and
women, and they will continue to be until there is the
freest industrial play in all occupations for women as
well as for men.   As long as household employments performed without remuneration are the only occupations
for women looked upon with favor by society at large,
just so long will this free industrial play be lacking.
One effect of this is seen in the case of very many
mothers who have been overworked and overburdened by
household cares.   The pendulum swings to the opposite
end of the arc, and they declare that their daughters shall
never work at all.   The children therefore grow up in
idleness and ultimately, when driven to work by necessity,
drift into shops and factories.   When household employments are removed from the domain of charity and sentiment and put on a business basis, when the interests of

[1] "The men of my family would consider it the greatest disgrace if
one of the women connected with it were to support herself."

women are broadened, when they are better able " to distinguish between infinity and infinitesimals," there will be a more intelligent understanding of the financial side of woman's work.

The general remedies therefore must include a wider prevalence of education in the true sense of the word, not its counterfeit, information ; that mental education which results in habits of accuracy, precision, and observation, in the exercise of reason, judgment, and self-control, and that education of character which results in the ability constantly to put one's self in the place of another. There must be scientific training and investigation in economic theory, history, and statistics, especially in their application to the household, and an increased popular knowledge of all scientific subjects concerning the home, those which secure the prevention of economic and material waste in the household as well as those which concern the questions of production for it. The educational forces must "pull from the top" and draw domestic service into the general current of industrial development.

CHAPTER XII

POSSIBLE REMEDIES — IMPROVEMENT IN SOCIAL
CONDITION

CERTAIN general principles have been suggested in
accordance with which it seems reasonable to expect improvement in domestic service to be made. Of specific
remedies, the first class to be suggested concerns the social
degradation as yet entailed by the occupation. For the
most part the oppressive conditions are the lack of all
social and educational advantages, the use of an obnoxious epithet applied to the individuals of the class, the
universal use of the familiar Christian name in address,
the requirement of livery, enforced servility of manner,
and the offering of fees to several large subdivisions of
the class. Every one of these must seem a reasonable
objection to one who can put himself in the place of
another; they are among the weightiest arguments
against entering the service; each one can be entirely
removed, or so modified as to become unobjectionable.
It is useless to look for any improvement in the character of domestic service until these oppressive conditions
have been removed; but it is not vain to hope for an
emancipation from them in time. The social ban has
been removed from other occupations in which women
have become wage earners — it has been removed from

teaching,[1] the practice of medicine and law, and business industries — women can engage in all of these without fear of being ostracized. The relative social position of different occupations in which men engage has also changed. In colonial New England, the minister, not the lawyer, had the social precedence ; in the Southern colonies the lawyer was an honored guest, while the chaplain of the plantation was a hireling who often married an indentured servant on the same plantation. Dentists, men " in trade," brewers, and veterinary surgeons have in other localities all felt the lack of an assured place in society. Social barriers against both men and women are everywhere breaking down in the presence of high character, ability, education, and technical training ; they will ultimately fall before men and women engaged in domestic service, who can bear these same tests of character, ability, education, and technical training.

In considering the specific social disadvantages, it must be conceded that the desire for greater social and intellectual opportunities is most reasonable. Mr. Higginson says in answer to the question, " Why do children dislike history ? " " The father brings home to his little son, from the public library, the first volume of Hildreth's *United States*, and says to him, ' There, my son, is a book for you, and there are five more volumes just like it.' He then goes back to his *Sunday Herald*, and his wife

---

[1] Mr. Charles Dudley Warner asserts that women teachers have no social position (*Harper's Monthly*, April, 1895). But his statements can apply only to some of the ultra-fashionable finishing schools in two or three large cities.

reverts to *But Yet a Woman*, or *Mr. Isaacs.*" The atti-
tude of society towards social opportunities for domestic
employees is much the same. Society demands the theatre, the opera, the parlor concert, the lecture, the dinner,
the afternoon tea, the yacht race, the tennis match, the
bicycle excursion, the coaching party, and expects the
class lacking at present all resources within themselves
to stay quietly at home and thus satisfy their desire for
pleasure and intellectual opportunity. Country life sometimes proves lonely and distasteful to employers educated
in the city. Is it less so to the employee lacking the
opportunity for change enjoyed by others? [1]

Comparatively little can be done in the ordinary private home to meet these difficulties; but even if much
could be done, it is at least an open question whether this
would be the true remedy. In large establishments sit-
ting-rooms can be provided for employees, but such establishments are few in number, and the fact that such
rooms are in the home of another prevents that "good
time," the craving for which is so natural. Many employers are glad to give personal instruction evenings,
but solitary instruction is even more defective for the
domestic than it is for the children of the family.
Enthusiasm must always come with numbers, and comparatively little can be done for employees through this
means. But social opportunities and intellectual advantages can be provided, as has been done so successfully

---

[1] It is the testimony of more than one employer that those domestics
remain longest in a place and are most content who have a taste for sewing
and reading. Those who are wholly dependent for pleasure on excitement and change form of necessity a restless class.

in the case of the employees of shops and factories.
Social life everywhere tends towards clubs, societies, and
organizations. Domestics can be encouraged to form
clubs and societies through which parlors can be provided for social intercourse, and reading-rooms where intellectual needs will be met. If the domestic employee
were taken from the home of the employer and encouraged to find for herself avenues of improvement and
entertainment, her social condition would be greatly
improved. She must be made to see that the reason
why she does not rise to the social position to which she
aspires, is not because her work is degrading, but because
her conversation is often ungrammatical and lacking in
interest, her dress sometimes untidy and devoid of taste,
and her manner not always agreeable. She must do her
part towards improving her social condition. It is true,
that probably at first comparatively few domestics would
avail themselves of such privileges, *but just as long as
social and intellectual advantages do not exist anywhere for
this class, just so long will the intelligent and capable young
woman most needed in this occupation shun it for others
where such opportunities do exist.*

The stumbling-block in the use of the word " servant " is
easily removed. The exclusive application of this word
to domestic employees must be abolished before the class
most desired in the occupation will enter it. As has
been done in every other occupation, a word like "employer" must be substituted for "master" and "mistress,"
— terms associated only with a system of apprenticeship or
slavery, — while "domestic," "housekeeper," or some other
descriptive term must be used for "general servant," the

words "cook," "waitress," and "maid" being unobjectionable for other classes of service.[1] As a matter of fact the
word as now used is inappropriate in characterizing the
work expected of an efficient domestic employee. Division
of labor has made her in reality, though not in position, not
a menial, a drudge, a slave, but a co-operator in the work
of the household. The cook who prepares the raw material for consumption is not more a servant than is the
farmer who produces the raw material; indeed her work is
justly considered skilled labor, while that of the agricultural laborer is often unskilled. The cook is the co-operator with her employer in the same sense as the farmer is
a co-operator in the industrial system; and the term "servant" as indicating a menial applies to her as little as it
does to him. New words are coined and pass into familiar usage in a short time, old words become obsolete, new
meanings are given old terms, and it is possible in the
course of a few years to substitute for the present objectionable usage of this word a term which will describe
more definitely the duties of the position and at the same
time remove one of the most serious obstacles in the way
of improving the character of the occupation.[2]

[1] The word "servant" has been used many times in this work, but it
has seemed unavoidable in the absence of any other generally recognized
term.

[2] It has been suggested that the word "homemaker" be applied to the
mistress of the house and "housekeeper" to the employee; "working
housekeeper" is often used of an efficient caretaker who does her work
without direction; "domestic" and "house helper" seem wholly unobjectionable. It certainly is not necessary in abandoning one objectionable
word to adopt another equally so. The Lynn, Massachusetts, papers, for
example, advertise under "wants" for a "forelady in stitching room,"
"a position as forewoman by a lady thoroughly familiar with all parts of

The inferiority implied in the use of the Christian name in address is less clearly seen and less easily removed because its effects are more subtile. It may not be possible to attempt any immediate or general change, but a compromise is possible in giving the title to married men and women in domestic service, since marriage is supposed to carry with it added dignity. The Japanese custom of addressing one's own employees by a familiar term, but the employees of another by a title of respect,[1] is also a possible compromise. It seems difficult to find weighty arguments in favor of refusing to a class of self-supporting men and women the title of respect accorded in all other occupations.

The cap and apron are in themselves not only unobjectionable, but they have certain very definite advantages. They are conducive to neatness and economy and moreover form a most becoming style of dress. The picturesque effect of both is appreciated by all young women who take part in public charitable entertainments, it was understood by the matrons of an earlier generation, and it has formed the theme of many letters written on foreign soil. No costume in itself could be more desirable or better adapted to the work of the wearers, and a more general rather than a more restricted use of this form of dress should be advocated on theoretical grounds. But the cap and apron as worn do not always indicate a desire on the part of the wearer for neatness, economy, and tasteful

shoe stitching," " on millinery an experienced saleslady." In other places one finds " a gentlewoman who desires employment at twenty-five cents an hour." The public has much to answer for in the misuse of both " servant " and " lady."

[1] *Japanese Girls and Women*, p. 304.

P

attire, nor always an appreciation of these things on the part of the employer. They are regarded as a traditional badge of servitude, and while so regarded it seems unwise to force them on those unwilling to wear them. Moreover the cap and apron while serving admirably their place within the house have no *raison d'être* out of doors; the cap affords no protection from heat, cold, or storms, and the apron is inappropriate for street wear. The cap and apron are appropriate and desirable in all places where they would be worn by the employer under the same circumstances, they are inappropriate elsewhere and hence out of taste. If employees as a class would recognize the many advantages of the costume within doors and adopt it universally, and if employers would accept its limitations out of doors and abandon the requirement of it there at all times, the vexed question of livery would seem to be answered.

The servility of manner demanded — at least in public — of all domestics is an anomaly in a country where there is no enforced recognition of social and political superiors. The price paid for it — high wages, poor service, constant change, household friction — seems a heavy one and the excuse for it small. As long as domestic service lacks the safety valve of personal independence and the outward expression of self-respect, just so long is there danger of too great repression and consequent explosion. No genuine reform in domestic service is possible while this theory of outward servility is enforced.

The most objectionable of all the manifestations of social inferiority — the feeing system — has its economic as well as its social side and will be considered by itself in the chapter on profit sharing in domestic service.

These social barriers that now prevent so effectually the entrance into domestic service of intelligent, well-educated, capable, and efficient persons can all be swept away if employers as a class are willing to make the effort. This effort will involve in some cases the relinquishing of a favorite theory that employees can be made a part of the family with which they are externally connected and, instead of this, assisting them to live their own independent lives as citizens of the community in a normal, happy way. It will involve in other cases abandoning the assumption that domestic employees belong to a separate and obnoxious class in society and cannot be met as individuals on the same plane as are other persons of like attainments. It will involve in still other cases the sacrifice of that personal vanity that is gratified by the constant presence of those deemed to be of an inferior station. If employers are willing to yield all of the points now often unconsciously maintained by them in opposition to the teachings of political and industrial history, the social objections that now hold against domestic service as an employment will disappear. Sir Henry Sumner Maine has well said, " The true equality of mankind lies in the future, not in the past." It is this true equality of the future, not the fictitious equality of the past, that must free domestic service from the social ill-repute it now bears.

CHAPTER XIII

POSSIBLE REMEDIES — SPECIALIZATION OF HOUSEHOLD EMPLOYMENTS

THE efforts to remove the social stigma that now brands domestic service will not alone accomplish the desired result. Another means of lessening the difficulties in the modern household is to put all household employments on the same business basis as are all employments outside of the household. The principles which lie at the foundation of modern business activities are division of labor and unconscious co-operation. This statement does not mean that both of these principles are carried out perfectly, but that industrial progress has been made and is being made along these lines, that the advance already made by household employments has been in the same direction, and that the reforms proposed for the household that diverge from these lines, however wise in themselves, cannot lead to the best results because they are out of the current of general progress.

In considering the historical phase of the subject, a long list of articles was suggested[1] which were formerly made within the household, but are now made out of the house both better and more cheaply than they could be made at home.

[1] *Ante*, Chap. II.

A list can be drawn up of other articles made out of the house, which if made in factories are inferior, and if purchased through the woman's exchanges, though as well or even better prepared, are more expensive because the demand for such articles made in the homes of others has up to this time been limited. The articles in this transitional state are vegetable and fruit canning, the making of jellies, pickles, and preserves, the baking of bread, cake, and pastry, the preparation of soups, pressed meats, cold meats, ice-cream, and confectionery, condensed, sterilized, and evaporated milk, and the making of butter not yet abandoned in all rural homes. The transitional list also includes the making of underclothes for women and children, which can be made more cheaply out of the house but not always so well; and millinery and dressmaking, which can be done better but at greater expense. There is every indication that all the articles in this transitional state must soon be enumerated among those articles made both better and more cheaply out of the house than within.

A third list can be made of articles that are now seldom if ever manufactured out of the house but which can be made elsewhere. This list includes in the first place bread and cake of every description; it is possible by taking all of this work out of the house to save, considered in the aggregate both as regards the individual and the community, an enormous waste of time and fuel and at the same time to secure through the application of scientific principles articles often more uniform and superior in quality to what can be produced in the home.[1] A

---

[1] This does not refer to ordinary baker's bread, but to that made

second class includes the preparation of all vegetables for cooking. It is not sentiment but economic principle that should release the human hand from performing this part of housework, more purely mechanical and more justly entitled to be called drudgery than any other work carried on in the house. A few years since coffee was roasted in every kitchen. If it has been found that an article requiring such delicate treatment as this can be prepared by business firms better than it can be in the household oven, there can be no serious obstacle in the way of delivering at the door all vegetables ready for cooking.[1] Compensation for the additional cost at first incurred would be found in the hygienic advantage of removing from many cellars the supply of winter vegetables. A third class of articles includes the preparation of all cold meats, half-cooked meats, as croquettes, all stuffed meats, as fowl and game, all "made" dishes, as salads and cold desserts, and the cooking of all articles which need only heating to make ready for use. The careful study of a large number of elaborate menus as well as of more simple bills of fare shows a very small proportion of articles which could not be made out of the house and sent in ready for use or requiring only the application of heat.

according to scientific principles, such as is sold at the New England Kitchen in Boston and by the Boston Health Food Company.

[1] A beginning in this direction has already been made in the case of vegetables canned for winter use. In the canning factories of Western New York an ingenious pea huller is in use which does away with much of the laborious process hitherto necessary. In a trial of speed it was recently found that one machine could shell twenty-eight bushels of peas in twenty minutes. In some of the largest cities the principle has been applied, and this vegetable is delivered ready for use; but such preparation should be made universal and all other vegetables added to the list.

The Aladdin oven constructed on scientific principles renders the cooking and heating of food a most simple matter. The sending of hot food to individual homes has in no case as far as can be learned proved a success, but the delivery of all articles ready for the final application of heat is possible through business enterprise and scientific experiment.

This partial, although not entire, solution of the problem of domestic service, by taking a large number of servants out of the house and by having a large part of the work now done by them in the house done elsewhere, is in direct line with the progress made in other occupations.

It was estimated by Mr. Gallatin in 1810 [1] that two-thirds of the clothing worn in the United States was the product of family manufacturing — then in a flourishing state. During the twenty years following, a part of this family weaving and spinning was transferred to factories, and this transfer created the great factory industry. Its rapid growth was due to the fact that the power loom and the factory took the place of the hand loom and of home manufacturing. A similar change has taken place in the manufacture of cheese. Until about 1830 all cheese was made at home, and in 1860 not more than twenty cheese factories had been built.[2] After that time factories multiplied rapidly, until now practically all cheese is factory made. The demand for ready-made clothing for men was a generation ago very small. It grew out of a demand on the part of sailors, and was increased in large proportions at the time of the Civil War;

[1] Cited by Bolles, p. 413.   [2] Bolles, p. 130.

the manufacture of such articles is now so firmly established in our industrial system that a return to the home system of manufacturing, even in the most isolated and primitive communities, would be as impossible as the revival of the spinning wheel. The demand for ready-made clothing for women is nearly as great and is annually increasing through the facilities offered by all large retail houses for shopping by mail. The tailoress and the maker of shirts have disappeared from the homes of their employers and have set up establishments of their own, or have become responsible to large business houses; the dressmaker and the seamstress are fast following in their footsteps, and the cook must set her face in the same direction.

The trend in this direction can be seen in many ways. The growing prevalence of camping has increased the demand for articles of food ready for use, and even tea, coffee, and soups are delivered hot for the benefit of pleasure seekers.[1] The development of Western resources by Eastern capitalists has also increased the demand for such articles, and at least one housekeeper among the Black Hills of South Dakota, one hundred miles from a railroad station, speaks casually of doing her marketing in Chicago, and a housekeeper in North Carolina gives frequent and elaborate lunches through caterers in Philadelphia. The tendency even among persons of moderate means is more and more towards the employment of

[1] The Oriental Tea Company of Boston sends out coffee and guarantees it to maintain a temperature of 150° Fahrenheit for twenty-four hours. The experiment has been tried of sending it from Boston to St. Louis, with the result of maintaining a temperature of 148° at the end of three days.

caterers for special afternoon and evening entertainments, although in villages and small towns this course as yet involves the employment of persons from large cities. The practice is not uncommon for the women connected with church organizations to hold every Saturday afternoon sales for the benefit of the society, of all articles of food that can be prepared the previous day for Sunday dinners and teas.[1]

The most important medium for the sale of such commodities is the Woman's Exchange.[2] It has already become an economic factor of some little importance, and it will become of still greater importance when it is taken out of the domain of charity and sentiment and becomes self-supporting on a business basis. One of its most valuable results is that it has set a high standard for work and has insisted that this standard be reached by every consignor, not only once or generally, but invariably. It has maintained this standard in the face of hostile criticism and the feeling that a charitable organi-

[1] The women connected with two churches in a city in Indiana have maintained for some time such sales, and they have proved very remunerative. In one city in New Jersey $1,200 was raised in a few weeks to pay a church mortgage. In a Long Island village several hundred dollars was raised for a similar purpose by the women of the church, who took orders for cooking and sewing. In an Iowa city funds were obtained in this way for missionary purposes. In a village of five hundred inhabitants, in Central New York, the women of one of the churches have sold, every Saturday afternoon for eight years, ices and ice-creams, and have cleared annually about seventy-five dollars. In another town, several women of limited incomes began paying their contributions to the church by baking bread and cake for other families, and finding it remunerative continued the work as a means of support. In one Western city an annual sale is held at Thanksgiving time, and about one hundred dollars netted for home missionary purposes.

[2] The Woman's Exchange, *The Forum*, May, 1892.

zation ought to accept poor work if those presenting it are in need of money. It has shown that success in work cannot be attained by a simple desire for it or need of it pecuniarily. It has taught that accuracy, scientific knowledge, artistic training, habits of observation, good judgment, courage, and perseverance are better staffs in reaching success than reliance upon haphazard methods and the compliments of flattering friends. It has raised the standard of decorative and artistic needle work by incorporating into its rules a refusal to accept calico patchwork, wax, leather, hair, feather, rice, splatter, splinter, and card-board work. It has taught many women that a model recipe for cake is not "A few eggs, a little milk, a lump of butter, a pinch of salt, sweetening to taste, flour enough to thicken; give a good beating and bake according to judgment."

But still more it has opened up to women what has been practically a new occupation. Domestic work within the house performed by members of the family without fixed compensation and by those not members of the family with compensation had been the previous rule. The Exchange has shown that it is possible for the women of a family to prepare within the house for sale outside many articles for table consumption, both those of necessity and luxury. Innumerable instances are on record of women who within the past fifteen years have supported themselves wholly or in part by making for general sale or on orders different articles for the table.[1]

[1] Many illustrations of this can be given outside of those connected with the Exchange:

It seems inevitable that eventually all articles of food will be prepared out of the house except those requiring the last application of heat, and that scientific skill will reduce to a minimum the labor and expense of this final stage of preparation. This change is in direct line with the tendency towards specialization everywhere else found in

Mrs. A, in Central New York, has made a handsome living by making chicken salad to be sold in New York City.

Mrs. B, in a small Eastern village, has for several years baked bread, pies, and cake for her neighbors, and in this way has supported herself, three children, and a father. She has recently built a separate bakehouse, and bakes from thirty to one hundred loaves daily, according to the season, and other things in proportion. She says she always had a "knack" at baking, and that when she employs an assistant she has nearly every afternoon to herself.

Mrs. C, in a Western city, supports herself, three children, and an invalid husband, by making cake.

Mrs. D makes a good living by selling Saratoga potatoes to grocers.

Mrs. E has cleared $400 a year by making preserves and jellies on private orders.

Mrs. F partially supports herself and family by making food for the sick.

Mrs. G supports a family of five by making jams and pickles.

Mrs. H has built up a large business, employing from three to five assistants, in making cake and salad.

Mrs. I, in a small Eastern city, began by borrowing a barrel of flour, and now has a salesroom where she sells daily from eighty to one hundred dozen Parker House rolls, in addition to bread made in every possible way, from every kind of grain.

Mrs. J, in a small Western city, sells salt-risings bread to the value of $30 a week; and Mrs. K, in the same place, Boston brown bread to the value of $75 a week.

Mrs. L, living on a farm near a Southern city, has built up "an exceedingly remunerative business" by selling to city grocers preserves, pickles, cakes, and pies. "One cause of her success has been the fact that she would allow no imperfect goods to be sold; everything has been of the best whether she has gained or lost on it."

Mrs. M supports herself by taking orders for fancy cooking.

Mrs. N, living in a large city, sells to grocers baked beans and rolls.

that it thus becomes possible for every person to do exclusively that thing which he or she can do best; it allows the concentration of labor and capital and thus by economizing both secures the largest results; it permits many women to retain their home life and at the same time engage in remunerative business; it improves the quality of all articles consumed, since they are produced under the most favorable conditions; it brings the work of every cook into competition with the work of every other cook by providing a standard of measurement now lacking and thus inciting improvement; it is the application of the principle of unconscious co-operation and therefore in harmony with other business activities. More definitely, as one illustration, it permits all fruits to be canned, pickled, and preserved in every way in the locality where they are produced at a cost ultimately less than can now be done when fruit is shipped

Mrs. O, in New York City, has netted $1,000 a year by preparing mince-meat and making pies of every description.

Mrs. P, in a small village on Lake Superior, has large orders from cities in Southern Michigan for strawberry and raspberry jam.

Mrs. Q, in a country village of five hundred inhabitants, sells thirty loaves of bread daily.

Mrs. R and two daughters last year netted $1,500 (above all expenses except house rent) in preparing fancy lunch dishes on shortest notice, and delicacies for invalids.

Mrs. S puts up pure fruit juices and shrubs.

Mrs. T prepares consommé in the form of jelly ready to melt and serve.

Mrs. U has made a fair income by preparing and selling fresh sweet herbs.

These illustrations can be multiplied indefinitely. They have come to notice in nearly every state in the Union, and in places varying in size from country villages without railroad stations to such cities as Chicago, Philadelphia, and New York.

to cities and there sold at prices including high rents;
it prevents a glut in the market of such perishable articles by providing for their preservation on farms and
in villages and subsequent transportation to cities at
leisure; it makes it possible to utilize many abandoned
farms in the East which could be used as fruit farms but
are too remote from shipping centres to permit the transportation of ripe fruit; it ultimately lightens the labors
of many women on farms by enabling them to purchase
in cities many articles now produced by them at a disadvantage. The canning in cities, by individual families,
of fruits, often in an over-ripe condition, is as anomalous
as would be to-day the making of dairy products in city
homes. The preservation of fruit is but one example of
articles that could be prepared better and more cheaply
in the country than in the city. Miscellaneous articles
of every description, as plum-pudding, boned turkey,
chicken broth, jelly, croquettes and salad, minced meat,
pressed veal, bouillon, calf's-foot jelly, pure fruit juices,
blackberry cordial, and a score of other articles, could be
added to the list.

It is sometimes objected that this plan of taking out of
the house to as great an extent as possible all forms of
cooking lessens the individuality of the home by requiring all persons to have the same articles of food. But the
objection presupposes a limited variety of articles, while
the method suggested must result in an unlimited variety,
as has been the case in regard to articles used for wearing
apparel since the custom has been established of having
so many made out of the house. It presupposes also
that individuality depends on externals. The gentleman

who wishes to preserve his individuality through his cook could also preserve it through employing a private tailor, but he gladly sacrifices it in the latter case for the better work of one who serves a hundred other customers as well. Individuality is preserved when a person builds his own house, but the doubtful benefit of the result is suggested by Oliver Wendell Holmes when he says, "probably it is better to be built in that way than not to be built at all." The individuality of the present generation is certainly not less than that of the preceding one when all clothing worn by a family was made up in the house, or of an earlier one when all cloth was spun and woven, as well as made up, in the house, or of a still more remote one when our ancestors troubled themselves comparatively little about either the weaving or the making. The very perfection of the principle of the division of labor makes possible the expression of the greatest individuality in that it offers the possibility of selection from a hundred varieties whereas before no choice was given. The ability to choose between the work of a hundred cooks permits a truer individuality than does the command of the services of but one. Whims, caprices, and eccentricities sometimes masquerade as individuality and are not always entitled to respect.

Another form of work now done in the house that could be done outside is laundry work. The inconveniences resulting from the derangement of the household machinery according to the present method have formed the theme of many jests; a serious consideration of the subject must lead to the conclusion that this system results in great waste as well as in unnecessary wear and tear of the household machinery. An objection on hygienic grounds is sometimes made to the proposal to have articles of clothing laundered out of the house together with articles sent by other families. But science has already accomplished much at the bidding of business enterprise, and this objection can be overcome. Even as it is the question may well be asked whether the price paid is not a heavy one for individual laundresses. The vast army of persons who board are compelled to send out articles to be laundried, and this is apparently done without serious results. A beginning has been made in many families where a competent laundress cannot be secured by sending to public laundries all starched clothing, especially all collars and cuffs. The laundries of Troy, New York, have branches for the reception and delivery of goods in all parts of the country, and laundry many articles better and more cheaply than can be done at home. The amount of space now occupied in cities for laundering purposes that could be used for business or for homes is far from inconsiderable. It seems not altogether unreasonable to believe that if the space now occupied by laundries in individual homes could be used for other purposes rents would be perceptibly lower. On economic grounds alone this generation should relegate the washing machine and the wringer to the attic or the front parlor, where it has already placed the spinning wheel of its ancestors.

Still another field is open for business enterprise in connection with the household. A very large part of the work connected with it concerns the care of the house and grounds. This includes the semi-annual house-cleaning and the cleaning of windows, floors, brass, silver, and lamps; the sweeping, dusting, and general care of rooms, including the special attention that must be given to books, pictures, and bric-a-brac; the care of lawns, walks, porches, and furnaces; the repairing of articles of clothing and furniture; table service and chamber service. Here again economic tendencies are showing themselves. Much if not all of this work can be done by the piece or by the hour, and men and women are everywhere taking advantage of the fact.[1] A very large part of the work of

[1] Mrs. A has for several years gone from house to house at stated times sweeping and dusting rooms containing fine bric-a-brac.

Mr. B cares for all of the lawns of a large number of gentlemen, each of whom pays him a fixed sum for the season in proportion to the size of his grounds.

Mr. C cares for all of the furnaces and clears the walks in a city block.

Mrs. D earns a partial support by arranging tables for lunches and afternoon teas.

Mrs. E washes windows once in two weeks for a number of employers.

Mrs. F takes charge of all arrangements for afternoon teas.

Mrs. G earns $3 a day as a cook on special occasions.

Miss H waits on a table in a boarding house three hours a day.

Miss I distributes the clothes from the laundry in a large city school.

Mrs. J is kept busy as a cook, serving as a substitute in kitchens temporarily vacant.

Mrs. K derives a considerable income from the supervision of party suppers. "Her social position is quite unaffected by it."

Mrs. L "makes herself generally useful" at the rate of ten cents an hour if regularly employed and twenty cents when serving occasionally.

Mrs. M goes out as a waitress at lunches and dinners.

Mrs. N employs a young man working his way through school to keep wood-boxes and coal-hods filled.

Many college students in cities partially pay their expenses by table service.

Hotels and restaurants frequently send out waiters on special occasions.

One employer writes, "I think a central office in this city at which competent waitresses could be hired by the hour would be largely patronized."

the household can be thus done, especially if house-keepers are willing to waive the tradition that silver must be cleaned on Thursdays, sweeping done on Fridays, and all sleeping-rooms put in order before nine o'clock in the morning.

One other measure of relief concerns the purchase of supplies. Marketing is a science and might be made a profession. At present it is usually done in a haphazard, makeshift fashion. It is done by the head of the house-hold on his way to business and thus done in haste; or orders are given through a clerk who goes from house to house and thus serves primarily the firm he represents, while at the same time the purchaser loses the benefit of competition in the markets; or commissions are given by telephone and the customer has no opportunity of inspecting the goods before purchase; or marketing is done by the mistress of the household, who is unable to reach the markets in time to make her purchases with the care that should be given; or it is done by the cook, who may know the best articles to purchase but is igno-rant of their money value. It requires time, skill, and experience to purchase judiciously the supplies for a household, and in many households time, skill, and ex-perience are lacking. It would seem possible for one person to do the marketing for fifteen or twenty families, taking the orders at night and executing them in the morning. Supplies could then be purchased in quan-

The Syracuse, New York, Household Economic Club publishes a *Household Register*, giving the names and addresses of all persons in the city who do by the piece, hour, or day all forms of household work. Thirty-five different classes of work are enumerated.

Q

tity, this gain would pay the commission of the purchaser, and marketing would be done in a much more satisfactory manner than it is at the present time. At the same time such a plan would relieve the members of individual households of the burden and care of a difficult part of household management.

All of these measures suggested must tend ultimately to take as far as possible the domestic employee out of the house, letting her perform her work through the operation of unconscious business co-operation. This method would enable a large number of women to go into household employments who have ability in this direction but who now drift into other occupations which permit them to maintain their own home life. It is generally assumed that an unmarried woman has no desire for a home and no need of a place that she can call her own. When she goes into domestic employment, therefore, she must merge her individual life into that of her employer and relinquish all the social instincts, although as strong in her as in another. But this is what many are not willing to do. If the opportunity were presented of performing housework and remaining at home, large numbers would in time enter the work. Many who have no homes would still be glad to share the home of an employer, but where no alternative is presented, as under the present system, except where negroes are employed, the requirement of residence becomes irksome and is a hindrance in this as it would be in any other industry. It is also true that many employees particularly dislike to live in flats. The sleeping accommodations are generally poor, with little

light or ventilation, and all parts of the household are
cramped and crowded. To take the employee out of
the modern flat and let her go to her own home or
lodging place would be a boon to both employer and
employee. The plan proposed also lessens materially
the amount of care and responsibility now incurred by
the employer, since it decreases the number of personal
employees. The presence of the employee in the family
is a disadvantage to the household of the employer as
well as to the employee. Again, it enables large numbers of women who have only a few hours each day or
week to give to outside work to do it in their own houses
or in the homes of others without neglect of their own
households. Moreover, it lessens much of the difficulty
that now exists owing to the migratory habits of the modern family. The question of what shall be done with the
employees of a household during the summer and how
new ones shall be secured in the autumn is answered
in a measure if the work performed by them can be
done by the piece, hour, or season and a large part of
the family supplies can be purchased ready for use.
Then, too, it renders both employer and employee more
independent. Whether the desire for independence is
right or wrong is not the question — it is a condition
and must be met.

It has often been pointed out that the aristocracy of
the Church broke down at the time of the Reformation,
that the aristocracy of the State was overthrown by the
Bastile mob, that aristocracy in education is yielding to
the democratic influences of university extension, and
that aristocratic economics are disappearing in the light

of the industrial discussions of the day. The aristocracy of the household must succumb to this universal desire for personal independence on the part of employees.

The plan suggested of specializing household industries to as great an extent as possible and encouraging the domestic employee to live in her own home has much in its favor. It substitutes for the responsibility to an individual employer, so irritating to many and so contrary to the industrial spirit of the age, the responsibility to a business firm. It throws the responsibility for success on the individual employees by bringing them into more immediate competition with other workers in the same field. It provides a channel through which advance becomes possible and also independent business life if executive ability is present. It reduces house rent in proportion as the number of employees is lessened, or it places at the disposal of the family a larger portion of the house than is now available for their personal uses. It simplifies the problem in all families where there is more work than can be done by one employee but not enough for two. It makes possible such a division of labor in the household as will discriminate between skilled and unskilled labor. Under the present system the employer expects to find in one individual for $3 per week and expenses, a French chef, an Irish laundress, a discreet waitress, a Yankee maid-of-all-work, a parlor maid a Quaker in neatness, all this, "with the temper of a saint and the constitution of a cowboy thrown in." Expectations are often disappointed and the blame is thrown, not on a bad system, but on the individual forced to carry it out. The separation of skilled and unskilled labor permits each one to do a few things well and prevents the friction inevitable when the skilled workman is called upon to do unskilled work, or the unskilled laborer to perform tasks requiring the ability of an expert. It is a more flexible system of co-operation than the one technically known as such, since all articles are purchased, not of a certain manufacturer or dealer whom it has been agreed upon by contract to patronize, but wherever it is most convenient. It is easily adapted to the present system of living in flats and apartment houses rendered almost necessary in some places by high rents; this way of living makes it difficult to employ a large number of domestics, but on the other hand it makes it possible to do without them. It enables the domestic employee to have the daily change in going back and forth from her work which the shop-girl and the factory-girl now have. The domestic employee now has out-of-door exercise not oftener than once or twice a week, and the effect is as deleterious physically, mentally, and morally as a similar course would be in other walks of life. It must decrease that pernicious habit, so degrading to the occupation as well as to the individual, of discussing the personal characteristics of both employers and employees, since the relationship between the two is changed from the personal to the business one. It elevates to the rank of distinct occupations many classes of housework now considered drudgery because done at odd moments by over-worked employees. It must in time result in many economic gains, one illustration of which is the fact that the kitchen could be heated by the furnace and all cooking done by kerosene, gas, or electricity; on the other hand, the necessities of employers would cease to be the gauge for measuring the minimum of work that could be done by employees without losing their places.

Two objections are sometimes raised to this plan. The first is that the cost of living would be increased. This would undoubtedly be the effect at first, but it is not a valid objection to this mode of housekeeping. The list of articles now made out of the house shows that every article of men's dress is made more cheaply and better than formerly when made at home. This is due to the fact that in the transitional period men of means were willing to pay a higher price for goods made out of the house for the sake of obtaining a superior article. Competition subsequently made it possible for men of moderate means to share in the same benefit. The same tendency is seen among wage-earning women. They could make their own dresses at less expense than they can hire them made, but it would be done at a loss of time and strength taken from their own work, and they prefer to employ others. Moreover cost of living is a relative term — an increase in the family income makes it possible to employ more service and therefore to live better than before. Families of wealth now have two alternatives, either to employ more domestics within the home, or to purchase more ready-made supplies. The alternative usually chosen is the former, but if such families would choose the second and instead of employing additional domestics would, as far as practicable, purchase ready-made supplies for the table and have more work done by the hour, day, or piece, as great ease of living would be secured as through the employment of additional service within the house under the present system. Though the cost of living might be increased, it is a price many would be glad to pay for a release from the friction of a retinue of domestics in the home. When it has become the custom for families of wealth to have few or no domestics under their own roofs, the great problem of how people of limited incomes can have comfortable homes will be solved.

The second objection is the fact that it would take from the women of the household much of their work. The problem, however, has not been to provide a means of excusing from their legitimate share in the work of the world one half of its population, but to use that labor at the least cost of time and strength. The argument that would maintain the present system because it provides women with work is the same as that which destroyed the machines of Arkwright and Crompton; it is the argument that keeps convicts in idleness lest their work should come into competition with the work of others; it is the opposition always shown to every change whereby the number of workers in any field is at first lessened. But the plan proposed does not contemplate abolishing household work for women, but changing its direction so that it may be more productive with less expenditure than at present. It calls for specialization of work on a business basis, rather than idleness or charity. It asks that the woman who can bake bread better than she can sweep a room should, through unconscious cooperation, bake bread for several families and hire her sweeping done for her by one who can do it better than she. It asks that the woman who likes to make cake and fancy desserts but dislikes table service should dispose of

the products of her labor to several employers, rather than
give her time to one employer and do in addition other
kinds of work in which she does not excel. It asks that
the woman who cannot afford to buy her preserves and
jellies at the Woman's Exchange but crochets for church
fairs slippers that are sold at a dollar a pair shall dispose
of the products of her industry at a remunerative rate
and buy her jellies put up in a superior manner. The
plan allows the person who has skill in arranging tables
and likes dining-room work, but dislikes cooking, to do
this special kind of work, when otherwise she would drift
into some other light employment. It provides that
women in their own homes who are now dependent for
support on the labors of others shall have opened to them
some remunerative occupation. The preparation of food
in small quantities always secures more satisfactory results than when it is prepared in larger amounts. Women
in their own homes can give foods the delicate handling
necessary for the best results and at the same time use
the spare hours that are now given to unprofitable tasks.
It makes every member of the family a co-operator in
some form in the general family life. What is needed
indeed in the household is more co-operation among the
different members of it rather than conscious co-operation
with different families. It has been recently pointed out
that the carrying of electricity as a motive power to individual houses may cause a partial return to the domestic system of manufacturing which will be carried on under more
favorable conditions than was the old domestic system.[1]

[1] See also article on the "Revival of Hand Spinning and Weaving in
Westmoreland," by Albert Fleming, *Century Magazine*, February, 1889.

This is in the future — its possibility is only hinted at. But the domestic system of housework, if that expression may be used to distinguish it from the present individual system, and the proposed system of unconscious co-operation, enables women to work in their own homes and, by exchange of such commodities and services as each can best dispose of, to contribute to the general welfare.

The plan of specialization of household employments has already been put into partial operation by many housekeepers and its success attested by those who have tried it.[1]   Conscious co-operative housekeeping has in

[1] One writes, " I find it much better to employ one servant and to hire work by the piece, and to purchase from the Exchange, rather than to employ an extra servant."

Another housekeeper writes: " I began housekeeping twelve years ago with three servants and had more than enough work for all. I now have two and have not enough work for them, although my family is larger than at first. The change has come from putting work out of the house and hiring much done by the piece."

A business man writes : " Our family is happier than it ever dared hope to be under the sway of Green Erin. We purchase all baked articles and all cooked meats as far as possible. A caterer is employed on special occasions, and work that cannot be done by the parents, three children, and two aunts, who compose the family, is hired by the hour. Since we signed our Declaration of Independence in 1886, peace has reigned."

Still another says: " I used to employ a laundress in the house at $4 per week and board. I was also at expense in furnishing soap, starch, bluing, and paid a large additional water tax. Now my laundress lives at home, and does my laundry there for $4 per week, and we are both better satisfied."

Several small families who do "light housekeeping," have found that they have in this way been able to live near the business of the men of the family, and thus have kept the family united and intact, as they could not have done had it been necessary to employ servants.

One employee writes, "If more housework were done by the day so that more women could be with their families in the evening, I think it would help matters."

nearly every case proved a practical failure, but the unconscious co-operation that comes through business enterprise has brought relief to the household in many directions and it is one of the lines along which progress in the future must be made.

CHAPTER XIV

POSSIBLE REMEDIES — PROFIT SHARING

DOMESTIC service, as has been seen, is accompanied by certain social conditions that prevent many from entering the occupation. The present unclassified state of household employments operates in the same way. But in addition to this lack of organization, other industrial disadvantages are found. These are the lack of all opportunity for promotion within the service, the lack of kindred occupations opening out from it, the irregularity of working hours, and confinement evenings and Sundays, the necessary competition between those of American birth and foreign born and colored employees, and the lack of personal independence. These, in addition to the unorganized condition of the work, are the industrial disadvantages that tell most strongly against the occupation; they are the economic maladies that can be alleviated only by the application of economic remedies.

The attempt has been made to show how the lack of organization in household employments can be partially met by taking out of the house a large part of the work now performed there, and having much of what must necessarily remain done by the piece, hour, day, or season, thus securing better specialization of work and directing it into the current of industrial progress. The second group of industrial difficulties enumerated must in a similar way be met by measures that have proved successful in similar fields.

The vexed questions of wages and hours of labor in the industrial world are still unsettled, but in certain industries some little progress towards a solution of those difficulties has been made through the introduction of the profit-sharing system. In order to answer the question whether profit sharing could be introduced with advantage into domestic service, it is necessary to consider somewhat in detail the question, What is profit sharing, and also the question, What have been its advantages in general economic society?

Profit sharing, as defined by Mr. Carroll D. Wright, is the term that "may be applied to any arrangement whereby labor is rewarded in addition to its wages, or in lieu of wages, by participation in the profits of the business in which it is employed. Benefits of various kinds — as insurance, schools, libraries, and beautiful surroundings, so far as maintained by employers out of their profits and enjoyed by employees as an addition to what their wages would purchase — would have to be regarded, in a strict analysis, as an indirect form of profit sharing." [1] Mr. Nicholas Payne Gilman defines it as "the method of rewarding labor by assigning it a share in the realized profits of business in addition to wages." [2] Mr. D. F. Schloss considers it "an arrangement under which an employer agrees with his employees that they shall re-

[1] *Seventeenth Annual Report of the Massachusetts Bureau of Statistics of Labor*, p. 157.
[2] *Profit Sharing between Employer and Employee*, p. 8.

ceive, in partial remuneration of their labor, and in addition to their ordinary wages, a share, fixed beforehand, in the profits of his business." [1] The International Congress on Profit Sharing, held in Paris, in 1889, declared it to be "a voluntary agreement, by virtue of which an employee receives a share, fixed beforehand, in the profits of an undertaking."

The history of profit sharing is short, and can easily be recalled. It began in 1842 with the *Maison Leclaire* in Paris, and has been subsequently introduced into many business houses in France and Switzerland, countries where the economic conditions lend themselves readily to its progress. Its adoption in Germany has been less extensive, while the English industrial system has hitherto seemed hostile to it, although Mr. D. F. Schloss in his recent Report claims that a larger number of experiments in profit sharing have been made in England than in any other country. Probably about one fourth of the business establishments conducted on this principle are found in the United States.

What are the advantages that have resulted from this fifty years of more or less extensive experience with the system? There is first the fact that it results in the development of what Mr. Carroll D. Wright has called "the group of industrial virtues." This group includes diligence, zeal, caretaking, vigilance, punctuality, fidelity, continuity of effort, willingness to learn, a spirit of cooperation, and a personal interest in all business affairs. In addition to these virtues, other positive advantages have been noted by those who have tried the system.

[1] *Methods of Industrial Remuneration*, p. 158.

"An appreciable percentage of the occasions of worry, which all large employers experience, have disappeared," writes Mr. T. W. Bushill, of Coventry, England.[1] M. Billon, of Geneva, states as one result of his experiment, "Superintendence became easy for us, and *from that time we could, without fear of offending any one, show ourselves exacting in details to which previously we were obliged to close our eyes.*"[2] The Peace Dale Manufacturing Company began profit sharing "not to make money in the positive sense, but to save waste."[3] This saving of waste is seen in the efforts to economize time and materials and in the additional care with which machinery and all appliances for work are used. Various English firms have been most successful in attaining this end, stating that they find "increasing care to avoid spoilt work and waste both of time and material"; that "waste is guarded against"; that there is care in handling materials, and that "especially waste of raw material is avoided."[4] Another gain is found in the identification of the interests of employer and employees and the consequent harmony between capital and labor; "the occurrence of a strike in a profit-sharing establishment is believed to have been a rare event," says Mr. Schloss.[5] The advantage to the employer of this identification of interest is seen in the ability to obtain "a steadier and superior class of workers" ; in the fact that "the knowl-

[1] Schloss, *Methods of Industrial Remuneration*, p. 173.
[2] Gilman, *Profit Sharing*, p. 189.
[3] *Seventeenth Annual Report of the Massachusetts Bureau of Labor*, p. 178.
[4] Schloss, *Report on Profit Sharing*, p. 157.
[5] *Ibid.*, p. 160.

edge that there is such a scheme brings all the best workmen" to the firm employing it; that "workers remain
year after year"; and that "it tends to secure and retain the best workers." Its good effects on the character of the work are seen when "an efficient man is very
soon pricked up to greater diligence by his fellow workers"; in securing through it "the maximum of effort";
"in a steady pulling up all around"; when it "makes the
men keener after business and sharper in keeping down
expenses." [1]

It would seem difficult to introduce the scheme into a
business like that of tea-blending, but a London firm that
has practised it thirteen years states that the effect is
"to make the clerks willing to exert themselves in an
especial manner, when the occasion arises, because they
know that if they show themselves unable to cope with
the mass of work to be done, then the staff must be
increased; and they do not care to see their bonus diminished by an augmentation of the numbers entitled to
participation." [2]

The question naturally arises as to how far these gains
reimburse the employer for the financial cost of profit
sharing. The chairman of the South Metropolitan Gas
Company of London writes, "I state unhesitatingly that
the Company is recouped the whole of the amounts —
some £40,000 — paid as a bonus since the system was
started." [3] The managing director of the New Welsh
Slate Quarry Company gives it as his personal belief

---

[1] Schloss, *Report on Profit Sharing*, pp. 158–159.
[2] Schloss, *Methods of Industrial Remuneration*, pp. 173–174.
[3] Schloss, *Report*, p. 158.

" that we are recouping every penny of bonus and more ; " and similar testimony comes from others.

Yet this is putting the matter on the lowest plane. The system " converts the industrial association of employer and employees into a moral organism, in which all the various talents, services, and desires of the component individuals are fused into a community of purpose and endeavor." [1] A natural result, moreover, is a general elevation in the standards of morals. Most of all, in an individual way it is of help to the employee ; " to assist a person in improving his condition by his own efforts is to make a man of him." [2]

What can be learned from these successful experiences in profit sharing that will be of value in domestic service? The usual difficulties that beset the employer of domestic labor are lack of interest, desire for change, negligence, waste of time, extravagance in the use of materials, in a word, the absence of the industrial virtues. If these very difficulties — all of which exist elsewhere — are partially or entirely obviated by the employer of other forms of labor through the system of profit sharing, may it not reasonably be expected that they could be met in domestic service by the employment of similar means?

Domestic service, it is true, is not a wealth-producing occupation, but it is wealth-consuming probably beyond any other employment. The profit, therefore, must be negative, that is, economy in the use of time, materials, and appliances for work. It is in precisely these ways that profit sharing has been most successful, and the wage

[1] Wright, *Massachusetts Bureau of Statistics of Labor, 1886*, p. 231.
[2] *Ibid.*, p. 172.

system most unsatisfactory. Under the wage system the employer of domestic labor pays for time rather than for quality of service, and employers therefore constantly complain that employees do not accomplish one half as much as they should, and employees that employers exact twice as much as can be done. Neither party to the contract under the wage system can have a true notion of the working value or the money value of time; thus it is not strange that the one requires more than can be performed, and the other does less than might be reasonably demanded. The same ignorance and carelessness prevails in the use of materials. The employer may provide the best the markets afford, but if the cook has never had brought home to her a realizing sense of the money value of these materials, she is not altogether to blame if she fries doughnuts in butter costing fifty cents a pound, and makes angel food daily when eggs are forty cents a dozen. The employer may also provide the finest of furnishings for the dining-room and china closet, but if the maid-of-all-work does not associate a money value with these furnishings, she uses table napkins for holders, and carelessly drops fine china into an iron sink. From the selfish point of view the chief interest of the employer is to keep the bills down and to get the greatest possible amount of service even at the cost of the greatest expenditure of human strength; among employees, it is to do sufficient work to retain a good place, and to use whatever materials are most convenient.

Mr. Nicholas Payne Gilman has well said, " The deficiency in the daily wage system as a motive power to procure the desirable maximum of effort and performance is

R

extreme." Precisely the same objections that hold in all other employments to the wage system hold as well in domestic service. In other occupations it has been seen that the almost universal testimony of those who have tried profit sharing is that the system results in economy in the use of materials, care in the handling of machinery and implements of work, and a feeling of partnership, the spur of which as a motive "is only excelled in sharpness by complete proprietorship." Mr. Gilman sums up the advantages of the system when he says, "Profit sharing advances the prosperity of an establishment by increasing the quantity of the product, by improving the quality, by promoting care of implements and economy of materials, and by diminishing labor difficulties and the cost of superintendence." In a word, whatever arguments can be advanced in favor of profit sharing in productive industries can be used with equal force in its favor in domestic service.

The application of the principle to the household is simple. It is possible to allow a fixed sum, as $50, $100, or $500 per month for living expenses, which shall include the purchase of all food for the table, fuel, lights, ice, breakages, and the replacement of worn-out kitchen utensils, and to allow a pro rata amount for guests during the month. If by care in the use of food materials, fuel, and kitchen and dining-room furniture, the expenses amount to $45, $90, or $450 per month, the $5, $10, or $50 saved can be divided according to a ratio previously agreed upon between the employer and the one or more employees. The cook is in the position to save the most, and therefore ought to receive the greatest percentage of the amount saved; but it is a part of the work of the waitress to be careful of glass and china, of the laundress not to waste fuel, soap, and starch, and of all, including parlor maid, seamstress, and nursery maid, not to waste gas, fuel, or food at the table, and therefore each employee is entitled to a share in the profits. Thus each keeps watch over the others to prevent undue waste, and the employees are given a personal interest in the establishment now so often lacking. In addition to this, it is possible to allow a gardener and a coachman who have taken special care in the improvement of lawns, gardens, and stables a small percentage on the annual appreciation of property. " Comprehension is wonderfully quickened by the payment of a bonus or two in cash, and there is no more efficient instructor than self-interest."

Moreover, it is possible to allow a fixed sum for service, as $18 per month, out of which the employee may choose to have a small sum spent in hiring by the day some one to wash windows and clean verandas, or she may choose to economize her time and strength and do this work herself. In either case the financial outcome to the employer is the same, while either arrangement makes the employee a partner in the domestic company and gives her an active interest in its welfare.

It is possible to apply the principle in still other ways. If the general servant likes to cook but dislikes other parts of housework, she may contribute to the Woman's Exchange and with part of the money received hire with her employer an assistant to come in a certain number of hours each day to care for the rooms, the silver and brass, and wait on the table. It is possible also to give the cook a certain amount of time for making articles to be sold at the Woman's Exchange, the employer furnishing capital and implements of work and receiving a certain share in the profits.   In employment bureaus it would be possible to give a certain percentage of the profits of the bureau to all employees who have kept their names on the books of the bureau and remained at least one year in the place found by them through its agency.

The ways indeed are numberless in which the principle of profit sharing can be applied; and if the ingenuity and fertility of resource possessed by so many employers were once turned in this direction, the good resulting would be incalculable.

Great as would be the gain for domestic service if this principle could be adopted in private families, the advantage would be if possible even greater could it be introduced into hotels, boarding houses, and restaurants, and also the dining-car, parlor-car, and sleeping-car service. In all hotels, restaurants, and public institutions the waste is enormous — perhaps proportionately greater than in private families, largely because as a rule the superintendents of such establishments are also employees on wages.   Ignorance is often the chief cause of waste, and the best corrective of this ignorance is the experience gained through profit sharing.

But the greatest advantage of profit sharing in restaurants and hotels, dining-cars and sleeping-cars, is that through it the feeing system could be abolished.   In all such business enterprises where the feeing system is established there is in effect a combination of the general public and the employees of the establishments against the proprietors of them. Such is the case because the feeing system prevents the proprietors from receiving a fair amount of patronage unless each employee is feed for performing the service he ought freely to give and for which he will presumably be paid by his employer. The money profit in all these establishments depends largely on the good service rendered by the employees, and thus it would be possible to divide a positive profit as well as a negative saving. The feeing system, if it prevails in any branch of personal service, drags down with it in the social and industrial scale every other branch of the service. The substitution of profit sharing in hotels and restaurants and in the dining-car and sleeping-car service for the system of fees so increasingly prevalent would do more than any other one thing to remove the social stigma from domestic service and make of all such employees self-respecting men and women.

It may be urged against the proposition to introduce profit sharing into domestic service that few employees are of such stability of character as to warrant making the experiment. But the great desideratum is to introduce into the service some principle that will develop the best qualities of those already in it, that will sift out the worthless and compel them to undertake unskilled labor, that will draw from other occupations, where they are less needed, able persons whose natural tastes and abilities would attract them to this. M. Levasseur is quoted as saying that of one hundred firms that begin business, ten per cent succeed, fifty per cent " vegetate," and forty per cent go into bankruptcy. The statement characterizes with possibly sufficient accuracy the result in the case of the establishment of a corresponding number of households. Could an industrial partnership be formed between employer and employee, with the agreement to divide, not positive profits, but negative savings, something might be done to save the forty per cent who now give up housekeeping and go into the bankruptcy of hotels and boarding houses, and also to lessen the fifty per cent who "vegetate" through the employment in the household of obsolete industrial methods.

It may also be said that profit sharing appeals to a selfish motive and therefore is objectionable. But much of the waste and extravagance in the household comes from ignorance; profit sharing is one way of teaching the value of raw materials. The comfortable theory is often entertained that to be born poor is to be born with a knowledge of all household affairs. As a matter of fact, there is doubtless far more waste and extravagance in the households of the poor than in those of the rich. But extravagance is in reality a relative term; "tenderloin steak for breakfast and rump roast for dinner," which may be simple fare in the household of the employer, becomes an impossible luxury to the employee in such a family when she goes to a home of her own. Profit sharing would be of value in the household not because it would appeal to a selfish motive, but because it would teach the value of materials used and incidentally do something to prevent this prevalent waste and extravagance.

Neither of these objections to profit sharing holds in the face of all that can be said in its favor. The general arguments for it are many. It is usually assumed that the interests of the employer and those of the employee are antagonistic. The introduction of profit sharing could easily prove that this assumption in domestic service is wrong, as it has already made similar proof in other occupations. If the employers of other forms of labor find themselves relieved of much of the worry and friction that have previously resulted from the mutual relation of employer and employee, it would seem reasonable to expect a like result in the household. If it has been found elsewhere that the extra services called out, and the manner in which they are called out, constitute an invaluable educational discipline, and promote zeal, efficiency, and economy, a similar result might be looked for here. If other employees have learned through it to be careful of their methods of work, punctual in the performance of their duties, and economical in the use of materials; if it has become "a moral educator, and substituted harmony and mutual good-will for distrust and contention in the relations of employer and employee," then, indeed, may it not be considered, not as a panacea, but as one measure among many that may be of help in lessening some of the serious difficulties that now attend domestic service?

At the present time a public discussion of domestic service meets with little else but jest and ridicule, while in private life the social stigma is cast on all engaged in it, as is the case in no other occupation. To attempt to dignify labor by saying, "we must dignify labor," savors of the old problem of trying to raise one's self by the boot-straps. No concrete method by which this is to be done is ever suggested, and until some plan is adopted by which the personal dignity and independence of the employee is recognized, and his industrial and financial independence is secured, domestic service will continue to be under the industrial and social ban. When this improved condition is brought about, there will be established what Professor Jevons considers the best of all trade-unions — that between the employer and employee.

It must be frankly said that the plan of adopting profit sharing in the household is a theoretical one; and to say it is "mere theory" is often considered an unanswerable argument with which to meet every new proposition. But theory lies at the basis of all successful action; difficulties have come in household service often because it has been conducted without theory — in a short-sighted, haphazard, hand-to-mouth fashion. It is known, however, that the experiment has been tried successfully in a private family, and this perhaps saves the proposition from the charge of being only theory. It has been tried by Mrs. X, a university graduate, after one and a half years' experience in housekeeping. The experiment was made in a college town where the cost of provisions was rather above than below the average. The family comprised four adults, including the Irish maid rather above the average in intelligence and ambition. The plan provided for an allowance of $40 a month for living expenses, including groceries, meats, fish, poultry, butter, milk, cream, ice, candles, kerosene oil, and incidental expenses. The last included breakage and the replacement of worn-out kitchen utensils. The best materials of all kinds were purchased, and practically nothing was ever thrown away. The food was simple but abundant.

The co-operation between employer and maid consisted
on the part of the employer in planning the menu, especially the making up of left-over materials, the pricing of
all articles in the market, and keeping the accounts accu-
rately; the maid gave all orders and carried them out.
The profit sharing consisted in dividing equally between
employer and maid whatever had been saved at the end
of the month out of the $40 allowed for running expenses.
The results of four months' experiment were as follows:

Average monthly expenses before profit sharing began $41.25
Expenses first month after 36.74
"   second "   "   . . . . 43.75 [1]
"   third   "   "   . . . . 41.58 [2]
"   fourth "   " 36.28

The plan for carrying on the dining association using
the Memorial Hall of Harvard University is essentially
one of co-operation, and contains some points that could
be tried with advantage elsewhere. The steward receives
a fixed salary and in addition a small sum each week for
every person who boarded that week at the hall; but
this "head money" is proportionately diminished as the
average weekly price of board exceeds the amount agreed
upon.

At Placid Club, a social club established in the Adiron-
dacks, all fees are prohibited, and the rule is strictly enforced; but the past season (1896) a dividend of ten per
cent on the wages received was declared out of the profits

[1] This included the purchase of two new labor-saving appliances for
the kitchen, costing $5.70. The maid was given the choice of having the
new utensils or dividing a surplus; she chose the former.

[2] This included the presence in the family of two guests for two weeks.

of the club, and this was given to all house employees who had remained throughout the season and whose services had been satisfactory to the manager. The financial success of the club depended largely on the efficiency, good-will, and ready co-operation of its employees, and the dividend declared was in recognition of this fact.

Beginnings in a small way have been made elsewhere.[1] They are indeed but beginnings, but they seem to indicate one direction in which progress is possible.

[1] One housekeeper reports that she gives her cook five cents for every new soup, salad, made-over dish, or dessert that proves acceptable to the majority of the family. She thus secures variety and economy in the use of materials.

One reports that she has a German cook who understands thoroughly the purchase and use of all household materials. The cook is given a fixed sum each week with which to make purchases, and she keeps whatever sum remains after these have been made. The family report that they have never lived so well, or with so much comfort and so much economy as since the plan has been tried.

Another states that she adds at the end of the month twenty per cent to the wages of her waitress if no article of glass or china has been nicked, cracked, or broken during the time.

These are all variations of the same principle.

CHAPTER XV

ONE of the greatest obstacles in the way of improving domestic service has been the prevailing lack of information in regard to household affairs and of careful, systematic education of housekeepers.

Information and education are often used as synonymous terms, but the two words carry with them entirely different ideas. Information concerning household affairs includes a ready knowledge of the history of all household employments and household service, of the economic basis on which the household rests, and of the economic principles on which it is conducted. Much of this information it is now difficult to obtain. Many houses are found in Southern Germany without windows looking towards the public highway. Light and air are admitted through openings in the rear or on a court, but no chance passer-by is permitted to look within. The household has always been constructed on the same plan. No outsider has been permitted to know the percentage of the family income that goes for service, fuel, gas and water-tax, groceries, meats, fruits, and vegetables. In the great majority of households not only is there no disposition to give others the benefit of such information, but the information itself does not exist. Each new generation of housekeepers practically begins its work where the previous generation began. Its only heritage is recipes for desserts, rules for making furniture polish, methods of dealing with moth and mildew, which are handed down like family property from one generation to another in a way as primitive as that in which books were preserved before writing was known. Advance is not thus made, as is evident from the course followed in other occupations that have shown greatest progress. A vast accumulation of knowledge in regard to law has come through the added experience of individual members of the profession. It is said that every lawyer owes a debt of gratitude to his profession which can be paid only by some personal contribution to the sum total of legal knowledge. The constant progress made by the profession of medicine is due to the untiring investigations carried on by its members, the wide publicity given the results of these investigations, and the fact that every discovery made by one member becomes the common property of all. Until every housekeeper is willing to recognize her obligations to her profession and to share with other members the results of her experience, of her acquired information, and of her personal investigations, no progress in household affairs can be expected.

Much of the information to be gained in regard to household affairs is a direct product of education, but education includes much more. Education gives a certain amount of information that is of direct service, and it gives a training that is of indirect but even greater value. The information more immediately gained comes through the study of art, chemistry, economics, physiology, psychology, and history. The study of art should enable the housekeeper to build and furnish her home with taste; of chemistry, to provide for its sanitary construction and for the proper preparation of all food materials; of economics, to manage her household on business principles; of physiology, to study the physical development of her children; of psychology, to observe their mental growth and base their training upon it; of history, to know the progress made in all these departments of knowledge and avoid repeating as experiments what others have advanced beyond the experimental stage. These are the gains on the side of information. The real work of education in supplying the needs of the household is far more important. There are constantly arising in every household emergencies for which the housekeeper is, and must be, totally unprepared as regards the amount of available information she possesses. There are demands made every hour, every moment, for the exercise of reason, judgment, self-control, alertness, observation, accuracy, ingenuity, inventive genius, fertility of resources. The training received by the housekeeper must be such as to prepare her to meet at any moment any emergency that may arise within her home. In all ordinary circumstances she avails herself of the information gained in school or college and through her general reading, but this is of no avail in the decision of questions which arise outside of the field of this information, and could by no possibility be anticipated by it. If progress is to be made in the household, it must be no longer assumed that an establishment can be well managed by a young woman whose reasoning powers have never been cultivated, who has never been taught self-reliance and self-control, who has no conception of accuracy, who has never acquired the habit of observation, and whose inventive genius and fertility of resource are expended in providing for the pleasures of a day.

No improvement is possible in domestic service until every part of the household comes abreast of the progress made outside of the household; until the profession of housekeeping advances, like the so-called learned professions, through the accumulated wisdom of its individual members; until it ceases to be merely a passive recipient of the progress made elsewhere, and becomes on its own part an active, creative force.

So much has progress up to this time been hindered by this inactivity in the household, and so great is the interdependence of all parts of the household, that it seems necessary to consider somewhat more in detail the causes of this condition.

Inactivity in all household affairs has largely come from three things. It has in the first place been generally believed that a knowledge of all things pertaining to the house and home, unlike anything else, comes by instinct. It is assumed that the housekeeper is born with an intuitive knowledge of the right proportions of all materials to be used in cooking—this knowledge sometimes supplemented by an inherited cook-book and one purchased to aid a benevolent society soliciting funds for a charitable purpose. Her knowledge of the mental, moral, and physical training to be given her children is also to be gained through instinct and experience and the traditions handed down with regard to her own family. Instinct may sometimes be dormant, and experience prove an expensive schoolmaster through the exaction of heavy fees, but no other avenue of information has been open to her. Again, a very large proportion of all moneys spent for legitimate household purposes passes through the hands of housekeepers; yet no thorough investigation on an extensive scale has ever been carried on in regard to the expenditure made within or for the household. Few women when they assume the care of a household know the exact value of the household plant; the amount to be deducted each year for wear and tear; the relative proportions expended annually for rent, fuel, food, clothing, and service; the number of meals served and the approximate cost of each; the amount of profit, waste, or unproductiveness that results from all expenditures made. Every manufacturer, every business man knows the value of his plant, its increasing or diminishing value, the cost of materials used and of service employed. This information constitutes a part of the intellectual capital with which he begins business; he does not acquire it by instinct or tradition, but by careful and exact study of all the factors involved. It is difficult to see how a household can be successfully carried on except through the application of the same principles. If we turn to the construction and decoration of the house, ignorance, masquerading as instinct, quite as often prevails. It is true we have houses in which we live, many of them expensive and artistic, yet as a rule little or no attention is paid in their construction to the specific use each of the several parts is to serve. Libraries are

built with little or no regard to the place to be occupied
in them by book-shelves, desk, or library table, and no
attention is paid to the question of the best methods of
providing them with natural and artificial light. Draw-
ing-rooms and parlors are built without a place for a
piano, dining-rooms without regard to the position of a
sideboard, butlers' pantries without an entrance to the
kitchen, kitchens with absolutely no regard to the conven-
iences of the work to be carried on there, and bedrooms
with no normal place for a bed, bureau, or dressing-table.
Something has of late been done in deference to public
sentiment towards applying the principles of sanitation
to the construction of public and private buildings, yet
much still remains to be done, both in the investigation
of the principles and in their application. Many of our
private homes are pleasing to the eye, yet if we accept
that definition of art which considers that it is its highest
province to serve best the useful, many of the so-called
artistic homes must be otherwise classed. Before improvement can be looked for in any of these directions,
the position must be abandoned that the household, or
any single part of it, can be managed by instinct.

A second explanation of the prevailing inactivity in
regard to household affairs arises from the fact that it is
always assumed that these subjects concern only women.
The husband of the family often excuses his absolute
ignorance of the affairs of his own household by the lame
apology, "I leave all these things to my wife and daughters." It is certainly not the intention in such remarks
to belittle the affairs of the household, yet that is the
natural and inevitable result. A knowledge of house-

hold affairs has never been considered a part of a liberal education as is a knowledge of literature, science, and politics, but when it is so regarded by men as well as by women a great gain will have been made. Moreover, it must be said that the natural tastes of some men would lead them to take up housekeeping as an occupation, as the natural tastes of some women lead them into different kinds of business. Inactivity in the household will cease when the arbitrary pressure is removed that now tacitly compels many women to become housekeepers in violence to their natural tastes, and at the same time prevents any man whose abilities lie in this direction from giving them scope. The time must come when each person will take up the work in life for which he or she is best adapted, be it the care of a house for a man or business for a woman, when it will cease to be a matter of odium for the husband to direct the affairs of the house and for the wife to be the breadwinner. When the fact is everywhere recognized that both men and women have a vital concern in the affairs of the house, the relation between the different parts of the household will become an organic one, and its highest development reached.

A third explanation of this inactivity in the household is the belief that all women have a natural taste for household affairs, which without cultivation grows into positive genius for carrying them on. But a young man with a genius for law or medicine is not only not expected, he is not permitted, to exercise his untrained genius in legal and medical cases. The greater the genius he gives promise of, the more careful, systematic, and prolonged is the training he receives. In a similar

s

way the woman with a natural taste for housekeeping
duties is the one who should have most training in them,
while in no other way can an interest in such duties be
created in women who have not an inborn love of them.

These three common errors — that a knowledge of
housekeeping affairs is a matter of inspiration, that men
have no active interest in the management of a household,
and that all women have a natural love for such affairs
which supplies the place of training — are perhaps sufficient explanation of the present lack of all opportunity for
the investigation of the household in a professional way.

It has always been assumed, and asserted without fear
of contradiction, that the best place to learn everything
pertaining to the household is the home. But the same
change must come here as has already come in the profession of medicine and in nearly every other department
of knowledge. The period is not remote when every
housekeeper made, as well as administered, the family
tonics, bitters, pills, salves, and liniments, and every
household contained a copy of *Every Man his Own
Practitioner*. Happily that day has passed and the era
of scientific investigation and practice of medicine has
dawned. It was once assumed that an adequate knowledge of law could be obtained by any young man who
spent six months in reading law in any lawyer's office.
But the leading members of the bar to-day have been
trained in less haphazard ways. It was formerly believed
that any person could be fitted for a librarian by doing
the routine work of librarian's assistant in a small country library. Such training has been supplanted by library
schools open only to college graduates and offering a two

years' course of study. Less than a hundred years ago boys and girls of sixteen or seventeen years of age began teaching without even a high school education, while the tendency to-day is everywhere to insist not only on advanced academic but also on professional training. The system of apprenticeship is everywhere being supplanted by systematic, technical training given by experts.

There is evidence that this same spirit is slowly invading the household. Cooking schools are springing up that teach all the intricacies of the science "in ten easy lessons," while the lecturer on cooking with her demonstration lessons has found her way into nearly every town. Sewing is taught in the public schools, and the free kitchen garden is following fast in the train of the free kindergarten. All this is good in its way, but it is superficial work. No permanent advance will be made as long as only those schools are found that teach simply the mechanical parts of housekeeping. New recipes for salads and puddings, new ways of cleaning brass and silver, new methods of caring for hard-wood floors — all these may be helpful in a sense, but the knowledge of these and a thousand other mechanical contrivances will never put the household on a scientific basis and turn its face towards progress.

One thing, and only one thing, will turn the household into the channels where every other occupation has made advancement. This is the establishment of a great professional school, amply equipped for the investigation of all matters pertaining to the household and *open only to graduates of the leading colleges and universities of the country*. This work cannot and should not be done by the college. The college offers courses in physiology and hygiene, but the college graduate is permitted to practice medicine only after a long and thorough course in a medical school. The college offers courses in constitutional law, but the college student is admitted to the bar only after technical training in the law school. The college offers courses in chemistry and economics, but the college student who expects to have the care of a home should prepare herself for this work by technical study of all that concerns the household. The mechanical parts of housekeeping can be learned in the home, providing the head of the household herself understands the intricacies of the mechanism over which she has charge, and has the gift of imparting knowledge. These assumptions, however, cannot always be made, nor can it be assumed that even all the mechanical parts of housekeeping can be learned in any single home any more than that all forms of library work can be learned from a single library. Some of these mechanical parts of housekeeping can be learned in the kitchen-garden, the public school, the cooking school, but progress is never made by treadmill methods, by mechanical repetition, by giving attention only to those things already known. Professional training and investigation must supplement home and collegiate instruction in the case of the housekeeper, as the professional school supplements private and collegiate instruction for the physician, the lawyer, and the clergyman.

The household has been up to this time a *terra incognita*. Until but yesterday absolutely nothing had been done in any educational institution towards investigating its past history, its present condition, its future needs.

The beginning has scarcely been made, although the field for such investigation is limitless. Comparatively little is known of artistic house-building and furnishing, scarcely more of household sanitation[1] and the chemistry of foods,[2] even less of the economic principles underlying the household; fashion, not art, governs every question of costume, while, with a few notable exceptions, Porter's *Development of the Human Intellect* contains the sum and substance of our knowledge of the mental development of children. Years of patient, laborious, unremitting investigation must be given to all household affairs before any appreciable advance can be made by them. The historical and scientific investigation of all the great subjects of art, economics, chemistry, physiology, and psychology in their application to the household, and the publication of the results of these investigations, would not indeed settle to-morrow all the difficulties that arise to-day in regard to household affairs; but such investigation and publication would take the subject out of the domain of sentiment and transfer it to a realm where reason and judgment have the control. Household affairs would in time come to receive the respect now accorded the learned professions. Household service, instead of being taken up as a last resort by those who themselves say "have not education enough to do anything else," would be dignified into a profession that would attract large numbers who now seek other occupations.

[1] An admirable work on *Household Sanitation* has been published by Miss Marion Talbot and Mrs. Ellen S. Richards.

[2] The work in this direction carried on by Professor W. O. Atwater of Wesleyan University has been of the greatest value, and indicates the lines along which future investigation must be made.

It has already been said that "educational forces do not push from the bottom, they pull from the top." When a strong educational force exerted from the top shall have pulled the household and all questions connected with it out of the slough of stagnation in which it has been for so long a time, then, and not till then, will training schools for domestic employees be successful. Progress in every other field of human activity has been made only through investigation and the widespread diffusion of the results of such investigation; on similar investigations rests the only hope of making progress in household affairs.

CHAPTER XVI

ANY study of the subject of domestic service must lead to the conclusion that household service and household employments do not occupy an isolated position; that while they may be indifferent to the political, industrial, and social changes constantly occurring, they cannot by virtue of this indifference remain unaffected by them; that the inventions of the past hundred years have revolutionized household employments, and that the present generation must adapt itself to these new conditions; that while a century ago domestic service had no competitors as an occupation for women, it now has hundreds; that the personnel in the domestic service of America has been transformed through industrial, political, and social revolutions; that it has been affected by the democratic tendencies of the age and by the commercial and educational development of the country; that because of these constantly recurring changes in the conditions surrounding domestic service the questions connected with it vary from year to year; that it is governed by the same general economic laws as are all other employments, and that it has developed within itself other economic laws peculiar to it; that the increasing wealth and luxury of the country are

introducing new complications into a problem already
far from simple; that both employer and employee are
heirs of conditions which their ancestors could not control, and that they are surrounded by difficulties which
no person single-handed and alone can hope successfully
to overcome.

It has been seen that many of these difficulties arise
from the failure to recognize domestic service as a part
of the great industrial questions of the day. It is not
so recognized because economic writers have not as yet
discussed the subject, and because those who come in
daily contact with it overlook its economic side. The
housekeeper who completes her round of morning shopping by a visit to an employment bureau where she
engages a new cook regards that and her other business
transactions all in the same light; she has both in
shopping and in securing a cook been guided solely by
her taste, her necessities, and her bank account. The
economist must include domestic service in his discussions of the labor question, and the housekeeper must
differentiate the various parts of her housekeeping duties
before improvement is possible.

It must also be recognized that another difficulty has
been the natural conservatism of many women — a conservatism arising from the isolated, home-centred lives
many housekeepers lead, and that prevents that intellectual hospitality which is the presager of all true
progress. The typical housekeeper, like the Turk, is
a born fatalist; because things are as they are, they
must always have been so and they must continue so
to be. Many persons take pride in being "old-time

housekeepers" and look with disfavor on any change. "That plan might succeed in some families, but it would not in mine" is for many others the final settlement of the question. This lack of mental elasticity and the dislike of taking the initiative in any movement must be another obstacle in the way of immediate improvement.

It has also been seen that other causes partially explain the difficulty — the love of ease and pleasure, the attempt to keep up appearances, a pretentious manner of living, the frequent desire of both employers and employees to get everything for nothing, the willingness of mistresses to find maids who will do their work half right and of maids to find mistresses who will treat them half right, the endeavor to get "the largest expenditure of woman for the smallest expenditure of money," a natural tendency among women toward aristocracy and a dislike of everything savoring of social democracy.

Some of the difficulty arises from conditions to be expected in a country comparatively new and possessing great possibilities of wealth. The growing luxury among the middle classes not only creates a demand for more employees but it also increases the requisitions upon those rendering service. Those who have lately acquired riches make increasing demands upon their employees, and they must become accustomed to their riches before these demands will be modified. Bishop Potter has said, "Luxury has its decent limits, and we in this land are in danger in many directions of overstepping those limits."[1] Persons with moderate means are the greatest sufferers from this thoughtless trans-

[1] *Letter to the Clergy of the Diocese of New York,* May 15, 1886.

gression of the bounds of luxury. The remedy lies in such education of the wealthy classes, especially where wealth has been suddenly acquired, as will give a more practical knowledge of general and household economics, a realization of the ethical as well as of the economic principle involved in paying high wages for poor service and abnormally high wages for good service, such an education as will result in greater simplicity in manner of living because it will be governed by ethical, economic, and hygienic principles.

It is true that in thousands of households no difficulty in regard to domestic service exists, but this fact does not relieve those in charge of such households from further responsibility in the matter. A political club recently formed to secure better municipal government in Montreal took as its watchword, "Every man is individually responsible for just so much evil as his efforts might prevent." [1] In a similar way the responsibility of the employer does not end with his own household, but he is responsible for as much evil in the general condition of domestic service as he could have prevented by his investigation and discussion of the subject.

The first result of this investigation, discussion, and action must be the attempt to remove from domestic service the social stigma attached to it. During the feudal period every occupation was inferior socially to that of warfare; physicians were leeches, clergymen were held in disrepute, bankers were usurers, and merchants and traders were tolerated only because they could furnish the ready money necessary for military campaigns

[1] *The Century*, June, 1894.

— social position belonged only to the profession of arms. The substitution of higher ideals for those of feudalism and the spread of democratic ideas have removed the social ban from every occupation except domestic service. Industrial and social evolution point to its ultimate removal from this employment as has been the case in others.

A second result of investigation and discussion must be the working out of ways and means for taking both work and worker out of the house of the employer. This must result in a simplification of household management and a greater flexibility in household employments. It simplifies the household because it takes out of it a cumbersome, unwieldy machine long since become antiquated. It is possible to arrange a series of mechanical contrivances operated by electricity that will enable a person to open any window or door in his house without rising from his chair, but it is as a rule easier to open a window without such assistance than it is to keep the batteries in running order. A retinue of employees in a household becomes like a complicated mechanism used to attain simple ends. Taking the employee out of the house of the employer brings flexibility into household employments, since it results in greater personal independence and in openings for specialized work. An ambitious and energetic office boy is pushed on by his employer into more responsible positions, but the domestic employee is held back by impassable barriers. Industrial promotion is impossible as the occupation at present exists. "I suppose there must be a screw loose somewhere, or a man of his age would not be my coachman," said a lawyer recently in reply to a question concerning a new employee. The industrial barriers within the occupation must be removed before domestic service will attract large numbers of capable, efficient persons; this can be at least partially accomplished by taking the employee out of the house and allowing him or her to become a self-reliant, independent, business person.

Another direction in which progress lies is in the effort to put the employment on a business basis. This must be accomplished if any improvement is to come. No man takes his watch to a blacksmith to be repaired, or employs a mason as bookkeeper, or a longshoreman as superintendent of a mill, or a hod-carrier as floorwalker, yet practically the same thing is done when a housekeeper employs an inexperienced young woman as seamstress, installs a girl just from Ireland as cook, takes a tenement-house woman into her home to care for her table linen and bric-à-brac, and then adds to the incongruity of the situation by paying high wages for this unskilled labor. Some agreement must be reached by employers in regard to standards of work and wages before domestic service can be classed as skilled labor.[1]

The suggestion of profit sharing is in line with the effort to put the occupation on a business basis. Only where there is absolute equality, when employer and employee stand on the same business level, can amiability of manner and a spirit of helpfulness on the part of the employee be prevented from being interpreted as

[1] An excellent classification of standards of work and wages has been drawn up by the committee on Household Economics of the Civic Club of Philadelphia. See Appendix III.

springing from a desire to curry favor with the employer. Not until the domestic employee feels he has no reason to court the favor of his employer for the sake of possible perquisites will he be self-respecting, and therefore entitled to respect from others. The practice in many private houses of subsidizing employees by numerous and valuable gifts is as subversive of the best interests of all concerned, as is the giving of fees in large establishments. It fosters subserviency rather than responsibility, and creates dissatisfaction among the employees in families where the custom does not and perhaps cannot prevail. Profit sharing appeals not to selfishness but to intelligence, and has in it elements that tend to make the employee a self-respecting and therefore a better man.

Improvement in all these directions, or in other ways far better, can come only through the investigation of all household affairs by both men and women. Travellers in other countries often lament the sight, still so common in some places, of a woman harnessed to a cart with a dog, or dragging the cart by her own efforts, or weighed down by the heavy burdens placed upon her back. But a more unfortunate condition in such countries than the woman harnessed to a cart is the fact that wherever this is found the highest opportunities for education are not open to women. The woman and the cart will remain in every country where university education is not made possible for her. Until university investigation of domestic affairs is made possible for every one having the proper qualifications, the woman and the cart — the overburdened, ignorant, and hopeless worker — will remain in the household.

If progress is to be made in the same direction that it has been up to this time, it must bring a still further readjustment of the work of both men and women. It must result in attracting every man and woman to the work for which he or she is best fitted. Just as other forms of work once held in low estimation have been elevated by scientific advancement, so the time will come when it will be honorable to do housework of any kind for remuneration. A woman with no talent for art has been known after four lessons in oil painting to offer for sale the products of her work without blushing for her audacity or incompetence. But though ignorant of art, she may have been competent in cooking, and if the way had been open to gain an honorable support by the exercise of this talent, she might have been saved the attempt to secure a living by means from which nothing but failure ought to result. The mistress of a large and costly establishment said recently, "One of the most difficult things about housekeeping is to dispose of old fancy work." Much of this work represents idle labor in boarding houses, done by women in various walks of life who will not keep house under present conditions, but who would be glad to do so if the conditions could be made more favorable.

It is in many ways difficult to deal with woman as an economic factor, since many elements of uncertainty enter into her life which do not hamper men. A young man is reasonably sure of two things in his future life, — that he will have to support himself and that he will marry. But many young women are not certain of either marriage or the necessity of self-support. If a young woman

marries, she is not permitted by the conventions of society to be a breadwinner; on the other hand, she may
find herself obliged, without preparation for it, to provide
support, not only for herself but also for her family. If
she marries and boards, she probably finds herself obliged
to become a drone, and leads an aimless life. If, without
deference to convention, she engages in business, her
occupation may be broken up through the removal of
her husband's business to another locality. For economic
reasons it is impracticable for the married woman to engage in any industry involving the use of capital that
cannot be readily transferred, unless this business is the
same as that of her husband, or unless she bears the
entire burden of support and has unrestricted control
of the business enterprises of the family. A thorough
knowledge of some one line of domestic work which
would yield compensation would often lessen many of
the perplexities surrounding a married woman. Moreover, it seems not unreasonable to consider marriage on
its practical side as a business partnership to which the
woman as well as the man is to contribute. If she con-
tributes a practical knowledge of housekeeping, the business agreement is a fair one; if she does not contribute
this knowledge, but brings a knowledge of other things
as valuable, it is also a fair arrangement; but if she
brings no knowledge of household affairs, and no equivalent for it, the partnership on its business side is unfair.
There should be a definite understanding when a woman
marries whether she is to keep house or not, and if so,
that she knows how. The time ought to come when, in
case she marries and boards, she will be willing and able,

and society will allow her, to contribute her share in a
business capacity to the life partnership.

Thousands of ambitious and talented women in the
upper and middle classes are crying for work, as women
in a lower walk cry for bread. It is impossible for society
to maintain the former in idleness and at the same time
to pay full wages for work to the army of working
women. The pay of wage-earning women will never rise
above the starvation point while the women of the upper
and middle classes are permitted to live without work.
The boycotting of dealers in ready-made clothing whose
names are not on the " white list " is but a sop thrown to
Cerberus, — until the cause of the evil is removed, until
women now living in idleness become co-operators in the
work of the world, all women who work for remuneration
must do their share of the work for half-pay. Women
want work for all the reasons that men want it, but as
long as so many of them, when they do work, persistently
give their work for nothing, just so long will women's
work in general be undervalued.

This readjustment of work and the willingness of
larger numbers of women to work for remuneration would
be as productive of improvement in all household affairs
as division of labor has been elsewhere. A more far-
reaching benefit is suggested by Maria Mitchell when she
says : " The dressmaker should no more be a universal
character than the carpenter. Suppose every man should
feel it his duty to do his own mechanical work and *all*
kinds, would society be benefited ? would the work be
well done ? Yet a woman is expected to know how to do
all kinds of sewing, all kinds of cooking, all kinds of any

woman's work, and the consequence is that life is passed in learning these only, while the universe of truth beyond remains unentered." [1]

In seeking for some measure of relief from the present oppressive conditions, it must be said in conclusion that little can be accomplished except through the use of means which already exist, developing these along lines marked out by industrial progress in other fields. In the foregoing suggestions, — that the historical study of the subject points to relief through the removal of the social stigma ; that the specialization of household employments in consequence of the removal of as much work as possible and the removal of the domestic employee as well from the home of the employer leads to a simpler and better manner of life for both employer and employee ; that the introduction of profit sharing is one means of placing household employments on a business basis ; that the establishment in connection with one of our great universities of a school of investigation open only to graduates of the leading reputable colleges is the only opportunity for the scientific advancement of the household and all questions connected with it ; and that together with the last, a recognition of the necessity for the readjustment of the work of both men and women must result in making any form of housework for remuneration honorable for any person, man or woman, — in these suggestions nothing either novel or original has been presented. Progress has been made through such means ; it seems not unreasonable to believe that further progress will be made through their use.

[1] Maria Mitchell, p. 26.

T

Yet this view of the subject does not diminish, it rather increases, individual responsibility. Sir James Stephen said, when civil-service reform was first agitated in England, that a moral revolution was necessary in that country before the reform sought could become an accomplished fact. For a reform in domestic service a moral revolution is everywhere needed, bringing with it to every person an appreciation of his responsibility to all connected with the employment, whether employer or employee.

Reforms begin at the top, revolutions at the bottom. It rests with the men and women of the so-called upper classes, whether raised to their position by birth, wealth, intellect, education, or opportunity, to work out in the best way a satisfactory solution of the vexed question of domestic service.

APPENDIX I

STATISTICS OF DOMESTIC SERVICE

THE graduates of Vassar College, Classes of '88 and '89, desire to collect statistics in regard to the subject of domestic service, and ask your assistance.

The work has grown out of a belief that a knowledge of some of the actual conditions of such service, as viewed from the standpoint of both employer and employee, is essential to an intelligent discussion of this question. It is hoped to tabulate the results obtained, showing the average wages paid in each occupation, the length of time employed, etc. The statistics, to be of value, must represent the experiences of many housekeepers in many localities, and the co-operation of all who are interested in the subject is earnestly solicited. Three schedules are sent you upon which to supply information.

SCHEDULE No. I. — For Employers (mistresses of households).

SCHEDULE No. II. — For Employees (domestic servants of all kinds).

SCHEDULE No. III. — For Educational Statistics (from teachers, etc., in the kinds of schools specified).

These schedules are sent to all housekeepers and their employees who can be communicated with by the members of the Classes of '88 and '89 and the Department of History.

Will you please fill out the following blank and return it to the person sending it to you, or to the address given below? Please complete all the columns relating to each person in your employ.

Only estimates can be given in reply to Questions 7, 10, and 12.

If any question — as No. 17 — is not applicable to you, this sign — X — may be used.

A prompt reply will be considered as a special favor.

All personal information will be treated as confidential. The name is asked as a guarantee of good faith, to avoid sending duplicates, and to render possible further correspondence in regard to special points of experience. It may, however, be omitted if desired.

Please return to — DEPARTMENT OF HISTORY,

VASSAR COLLEGE,

December 1, 1889. POUGHKEEPSIE, N. Y.

OCCUPATIONS	NUMBER ETC.			WAGES			LABOR			
	I	II	III	IV	V	VI	VII	VIII	IX	X
	Number engaged in each occupation	Place of birth [1]	Time in your employ	Paid by the day, week, or month	Amount	With or without board	Actual working hours per day	Time allowed each week	Vacation time allowed during year	With or without loss of wages
WOMEN GENERAL SERVANTS					$					
SECOND GIRLS					$					
COOKS AND LAUNDRESSES					$					
COOKS					$					
LAUNDRESSES					$					
CHAMBERMAIDS AND WAITRESSES					$					
CHAMBERMAIDS					$					
WAITRESSES					$					
NURSES					$					
SEAMSTRESSES					$					
					$					
					$					
MEN BUTLERS					$					
COACHMEN AND GARDENERS					$					
COACHMEN					$					
GARDENERS					$					
					$					
					$					

[1] If foreign born, state the number of years each employee has resided in this country.

1. Name of Employer, _____

2. Post Office, _____   3. County, _____.

4. State, _____   5. Date, _____.

6. Do you live in a city, in a town, or in the country ?

_____

7. Estimated present population of city or town, _____.

8. Leading industries of city or town, _____

_____

9. Are women and girls employed in these industries ?

_____

10. Estimated total number so employed, _____

11. Are women and girls employed as clerks ? _____

12. Estimated total number so employed, _____

13. Length of time you have been housekeeping, _____.

14. Total number of domestic servants employed during that
    time, _____

15. Length of time without servants, _____

16. Length of time you have boarded, _____

17. Length of time you have boarded since marriage,

_____

18. Number of persons in your family, _____

19. Name any special privileges granted your servants, such
    as single rooms, the use of a sitting-room, etc., _____

_____

20. Have you paid, as a rule, higher or lower wages this year than last year, and in what branches of occupation, respectively? _____

_____

_____

21. Nature of the service rendered. Is it "Excellent," "Good," "Fair," or "Poor"? Please specify by kinds of employment, _____

_____

_____

22. Have you found it difficult to obtain good domestic servants? _____

23. What explanation of the difficulty can you give? _____

_____

_____

24. How do you think the difficulty can be lessened or removed? _____

_____

_____

SCHEDULE No. II.—EMPLOYEES

STATISTICS OF DOMESTIC SERVICE

1. Name, _____

2. Place of birth, _____

3. Present residence (city or town, and state), _____

4. Name of present employer, _____

5. Present occupation, _____

6. Years of service in present occupation, _____

7. Years of service with present employer, _____

8. Number of previous employers (domestic occupations),

_____

9. Whole number of years engaged in domestic occupations,

_____

10. Present wages received, per week, $ _____ ;

    per month, $ _____

11. Highest wages received from previous employers, per

    week, $_____; per month, $_____

12. Lowest wages received from previous employers, per

    week, $_____; per month, $_____

13. Have you ever had any regular employment other than

    housework ? _____

14. Name such kinds of employment, _____

15. Highest wages received in other than domestic occupa-

    tions, per week, $ _____; per month, $ _____

16. Lowest wages received in other than domestic occupa-

    tions, per week, $ _____ ; per month, $ _____

17. Why do you choose housework as your regular employment? _____

_____

_____

18. What reasons can you give why more women do not
choose housework as a regular employment? _____

_____

_____

19. Would you give up housework if you could find another
occupation that would pay you as well? _____

_____

_____

NOTE. — All personal information will be treated as confidential.

Please return the Schedule to the person giving it to you,
or to —

DEPARTMENT OF HISTORY,

VASSAR COLLEGE,

December 1, 1889.   POUGHKEEPSIE, N. Y.

SCHEDULE No. III. — SCHOOLS, ETC.

STATISTICS OF DOMESTIC SERVICE

SCHOOLS FOR TRAINING DOMESTIC SERVANTS

1. City or Town, and State, _____

2. Number of such schools, _____

3. How supported, _____.

4. Number that can be accommodated at the present time,

_____

5. Present number in attendance, _____

6. Greatest number ever in attendance, _____

7. Total number in attendance since organization, _____

PUBLIC SCHOOLS WHERE HOUSEHOLD EMPLOYMENTS ARE
TAUGHT

8. City or Town, and State, _____

9. Number of such schools, _____

10. Kinds of employment taught, _____

11. Is instruction compulsory or optional? _____

12. Is the object of such instruction technical or general?

_____

13. Present number receiving such instruction, _____

PRIVATE SCHOOLS WHERE HOUSEHOLD EMPLOYMENTS ARE
TAUGHT

14. Names of schools, _____

15. City or Town, and State, _____

16. Present number receiving such instruction, _____

WOMEN'S EXCHANGES, ETC.

17. Please give, below, instances with which you are acquainted of

    1. Women's exchanges.

    2. Co-operative housekeeping.

    3. Food prepared at home for sale outside.

    4. Housework, not including ordinary day labor or sewing done by persons other than regular servants,

and state also how far the results in these cases have been remunerative,

----

Name, --

Address, --

    Please return the Schedule to the person giving it to you, or to

DEPARTMENT OF HISTORY,

VASSAR COLLEGE,

POUGHKEEPSIE, N. Y.

December 1, 1889.

APPENDIX II

THE following table shows the geographical distribution of the replies received to the schedules sent out.

STATES	NUMBERS		
	CITIES AND TOWNS REPRESENTED	EMPLOYERS	EMPLOYEES
Alabama	2	2	11
California	13	30	76
Colorado	2	2	2
Connecticut	18	37	86
District of Columbia . .	1	13	32
Florida	3	3	8
Illinois	27	58	146
Indiana	11	45	94
Iowa	14	38	68
Kansas	4	6	9
Kentucky	2	5	9
Louisiana	2	2	2
Maine	4	6	6
Maryland	1	5	16
Massachusetts	53	199	486
Michigan	21	45	80
Minnesota	5	6	12
Mississippi	1	1	1
Missouri	4	26	90
Nebraska	4	12	21
Nevada	1	2	2
New Hampshire . . .	5	5	6
New Jersey	16	42	126
New York	58	231	606
North Carolina	2	2	2
Ohio	10	30	81
Pennsylvania	18	58	202
Rhode Island	4	8	32
South Carolina	8	23	94
South Dakota	2	2	2
Tennessee	1	1	3
Texas	5	31	72
Utah	1	2	4
Vermont	3	3	8
Virginia	2	3	9
Washington	2	2	3
Wisconsin	9	19	38
Total	339	1005	2545

APPENDIX III

THE following circular letter was sent out in November, 1895, to the members of the Civic Club of Philadelphia:

The Committee on Household Economics to the Members of the Civic Club:

The following standards of work and wages are submitted by the Committee on Household Economics to the members of the Civic Club for their consideration, with a view to taking some action on the subject during the next season.

If any amendments or additions suggest themselves to the members of the Club, will they please note them in the blank space left for that purpose, and send the paper to the Chairman of the Household Economics at the address given below?

In case an applicant for service fails to come up to these standards, the employer agrees to furnish instruction in the points of failure, the employee agreeing to share half the expense of such instruction by accepting a corresponding reduction of weekly wages until skill is attained. It is understood, of course, that the employer furnishes the proper materials and utensils for the performance of the labor.

STANDARDS OF WORK AND WAGES IN HOUSE-HOLD LABOR

COOKS AT $3.50 OR $4.00 PER WEEK

Must understand care of range or stove.

Must understand care of sinks and drains.

Must understand care of kitchen, cellar, and ice-chest.

Must understand care of utensils.

Must understand making bread, biscuit, muffins, and griddle cakes.

Must understand making soup stock.
Must understand roasting, boiling, and broiling meats.
Must understand dressing and cooking poultry.
Must understand cooking eggs, fish, and oysters.
Must understand cooking vegetables, fresh or canned.
Must understand making tea and coffee.
Must understand making plain desserts.

WAITRESSES AT $3.00 OR $3.50 PER WEEK

Must understand care of dining-room.
Must understand care of silver, glass, and china.
Must understand care and attention in waiting on the table.
Must understand care of parlor and halls.
Must understand answering the door-bell properly.

CHAMBERMAIDS AT $3.00 OR $3.50 PER WEEK

Must understand care of bedrooms.
Must understand care of beds and bedding.
Must understand sweeping and dusting.
Must understand care of toilet and bath-rooms.
Must understand care of hard-wood floors.

CHILD'S NURSE AT $3.00 OR $3.50 PER WEEK

Must understand washing, dressing, and feeding of children.
Must understand general care of the health and well-being of children.

LAUNDRESS AT $3.50 OR $4.00 PER WEEK

Must understand washing and ironing.
Must understand general care of bed- and table-linen and clothes.

SEAMSTRESS AT $3.50 OR $4.00 PER WEEK

Must understand plain sewing.
Must understand mending and darning.
Must understand use of sewing machine.

BIBLIOGRAPHY

FULL TITLES OF WORKS REFERRED TO IN THE TEXT

ALSOP, GEORGE. *A Character of the Province of Maryland.* New York, 1869.

ANBUREY, THOMAS. *Travels through the Interior Parts of America.* 2 vols. London, 1789.

Arrivals of Alien Passengers and Immigrants in the United States from 1820 to 1890, see UNITED STATES TREASURY DEPARTMENT.

ARUSMONT, MADAME FRANCES WRIGHT D'. *Views of Society and Manners in America, 1818–1820, by an Englishwoman.* New York, 1821.

BACON, ALICE M. *Japanese Girls and Women.* Boston, 1891.

BACON, THOMAS. *The Laws of Maryland at Large.* Annapolis, 1765.

BARBER, J. W. *Connecticut Historical Collections.* New Haven, Conn., 1838.

BIRD, ISABELLA. *The Englishwoman in America.* London, 1856.

BOLLES, ALBERT S. *Industrial History of the United States.* Norwich, Conn., 1879.

BOOTH, CHARLES. *Life and Labour of the People in London.* Vol. VIII. London, 1896.

BOUNICEAU-GESMON. *Domestiques et Maîtres.* Paris, 1886.

BRADFORD, WILLIAM. *History of Plymouth Plantation.* Boston, 1856.

BRECK, SAMUEL. *Recollections.* Edited by Horace E. Scudder. Philadelphia, 1877.

BROWN, ALEXANDER. *Genesis of the United States.* 2 vols. Boston, 1890.

BROWNE, WILLIAM HAND. *Archives of Maryland; Proceedings and Acts of the General Assembly of Maryland, 1684–1692.* Baltimore, 1894.

BRUCE, PHILIP ALEXANDER. *Economic History of Virginia in the Seventeenth Century.* 2 vols. New York, 1896.

Calendar of State Papers, Colonial Series, see SAINSBURY.

CAMDEN SOCIETY. *Publications.* London, 1849–.

CAREY, M., and BIOREN, J. *Laws of the Commonwealth of Pennsylvania, 1700–1802.* Philadelphia, 1803.

CHEVALIER, MICHEL. *Society, Manners, and Politics in the United States.* Boston, 1839.

CHILD, SIR JOSIAH. *A New Discourse of Trade.* London, 1694.

COBBETT, WILLIAM. *A Year's Residence in the United States of America.* London, 1828.

COMBE, GEORGE. *Notes on the United States of North America.* Philadelphia, 1841.

CONNECTICUT BUREAU OF LABOR STATISTICS. *First Annual Report.* Hartford, Conn., 1885.

Connecticut Historical Collections, see BARBER, J. W.

COOK, E. *The Sot-Weed Factor,* in Shea's *Early Southern Tracts.* Baltimore, 1865.

DALY, CHARLES P. *Reports of Cases in the Court of Common Pleas for the City and County of New York.* New York, 1874.

DAVENANT, CHARLES. *Political and Commercial Works.* 5 vols. London, 1771.

DEFOE, DANIEL. *The Great Law of Subordination Considered; or, the Insolence and Unsufferable Behaviour of Servants in England, Duly Inquired Into.* London, 1724.

DORSEY, CLEMENT. *General Public Statutory Law of Maryland, 1692–1839.* 3 vols. Baltimore, 1840.

DOYLE, J. A. *English Colonies in America.* 3 vols. New York, 1882–1887.

Duke of Yorke's Book of Laws, 1676–1682. Harrisburg, Pa., 1879.

EDDIS, WILLIAM. *Letters from America, Historical and Descriptive; Comprising Occurrences from 1769 to 1777, Inclusive.* London, 1792.

FORCE, PETER. *Tracts and Other Papers, Relating Principally to the Origin, Settlement, and Progress of the Colonies in North America.* Washington, 1838–1846. 4 vols.

GILMAN, NICHOLAS PAYNE. *Profit Sharing between Employer and Employee.* Boston, 1893.

GRATTAN, THOMAS COLLEY. *Civilized America.* 2 vols. London, 1859.

GRUND, FRANCIS J. *The Americans in their Moral, Social, and Political Relations.* 2 vols. Boston, 1837.

HAMILTON, THOMAS. *Men and Manners in America.* Philadelphia, 1833.

HAMMOND, JOHN. *Leah and Rachel, or the Two Fruitful Sisters, Virginia and Mary-land.* 1656, in FORCE, *Tracts,* Vol. III.

HENING, WILLIAM WALLER. *Statutes at Large ; Being a Collection of all the Laws of Virginia.* 13 vols. Richmond, Va., 1809–1823.

HILDRETH, RICHARD. *History of the United States.* 6 vols. New York, 1882.

HOWELL, T. B. *State Trials.* 34 vols. London, 1813.

Indian Narratives. Claremont, N. H., 1854.

IREDELL, JAMES. *Laws of the State of North Carolina.* Edenton, 1791.

KALM, PETER. *Travels into North America.* 3 vols. Warrington, 1770–1771.

KEMBLE, FRANCES ANNE. *Journal of a Residence in Georgia in 1838–1839.* New York, 1864.

KENT, JAMES. *Commentaries on American Law.* 3 vols. New York, 1836.

KNIGHT, SARAH. *The Private Journal of a Journey from Boston to New York in 1704.* Albany, 1865.

LEAMING, AARON, and SPICER, JACOB. *The Grants, Concessions, and Original Constitutions of the Province of New Jersey.* Philadelphia, 1752.

LECHFORD, THOMAS. *Note-book,* 1638–1641. Cambridge, Mass., 1885.

MACKAY, CHARLES. *Life and Liberty in America.* 2 vols. London, 1859.

MAINE HISTORICAL SOCIETY. *Collections. Second Series.* 4 vols. Portland and Cambridge, 1869–1889.

MARTINEAU, HARRIET. *Autobiography.* 2 vols. Boston, 1877.

—— *Society in America.* 2 vols. New York, 1837.

MASSACHUSETTS BODY OF LIBERTIES, *see* WHITMORE.

MASSACHUSETTS BUREAU OF STATISTICS OF LABOR. *Seventeenth Annual Report.* Boston, 1886.

MASSACHUSETTS. *Census for* 1885. 4 vols. Boston, 1887–88.

MASSACHUSETTS HISTORICAL SOCIETY. *Collections.* 58 vols. Boston, Mass., 1806–1896.

—— *Proceedings.* 31 vols. Boston, Mass., 1859–1896.

MOORE, GEORGE H. *Notes on the History of Slavery in Massachusetts.* New York, 1866.

MORTON, THOMAS. *New English Canaan,* in *Prince Society Publications.*

U

290 DOMESTIC SERVICE

Mrs. Johnson's Captivity, in *Indian Narratives.*

MUNBY, ARTHUR J. *Faithful Servants; being Epitaphs and Obituaries Recording their Names and Services.* London, 1876.

NEILL, EDWARD D. *The Founders of Maryland.* Albany, 1876.

—— *Terra Mariæ.* Philadelphia, 1867.

—— *Virginia Carolorum.* Albany, 1886.

NEW HAMPSHIRE HISTORICAL SOCIETY. *Collections.* 9 vols. Concord, N. H., 1824–.

NEW YORK HISTORICAL SOCIETY. *Collections.* 9 vols. New York, 1811–1859.

Nova Britannia, in FORCE, *Tracts*, Vol. I.

O'CALLAGHAN, E. B. *Documentary History of the State of New York.* 4 vols. Albany, 1865–1866.

PARSONS, THEOPHILUS. *The Law of Contracts.* Boston, 1873.

PURDON, J. W. *Digest of the Laws of Pennsylvania from 1700 to 1830.* Philadelphia, 1831.

A Relation of Maryland. Edited by Francis L. Hawks. New York, 1865.

Report of a French Protestant Refugee in Boston, 1687. Brooklyn, 1868.

SAINSBURY, W. N. *Calendar of State Papers, Colonial Series* (1574–1676). 9 vols. London, 1860–1893.

SCHARF, J. THOMAS. *Chronicles of Baltimore.* Baltimore, 1874.

SCHLOSS, D. F. *Report on Profit Sharing.* London, 1894.

—— *Methods of Industrial Remuneration.* London, 1894.

SCHOULER, JAMES. *Law of the Domestic Relations.* Boston, 1874.

SMITH, J. F. D. *Tour in the United States.* 2 vols. London, 1784.

SMITH, WILLIAM. *The History of the Province of New York from its Discovery to 1762.* 2 vols. New York, 1829–30.

Sot-Weed Factor, see COOK, E.

STARKIE, THOMAS. *A Treatise on the Law of Slander and Libel.* Edited by H. C. Folkard. Albany, 1877.

STILES, HENRY R. *History of the City of Brooklyn.* 3 vols. Brooklyn, N. Y., 1867.

STILES, WILLIAM H. *Austria in 1848–49.* 2 vols. New York, 1852.

STIMSON, F. J. *American Statute Law.* 2 vols. Boston, 1888–1892.

TEELE, A. K. *History of Milton, Massachusetts, 1640–1887.* Boston, 1888.

TOCQUEVILLE, ALEXIS DE. *Democracy in America.* 2 vols. New York, 1841.

TRIPIER, L. *Constitutions qui ont regi la France depuis* 1789. Paris, 1879.

TROLLOPE, MRS. FRANCES E. M. *Domestic Manners of the Americans.* 2 vols. London, 1832.

TRUMBULL, J. HAMMOND. *The True Blue Laws of Connecticut.* Hartford, Conn., 1876.

—— *Public Records of the Colony of Connecticut from* 1665 *to* 1678. Hartford, Conn., 1852.

TROTT, NICHOLAS. *Laws of the Province of South Carolina before* 1734. 2 vols. Charleston, 1736.

UNITED STATES. *Tenth Census.* Washington, 1883–1888.

—— *Eleventh Census.* Washington, 1892–1897.

—— TREASURY DEPARTMENT. *Arrivals of Alien Passengers and Immigrants in the United States from* 1820 *to* 1890. Washington, 1893.

WALKER, FRANCIS A. *The Wages Question.* New York, 1886.

WATSON, ELKANAH. *Men and Times of the Revolution.* New York, 1857.

WATSON, JOHN F. *Annals of Philadelphia.* Philadelphia, 1830.

WHITMORE, WILLIAM H. *The Colonial Laws of Massachusetts.* Reprinted from the edition of 1672 with the Supplements through 1686. Boston, 1890.

WINSOR, JUSTIN. *Narrative and Critical History of America.* 8 vols. Boston, 1889.

WINTHROP, JOHN. *The History of New England.* 2 vols. Boston, 1853.

INDEX

293

Camping, prevalence of, has increased demand for prepared articles of food, 216.

Canadians, Irish in factories displaced by, 11; number of, in the United States, 78; in domestic service, 79.

Cap and apron, as badge of servitude, 157, 210; not mark of attainment or desire for neatness, 157, 209; not necessarily badge of servitude, 209, 210; regulations for wearing should be reasonable, 210.

Caterers, services of, growing in demand, 217.

Chambermaids, average wages of, statistics, 89, 94–97.

Chambermaids and waitresses, average wages of, statistics, 89, 94–96.

Charleston, S.C., Employment Bureau, 173, n.

Cheese, manufacture of, transferred from home to factories, 215.

Chevalier, Michel, on Sunday privileges of servants, 1839, 58.

Child, Sir Joshua, on benefit to England of shipping convicts to America, 17.

Chinese, in domestic service, number of, 64, n.; have lowered its social position, 147, n.

Chinese domestics, character of service, 176, n.

Chinese immigration, 64.

Chinese treaty, 1844, effect on domestic service in America, 64.

Choremen, average wages of, statistics, 89, 95, 96.

Christian name, use of, in case of domestic employees, 156; applied to no other class of workers, 156; implies lack of dignity, 156; allows unpleasant familiarity, 156; custom should be abandoned or modified, 209.

Church sales of articles of food, 217.

Cities, majority of foreign born found in, 77, 78; majority of domestic employees found in, 83; manufacturing, have smallest relative number of domestic employees, 84.

City life, attraction of, for domestic employees, 83.

Clothing, men's, manufacture of, transferred from the home to business houses, 215.

Clothing, women's, increase of its manufacture outside the home, 213, 216.

Clubs and societies, among domestic employees, 207.

Coachmen, average wages of, statistics, 89, 94–96.

Coachmen and gardeners, average wages of, statistics, 89, 94–96.

Cobbett, William, on self-respect of servants in America, 1828, 57, 58.

Coffee, roasting of, transferred from the kitchen to business firms, 214.

Coffee, sent hot from Boston to St. Louis, 216, n.

College students, experiments of, in co-operative boarding, 191.

College students, table service performed by, 142.

Colonial laws, regarding servants, 22–48; law in Virginia binding servants coming without indenture, 23, 24; in North Carolina, 24, n.; in Maryland, 25, n.; in West New Jersey, 25, n.; laws regulating wages, 30, 31; to prevent pilfering on part of servants, 32; laws not specifically for household employees, but for all servants, 37; law to protect servants against ill-treatment from masters, 38–40; to protect masters, 40–46; latter more specific, 40; relate chiefly to runaways, 40; penalties for harboring runaways, 41–43; rewards for capture of runaways, 43, 44; means for prevention of runaways, 44; laws for infliction of corporal punishment upon servants, 45; for prevention of bartering with servants, 45, 46; examples of laws placing oppressive restrictions upon servants, 47; laws to prohibit freeing servants, 47, 48.

Colonial period of domestic service, see Domestic service.

Colored servants, see Negro domestic employees, Negro slaves.

Competition of other industries with domestic service, 68.

296 INDEX

employees, 64, 65; change in kind at the South through abolition of slavery, 65; lack of political privileges of, in Europe, 72, n.; mostly of foreign birth, 74–77; geographical distribution of, in the United States, 76; number of Irish, 79; number of German, 79; number of English, 79; number of Canadian, 79; number of Swedish and Norwegian, 79; few in agricultural and thinly settled states, 80; relative number large in states containing large cities, 80; smallest relative number in Oklahoma, 81; greatest relative number in District of Columbia, New York, Massachusetts, and New Jersey, 82; relative number unaffected by aggregate wealth of state, 82; affected by per capita wealth of state, 82; high relative number in cities, 83; relative number most affected by prevailing industry, 84, 87, 88; relative number small in manufacturing towns, 84; relative number large in the South, 84; foreign born receive higher wages than native born, 91, 92; savings, 102, 103; small number of unemployed, 104, 105; number in average family, 107; nationalities represented in schedules forming basis of this work, 108, n.; foreign born an extraneous element difficult to assimilate into household, 109; brief tenure of service, 109–112; ignorance of, 112, 113; dislike of occupation, 127; industrial independence of, 130; other occupations engaged in, 130, n.; reasons for entering service, 131; special privileges given, 133, 134; hours of work, 143; *disadvantages — social deprivations*, 152–154; enforced loneliness, 154, n.; obnoxious term "servant," 156; address by Christian name, 156; wearing of livery, 157; servility of manner expected, 158; ignored socially, 158; required to obey absurd orders, 158; degraded by offering of fees, 158–162; often required to go out at night unprotected, 162; exposed to contamination in intelligence offices, 162; do not care to be treated as members of the family, 170–172; desire opportunity to live their lives in their own way, 172; their demand for more social opportunities reasonable, 206; demand cannot be met in private home, 206; solitary instruction unsatisfactory, 206; social opportunities more satisfactory if provided by them than for them, 207; taken from the home of employer through specialization of household employments, 213–234; independence of, secured through specialization of household employments, 228; moral education acquired through profit sharing, 247. See also Hours of work, Wages.

Domestic employments, see Household employments.

Domestic service, "the great American question," 1; discussed frequently, in a popular manner, 1; has been omitted from economic discussion, 2; omitted from theoretical discussion, 2; reasons — capital not involved, 2; no combinations formed, 2; products of labor transient, 2; omitted from official statistics because of no demand by public for its investigation, 2, 3; references to partial discussions, 3, n.; subject has not been considered historically, 3; an important question, considering numbers involved, 3; nature of, has been regarded as personal only, 4; regarded as an isolated form of industry, 5; difficulties in domestic service due partly to incomplete division of labor, 15; three phases of, in America, 16; in the colonial period, 16–53; implied social inferiority even more than now, 53; unsatisfactory to both master and servant, 53; accompanied by definite legal exactions, 53; in New England, early part of century, 54; described by Harriet Martineau, 55, 56; since 1850, 62–68; at the North, change of personnel from native born to foreign, 62–65; at the South, no change till later, 62; causes of change — Irish famine, 62, 63; German Revolution, 63, 64; treaty between United States and China, 1844, 64; effect of change, lowering of social status, 65; at the South, condition changed with abolition of slavery, 65; foreign born domestics introduced, 65; the employment as affected by development of material resources, 66, 67; mobility of, 67–69; new rival occupations to compete with, 68; changes indicated by history of "servant," 69–71; *economic phases of domestic service*, 74–106; the occupation includes more foreign born women than any other occupation, 77; includes majority of foreign born wage-earning women, 77; employees prefer city to country life, 77, 78, 83; nationalities most represented, 79; effect of aggregate wealth of state upon number, 82, 83; statistics representing effect of locality, 85; effect of per capita wealth, 86–88; effect of prevailing industry greatest, 87; character of service rendered, 91; wages higher than average wages in other occupations, 93; average annual earnings, 98; remuneration compared with that in teaching, 101, 102; wage limit sooner reached, 103, 104; offers constant occupation and least loss of time, 104, 105; free from strikes and combinations, 105; conforms to economic conditions, 106; *difficulties of employer*, 107–129; not confined to America, 128, 129; cannot be remedied without economic treatment, 129, 264; *advantages in domestic service*, 130–139; reasons given for entering, 131; high wages, 132; healthful occupation, 132; externals of a home, 133; free hours and vacations without loss of wages, 134–136; useful training, 137; the employment congenial to many, 137; legal protection in, 138; legal rights — freedom from physical punish-

ment, sufficient food, support during illness, good character, wages, damages for discharge, 138; advantages are inherent in the occupation, 139; summed up, are those of "wages, hours, health, and morals," 139; advantages unavailing to attract, 139; *industrial disadvantages*, 140–150; independent of personal relationship, 140; list of reasons given for not entering service, 140, 141; little chance for promotion, 141; lack of stimulus for the efficient and ambitious, 141, 142; "housework never done," 142, 143; lack of organization in housework, 143; irregularity of working hours, 143–146; limited free time, 146; in case of Americans, competition with foreign born and negroes, 146, 147; strictures on personal independence, 147–149; summary of industrial disadvantages, 149, 150; *social disadvantages*, 151–166, 204–211, 266, 267; no real home life for employees, 151; being *in* a family and not *of* it, 152; regulations in regard to visitors necessary, 152; lack of opportunity to receive or give hospitality, 152; exclusion from general social life of community, 153; deprivation of opportunities for personal improvement, 153, 154; appellation of "servant," 155; use of Christian name in address, 156; requirement of livery, 157; requirement of servility of manner, 158; custom of offering fees, 158–162; lack of protection and exposure to vice, 162; discrimination according to ordinary social standards not expected, 163, n.; social inferiority weighs more than anything else against the employment, 163; other disadvantages, 164; advantages and disadvantages compared, 165; latter outweigh former, 166; remedies adapted to nature of difficulties required, 168; no panacea, 168; reform must be in line with industrial progress, 168; must be an evolution, 168; cannot be immediate, 168, 169; real problem of domestic service, 198; the subject neglected by economic students and writers, 199; its importance underestimated in public sentiment, 200, 201; improvement dependent on wider general education and more scientific investigation, 203; social disadvantages can be removed or modified, 204; removal of social barriers will remove social ban, 211; improvement impossible, till housekeeping as a profession advances, 254; improvement hindered by partial treatment of labor question, 264; by conservatism of many women, 264, 265; by tendency of women toward aristocracy, 265; by tendency to display of wealth, 265, 266; responsibility of introducing improvement rests on all, 266; investigation and discussion will result in removal of social stigma, 266, 267; in removal of work and worker from home of employer, 267; in placing the employment on a business basis, 268; in readjustment of work of both men and women, 270; suggestions as to means of attaining results, 273. See also Convicts, transported, Freewillers, Redemptioners, Remedies, Wages.

Domestic system, see Home manufactures.

Dudley, Mrs. Mary Winthrop, description of a refractory servant by, 35.

Earnings of domestic employees, 98. See also Wages.

Economic discussion of domestic service neglected, 2, 199.

Economic gains from specialization of household employments, 229.

Economic laws, disregard of, by employers of domestic service, 117-122.

Economic phases of domestic service, 74-106.

Economic tendencies, see Industrial tendencies.

Education, views of effect of, on domestic service, 179.

Education in household affairs, 251-262.

Electricity in the household, 9, 232.

"Employer," use of, for "master" and "mistress," 207.

Employers, their personal point of view, 4; difficulties of, 107-129; assimilation into household of foreign and ignorant employees, 109; restlessness of domestic employees, 109-112; ignorance of domestic employees, 112, 113; the choice of a domestic a lottery, 114-117; general disregard among employers of economic principles, 117-122; individual irresponsibility of employers, 121, 122; difficulties of, increasing, 125, n.; fewer under certain conditions, 126; difficulties also in England, Germany, and France, 127; due to a defective and antiquated system, 129; individual standpoint of many employers, 170; each responsible to all, 266. See also Housekeepers.

Employment bureau, unsatisfactory, 115-117; application of profit sharing to, 244.

Employments of men and women need readjustment, 270-272.

England, domestic service in, unsatisfactory, 127, 128.

English custom of using surname for domestics, 157.

English in the United States, number of, 78; in domestic service, number of, 79.

Ethics of domestic service given too exclusive attention, 167.

Evans, Elizabeth, wages of, 28.

Extravagance of domestics checked through system of profit sharing, 241, 242.

Extravagant habits acquired in domestic service, 150.

Factory system, substituted for the domestic system, 8-15; agencies which brought about, 8; released labor from the home, 10; changed personnel of domestic service, 11; diverted labor into other channels,

Leclaire, M., on knowledge of the workman, 200.
Leclaire, Maison, 237.
Legal status of domestic employees, 138.
Levasseur, M., on proportion of failures among business firms, 245.
Library strictures in regard to domestic employees, 154, n.
Licenses for domestic employees, 177, 178.
Livery, absence of, in early times at the North, 57, 61. See also Cap and apron.
Living, cost of, affected by specialization of household employments, 230.
London, domestic service in, 128, n.
London South Metropolitan Gas Company, profit sharing in, 239.
Lowell, J. R., on Indian servants, 51, n.; on "help," 55; on influx of Irish domestic employees, 63.
Lyman, O. E., on legal status of domestic employees, 138, n.

MACKAY, CHARLES, on "help," 58, n.
"Maid" as substitute for "servant," 156; unobjectionable, 208.
Maid-of-all-work, present requirements of, 228.
Maine, high wages of redemptioners in, 28, n.; instance related by John Winter of unsatisfactory service in, 33, 34.
Maine, Sir Henry Sumner, on equality, 211.
Maison Leclaire, 237.
Manufacturing industries, number of women in, in Massachusetts, 10, n.; women employees in, largely outnumber men, 10, n.; greater demand for servants created by increase of, 11; manufacturing industries utilize ignorant labor, 14; relative number of domestic employees diminished by, 87.
Marketing, made a specialty by one person for many families, 225, 226.
Martineau, Harriet, on democratic condition of service in America, 55, 56.

Maryland, transported convicts in, 18; free willers in, 19; redemptioners in, 21, 25; colonial law regulating wages of redemptioners in, 31; to protect servants in, 38, n.; concerning runaways in, 41; concerning those who harbored runaways in, 43; fixing reward for capturing runaways in, 44; preventing barter with servants in, 46; redemptioners who rose to distinction in, 48, n.
Massachusetts, number of women in manufacturing industries in, 10, n.; redemptioners in, 20; colonial law concerning wages of redemptioners in, 30; to protect servants in, 38, n.; in regard to punishment of servants in, 45; to prevent barter with servants in, 46; debarring servants from holding public office in, 47; concerning wearing apparel of servants in, 47; prohibiting setting servants free in, 47; proportion of foreign born domestic employees in, 77; large relative number of domestic employees in, 82.
Massachusetts Bureau of Labor Statistics, returns from schedules collated by, preface, ix, x.
"Master," as a term should be abolished, 207.
Meats, stuffed, delivered ready for final application of heat, 214.
Michigan, University of, women graduates of, assistance of, in obtaining statistics, preface, vii.
"Mistress," as an appellation should be abolished, 207.
Mitchell, Maria, on woman's work, 272.
Mobility of labor made possible, 67; developed to an inconvenient extent, 68.
Morton, Thomas, use of word "servant," 69, n.
Munby, A. J., *Epitaphs of Servants*, 55, n.
Music lessons, desire for, ridiculed, 153, n; of a domestic, 154, n.

NEGRO domestic employees, their in-

x

Sunday, free hours on, in domestic service, 134, 146, 147.

Sunday privileges of domestics in early part of century, 58.

Swedes and Norwegians in the United States, number of, 78; number in domestic service, 79.

Syracuse, N.Y., Household Economic Club, 225, n.

TABLE service an art, 142; may be performed by specialist, 224.

Talbot, Marion, and Richards, Mrs. Ellen S., *Household Sanitation,* 261, n.

Taylor, George, signer of the Declaration of Independence, a Pennsylvania redemptioner, 48, n.

Tea Company, Oriental, Boston, 216, n.

Teachers, wages of, compared with wages of domestics, 99–102; salaries of, statistics, 99, 100.

Technical training, demand for, an industrial tendency, 195.

Texas, preference in, for German and Swedish domestics, 173, n.

Thatcher, Rev. Peter, Indian servant of, 51.

Tips, see Feeing.

Tocqueville, A. de, on democratic condition of service in America, 57.

Training schools for domestics, 180–186; possible benefits from, 180, 181; demand for, from employers, 181; scheme for their establishment in connection with World's Fair, 1893, 181; few established and those unsuccessful, 181; reasons for their failure, 182–186; admit pupils too young, 182; course too short, 182; attendance not voluntary, 182, 183; ignorance of employers, 183; not analogous to training schools for nurses, 183, 184; methods superficial, 184, 185; undemocratic, 185, 186.

Trollope, Mrs., on difficulty in obtaining servants, 58.

Troy, N.Y., laundries, 223.

Tutwiler, Julia R., on feeing, 162, n.

UNCONSCIOUS co-operation, characteristic of modern industry, 212.

Unemployed, number of, among domestic employees, very small, 104, 105.

University education in household affairs needed, 259–262, 269.

VACATIONS, of domestic employees, 135, 136.

Vassar College, Associate Alumnæ of, assistance of, in obtaining statistics, preface, vii; Classes of 1888 and 1889, assistance of, in obtaining statistics, preface, vii.

Vegetables, preparation of, for cooking, 214; canning of, 214, n.

Verney, Thomas, a redemptioner, 21, n.

Virginia, transported convicts in, 18; General Court of, prohibits introduction of English criminals, 19, n.; redemptioners in, 21, n., 23, 25, 27, 48, n.; colonial law of indenture in, 23, 24; laws binding servants not indented in, 23, 24; law regulating wages of redemptioners in, 30; to punish pilfering of bakers in, 32, n.; fixing reward for capturing runaways in, 44.

WAGES in domestic service, total aggregate paid, 3, n.; average paid in 1817, cited by Breck, 58, n.; present average of, statistics, 88, 90, 94–97; by geographical sections, 88; by occupations, statistics, 90, 94–97; highest for skilled labor, 89; higher paid to foreign born than to native born, 91, 92; higher paid to men than to women, 92; tending to increase, 93; exceed average wages in other occupations, 93; compared with wages of teachers, 99–102; maintained without strikes, 105; conform to economic laws, 106; in average family, 108; underrated in popular estimate, 164, n.; not officially investigated as are wages in other occupations, 198.

Wages of redemptioners, 28–31.

"Waitress," as an appellation unobjectionable, 208.

Waitresses, average wages of, statis-

American Women: Images and Realities

An Arno Press Collection

[Adams, Charles F., editor]. **Correspondence between John Adams and Mercy Warren Relating to Her "History of the American Revolution," July-August, 1807.** With a new appendix of specimen pages from the **"History."** 1878.

[Arling], Emanie Sachs. **"The Terrible Siren": Victoria Woodhull, (1838-1927).** 1928.

Beard, Mary Ritter. **Woman's Work in Municipalities.** 1915.

Blanc, Madame [Marie Therese de Solms]. **The Condition of Woman in the United States.** 1895.

Bradford, Gamaliel. **Wives.** 1925.

Branagan, Thomas. **The Excellency of the Female Character Vindicated.** 1808.

Breckinridge, Sophonisba P. **Women in the Twentieth Century.** 1933.

Campbell, Helen. **Women Wage-Earners.** 1893.

Coolidge, Mary Roberts. **Why Women Are So.** 1912.

Dall, Caroline H. **The College, the Market, and the Court.** 1867.

[D'Arusmont], Frances Wright. **Life, Letters and Lectures: 1834, 1844.** 1972.

Davis, Almond H. **The Female Preacher, or Memoir of Salome Lincoln.** 1843.

Ellington, George. **The Women of New York.** 1869.

Farnham, Eliza W[oodson]. **Life in Prairie Land.** 1846.

Gage, Matilda Joslyn. **Woman, Church and State.** [1900].

Gilman, Charlotte Perkins. **The Living of Charlotte Perkins Gilman.** 1935.

Groves, Ernest R. **The American Woman.** 1944.

Hale, [Sarah J.] **Manners; or, Happy Homes and Good Society All the Year Round.** 1868.

Higginson, Thomas Wentworth. **Women and the Alphabet.** 1900.

Howe, Julia Ward, editor. **Sex and Education.** 1874.

La Follette, Suzanne. **Concerning Women.** 1926.

Leslie, Eliza. **Miss Leslie's Behaviour Book: A Guide and Manual for Ladies.** 1859.

Livermore, Mary A. **My Story of the War.** 1889.

Logan, Mrs. John A. (Mary S.) **The Part Taken By Women in American History.** 1912.

McGuire, Judith W. (A Lady of Virginia). **Diary of a Southern Refugee, During the War.** 1867.

Mann, Herman . **The Female Review: Life of Deborah Sampson.** 1866.

Meyer, Annie Nathan, editor.**Woman's Work in America.** 1891.

Myerson, Abraham. **The Nervous Housewife.** 1927.

Parsons, Elsie Clews. **The Old-Fashioned Woman.** 1913.

Porter, Sarah Harvey. **The Life and Times of Anne Royall.** 1909.

Pruette, Lorine. **Women and Leisure: A Study of Social Waste.** 1924.

Salmon, Lucy Maynard. **Domestic Service.** 1897.

Sanger, William W. **The History of Prostitution.** 1859.

Smith, Julia E. **Abby Smith and Her Cows.** 1877.

Spencer, Anna Garlin. **Woman's Share in Social Culture.** 1913.

Sprague, William Forrest. **Women and the West.** 1940.

Stanton, Elizabeth Cady. **The Woman's Bible** Parts I and II. 1895/1898.

Stewart, Mrs. Eliza Daniel . **Memories of the Crusade.** 1889.

Todd, John. **Woman's Rights.** 1867. [Dodge, Mary A.] (Gail Hamilton, pseud.) **Woman's Wrongs.** 1868.

Van Rensselaer, Mrs. John King. **The Goede Vrouw of Mana-ha-ta.** 1898.

Velazquez, Loreta Janeta. **The Woman in Battle.** 1876.

Vietor, Agnes C., editor. **A Woman's Quest: The Life of Marie E. Zakrzew-ska, M.D.** 1924.

Woodbury , Helen L. Sumner. **Equal Suffrage.** 1909.

Young, Ann Eliza. **Wife No. 19.** 1875.